POLITICAL CHANGE IN LATIN AMERICA

John J. Johnson

POLITICAL CHANGE IN LATIN AMERICA

THE EMERGENCE OF THE MIDDLE SECTORS

STANFORD UNIVERSITY PRESS

STANFORD, CALIFORNIA

Stanford University Press
Stanford, California

© 1958 by the Board of Trustees of the
Leland Stanford Junior University

Printed in the United States of America

Cloth SBN 8047-0528-3
Paper SBN 8047-0529-1

First published 1958

Last figure below indicates year of this printing:

78 77 76 75 74 73 72 71

To Michael

Preface

In Latin America a continuing economic revolution dating from the late nineteenth century has brought to the surface the politically ambitious urban middle groups that have in several republics successfully challenged the historically dominant ruling elements. This study seeks to develop, first, the circumstances under which the urban middle groups rose to political prominence and, second, how their influence upon decision-making on the national level has contributed to the current socioeconomic orientation of the governments of five of the twenty Latin American republics. I undertook it because I believed that an appraisal, although it could not fail to be inconclusive in some respects, was needed at this time. The groups with which the volume deals appear determined to enlarge their role in society, and they give no indication of waiting to have their present strengths and weaknesses or their future capabilities definitively analyzed before they take their next step on the way to greater influence and power.

As for the impact of my present efforts upon the long-range course of the scholarly study of the Latin American area, I can only hope that they will stimulate further research on the many questions I have raised and only partially answered. In the meantime, I feel, my findings give the volume considerable pertinence as a document on the political implications of socioeconomic change in a so-called underdeveloped area. Also, certain of my conclusions call into serious question a number of views that have long been current.

I hold that the urban middle groups are vitally, if not decisively, important in an area where one still commonly hears and reads that there is "no middle class to speak of"—a statement that is both partially true and dangerously misleading. It is true in terms of the number of republics in which the urban middle groups play a major political role. It is misleading in terms of the area, population, gross product, and international importance of the republics in which these groups are a significant factor in politics.

I emphasize social groups in a region where, in the view of traditional scholarship, individuals hold the center of the stage. The chief executives, the caudillos, and the colonels who shoot their way into the presidential chair are no longer the effective agents of all political change.

Further, I propose that for over a quarter of a century the social and economic problems, not the historical, political, and religious ones, have been the primary concern of all but the most reactionary of those belonging to the politically articulate elements.

Finally my study places stress upon five countries—Argentina, Brazil, Chile, Mexico, and Uruguay—that have experienced significant social and economic change and have in some instances achieved considerable political progress in recent decades. These five nations, whether one finds them repugnant or attractive, will set the pattern of tomorrow for the present feudally held Dominican Republics, the socially retarded Paraguays, the poverty stricken Haitis, and the strife-torn Venezuelas which so often capture the headlines.

The terms used to identify the urban middle groups were difficult to decide upon and are not completely satisfactory. First of all it seemed necessary to avoid the words "classes" and "strata," which have come, in the minds of the people of Western Europe and Anglo-America, to have an essentially economic connotation, whereas in Latin America it is only in recent years that income and wealth have successfully vied with learning, prejudices, conduct, way of life, background, and esthetic and religious sentiments as social determinants. Today certain of these cultural determinants still play a much greater part in establishing social status than they do, for example, in the United States. As the alternatives to "classes" and "strata"

the terms "middle sectors," "middle groups," "middle segments," "middle components," "middle elements," used inter-
changeably, were settled upon to convey the idea of "middleness" without paralleling any fixed criteria of "middleness" employed in areas outside Latin America.

A closely related problem was whether to use the singular
or plural form of the terms. The plural was settled upon because socially and economically the groups dealt with are highly
fluid and widely disparate. In Spanish the verb *estar* applies to
them better than does the verb *ser*. Their membership ranges
upward from the poorly paid white-collar employee in government, with a limited education and often a lack of helpful family connections, to the wealthy proprietors of commercial and
industrial enterprises on the one hand and to the educated
professional men, teachers, and high-level government bureaucrats, usually from old established families, on the other.

Statistics are relied upon rather heavily for comparative
purposes in several portions of the study. The unreliability of
statistics from most private and public agencies in Latin America is well known. I recommend an allowance of 10 to 15 per
cent for error.

Although the decision was to keep footnotes to a minimum
I am no less indebted to the hundreds who compiled the statistics and wrote the studies that I used. The Bibliography of
more than nine hundred entries, a majority of which are annotated, pays credit in a small way to those upon whom greatest
reliance was placed.

I first became fully aware of the importance of the urban
middle sectors in Latin American politics during the fifteen
months in 1952–53 that I was with the State Department as
Acting Chief of the South American Branch of the Division of
Research for the American Republics. I am deeply grateful
to the members of the Division, most especially Elizabeth
Hyman, James S. G. Cunningham, and Rollie E. Poppino, who
then and subsequently gave generously of their time and experience. The then Chief of the Division, the late Miron Burgin,

gave me every encouragement and the benefit of his unequaled knowledge of contemporary Latin America. My warm thanks go to my colleagues Thomas A. Bailey, Claude A. Buss, and George H. Knoles who read large parts of the manuscript.

JOHN J. JOHNSON

Guadalajara, Mexico
July 5, 1958

Contents

POLITICAL CHANGE IN LATIN AMERICA

I *Introduction*

In the late nineteenth century a number of the republics of Latin America began to undergo technological transformations. By 1920 the impact of those transformations was widely felt. One of the most profound developments to come from them was the emergence of the urban middle sectors of society as an aggressive political force. Today these groups hold a prominent position in the social-political amalgams that control Argentina, Brazil, Chile, Mexico, and Uruguay. These five countries contain two-thirds of the land area and two-thirds of the population, and produce more than two-thirds of the gross product, of the twenty Latin American republics.

The behavior of the urban middle sectors as political entities has been determined by the changes they have undergone as a result of the technological transformations and by their bid for popular support outside their own groups—a support that has ordinarily come from the industrial proletariat. The constant search for a balance between values they hold to be basic and those dictated by political expediency has been a primary characteristic of their political conduct in this century.*

Before the five republics began the transition from neofeudal agriculture to semi-industrial capitalism, the composition of the middle sectors was essentially static: they were members of the liberal professions, such as law and medicine; they were writers, publishers, and artists; they were professors in secondary schools and institutions of higher learning; they were bureaucrats; they were members of the secular clergy of the

---

* The reasons for using the terms middle sectors, middle elements, and so on, rather than middle classes or middle strata are discussed in the Preface.

Catholic Church, and of the lower and middle echelons of the officer corps. This composition began to change as soon as the technological transformations gained momentum, and it continues to change as the component groups remain fluid and as movement in and around them accelerates. Before 1900, representatives of commerce and industry were notably absent from the composition of these middle sectors; the same technological developments that gave the other components an opportunity to improve their political status also created the conditions for the emergence of the commercial and industrial elements—owners as well as managers, applied scientists, and highly trained technicians.

Numerically, the middle sectors formed, until well into this century, a small minority. Until 1900 they might be described as a thin intermediate layer separating the elite from the inarticulate masses; their growth after 1900 was stimulated by the requirements of technology and by the expansion of education and of the functions of the State. Even so they remained, for the first two decades of this century, a small percentage of the total population in each of the five republics. The sharp upswing in their growth curve coincided with World War I. Since 1919 their numerical expansion has been large both in absolute figures and relative to the other elements of society, except the industrial proletariat. Today the middle sectors probably constitute at least 35 per cent of the population in Argentina, 30 per cent in Chile and Uruguay, and 15 per cent in Brazil and Mexico.

In the course of the middle sectors' rapid expansion since World War I their ranks have been infiltrated by appreciable numbers from other levels of society. As long as the demand for their skills rose gradually, as was the case throughout the colonial period and the nineteenth century, the increments to middle sector positions came almost wholly from the middle elements themselves, although occasionally individuals from the elites would drift down and become permanent members, and isolated individuals belonging to the working groups could and did lift themselves up—usually via the Catholic Church or the military. Generally, though, the sons of middle sector families followed in the footsteps of their fathers or moved horizontally within the middle groups. There was nothing approaching the vertical social mobility, limited as it remains, found in the republics today.

When the members of the middle sectors could no longer satisfy the increased demands for skills associated with their status, individuals from other groups began to bid successfully for recognition. In Argentina, Brazil, Chile, and Uruguay many naturalized citizens or sons of immigrants entered the ranks of the middle sectors as the owners of commercial and industrial establishments. Others came from the old rural families who for various reasons—as, for example, scarcity of land in Chile—had invested in urban industry and commerce. The salaried elements — teachers, bureaucrats, technicians, managers—drew an important share of their accretions from the working groups.

Clearly, the middle sectors are anything but a compact social layer. They do not fulfill the central condition of a class: their members have no common background of experience. On the contrary, among them are representatives of nearly the entire cultural and economic range. Members of old Spanish and Portuguese families co-exist with mestizos, mulattoes, Negroes, and newcomers from Europe. Some are members of the middle sectors because of their intellectual attainments; some, because they have combined education and manual labor in proportions that meet the standards of those middle sector elements that still look askance at men who depend upon their hands for a livelihood; others, more because of their wealth than because of their learning. Property owners are associated with persons who have never possessed property and have little prospect of ever operating their own businesses. Some members are strongly committed to the defense of personal initiative and private property; others may be little concerned with property rights or infringements upon what are often considered the domains of private enterprise. Some take their status for granted: their lives are organized, they know where they are headed and what they want when they get there. Others are undergoing the frustrating and unsettling experi-

ences and tensions inherent in passing from one socioeconomic
group to another. Some have only a paternalistic interest in,
and a theoretical understanding of, the working elements.
Others know the lower levels of society because they have risen
from them, and their feeling for those groups is likely to be
highly personal.* They are all the more aware of the existing
social and economic inequities because as new members of the
middle sectors they are more often confronted by them than
they were as members of the lower levels. Some have inherited
an almost congenital abhorrence for the labor movement, while
others come from families that have depended upon the labor
leader as their sole representative before their employers and
public officials.

The differentiations in their social backgrounds and economic interests have prevented the middle sectors from becoming politically monolithic. Individual members have reserved the right to act independently. At times large components find the prevailing middle sector attitudes unacceptable
and either refuse to exercise the suffrage or make *ad hoc* arrangements with the elites or the workers, or both, in order to
oppose the dominant elements. But the differences have not
prevented large and ordinarily major segments of the middle
sectors from finding common ground for joint political action.

* In Latin America the privileged groups are strongly inclined to
look for cultural symbols rather than biologically inherited characteristics. Race, consequently, tends to be subordinated to human and social
values. For this reason racial differentiations are dealt with only ob-
liquely in this study. In any event, only in Brazil was the racial composition of the middle sectors notably changed when workers began to find
their way into them. There, although most of those entering the middle
sectors from the working elements have been European in racial origin,
for the first time the mestizos, mulattoes, and Negroes in substantial
numbers have been provided opportunities to improve their social status.
In Argentina, Uruguay, and Chile the new members of the middle sectors have been almost wholly European or mestizos with a decided pre-
ponderance of European blood. In Mexico, the new elements entering
the middle sectors from the laboring groups have been basically mestizo,
but the mestizo has been entrenched in the middle sectors there at least
since the mid-nineteenth century. (The term "mestizo" in Spanish
America is used to refer to persons of mixed European-Indian blood. In
Brazil those of mixed European-Indian descent are normally referred to
as *caboclos*.)

To the extent that the middle sectors have had political cohesiveness and a continuity of common interests, this cohesiveness and continuity seem to have been due to six characteristics they hold in common. They are overwhelmingly urban. They not only have well above average educations themselves but they also believe in universal public education. They are convinced that the future of their countries is inextricably tied to industrialization. They are nationalistic. They believe that the State should actively intrude in the social and economic areas while it carries on the normal functions of government. They recognize that the family has weakened as a political unit in the urban centers, and they have consequently lent their support to the development of organized political parties.

1. *Urbanization.* Whether they are salaried persons, self-employed professionals, or property owners and *rentiers*; whether they belong to the middle sectors because of their learning or their wealth, the members of the intermediate groups are almost solidly urban. It has been thus historically. The great and rapidly expanding centers—Mexico City, Rio de Janeiro, Buenos Aires, Montevideo, Santiago—where the middle sectors are presently found in large numbers were, from their beginning, the centers of concentration for professionals, educators, bureaucrats, and other components of the early middle sectors. The metropolises were first of all administrative centers with revenues that provided the means for their becoming oases in what was otherwise largely a cultural and intellectual void. As industry developed it too has, in general, concentrated in cities, and thus the new components of the middle sectors have been added to the old. Since the middle sectors are predominantly urban, they favor, as they traditionally have, national policies that promote urban growth and economic development and assign a disproportionately large per capita share of public revenues to the urban centers.

2. *Public education.* Before 1900 all other determinants of middleness paled before the educational requirement. It was assumed that the student who entered school would eventually go on for a higher degree. Consequently primary and secondary schools were viewed not as ends in themselves but as step-

pingstones on the way to a university. In the universities logic and dialectics were emphasized. Empiricism and pragmatics were slighted in favor of deductive reasoning. A humanistic education was the trade-mark of nearly every member of the middle sectors. The rigid quantitative and qualitative requirements of education gave ground to the conditions created by the economic transformation and the entrance into the middle sectors of the commercial and industrial elements. Members could no longer be expected to hold a degree from an institution of higher learning. The needs of industry and commerce provided the impetus that made scientific training an acceptable substitute for the traditional humanistic training. Trade schools and high schools began to turn out semiprofessionalized graduates able to use their limited educations along with their other qualifications to achieve middle sector status.

Although middle sector families have themselves shown a strong preference for private schools, their leaders have for a century used the political forum to champion mass public education. In the nineteenth century they associated education with representative government and national progress. As industrial and commercial proprietors began to wield their influence upon political thinking, they added a demand that public schools provide the trained personnel needed to operate their plants more efficiently. Political leaders of the middle sectors have continued their demands for public elementary and secondary schools to ensure a literate electorate and a supply of semiskilled and skilled industrial artisans.

3. *Industrialization.* Industrialization has become an obsession within the middle sectors. The urgent need to industrialize further is accepted as a self-evident truth by all components, although in periods of stress differences may arise as to the degree of urgency. The cries for industrialization have mounted to a crescendo since World War II. Today it would be political suicide for a member of the middle sectors publicly to recommend a national policy founded on the economic doctrine that holds that each geographic area should produce only what it can turn out most efficiently. In each of the republics

such a position would be interpreted by the political opposition as advocating that the nation remain a producer of unfinished goods and hence an economic colony of the industrial powers.

The middle sectors reached their present views on industrialization in four stages. In the late nineteenth century those concerned with industrial development were by and large content to promote the extractive and processing industries and to support technological development as requisite to continued industrial expansion. Ordinarily, the major enterprises were foreign financed and managed. In the second stage came the clamor for more processing industries. The breakdown of normal trade channels during World War I showed the inconveniences that nonindustrial countries could expect in periods of international catastrophe. The politicians made capital of proposals to avert any recurrence of widespread shortages resulting from dependence upon outside sources of supply. Meanwhile the economics of industrialization remained largely unaltered, although the nature of the new enterprises, many of which required only limited amounts of capital, opened the way for considerably greater domestic financial and managerial participation.

Industrialization and politics became increasingly entwined in the third stage, which corresponded to the world depression of the 1930's. Domestic ownership of natural resources and industry was the cliché of politicians in Uruguay and Mexico and to a lesser extent in the other republics. Substantial expansion in the production of semidurables requiring raw materials as well as capital goods from abroad increasingly involved the politicians in the economic sphere, particularly when foreign-exchange shortages developed. But the important increment to the industrial environment in this phase was the politicians' discovery of the power and appeal of their solicitude for the protection and welfare of the industrial workers. The new concern for the workingman had many facets. He had won a new status throughout the Western World. An aggressive labor movement in Europe had spread to other nations and had helped to strengthen the bargaining power of working groups in Latin America. The laborer had become more politically articulate. His vote was in large part responsible for the success of the political amalgams that the middle sector leadership headed.

Since World War II, in the fourth stage, two aspects of the political-industrial scene have become particularly pronounced. The demands that industry be expanded to include heavy industry have become incessant. The iron and steel plant has become the symbol of progress. On the other hand, serious doubts have been raised whether the republics can achieve the industrial development they seek without a greater price to labor than it has been asked to pay since the 1930's. Differences of opinion on this question have provided the fuel for political fireworks, particularly in Argentina, Brazil, and Chile.

4. *Nationalism.* Nationalism of an assertive xenophobic nature is for all intents and purposes a twentieth-century phenomenon in Latin America. In the course of their drives to power, the middle groups in the five republics have raised nationalism to the level of a major political ideology. Its effectiveness in arousing the emotions of a broad segment of the electorate gives every indication that it will remain a weapon or a potential weapon in the arsenal of the middle sector politician.

During the relatively brief period that it has enjoyed currency, the concept of nationalism has had several dimensions as it has responded to stimuli originating at home and abroad. It was initially nourished by individuals acting in a private capacity. In that stage its juridic and cultural features were presented in abstract terms by intellectuals. The two aspects were often viewed as independent.* Not unusually, the advocates of cultural and juridic nationalism condoned the alienation of natural resources and the granting of long-term concessions of a monopolistic nature to foreigners as the price of technological development. As long as private individuals supplied the driving force and the concept remained abstract, nationalism was largely devoid of political appeal because of the narrow audience reached.

* Economic nationalism commanded only sporadic attention at that stage.

In Uruguay and Mexico between 1910 and 1920 and in Argentina, Brazil, and Chile in the 1930's the State replaced the intellectual as the chief propagandist for nationalism. Under the sponsorship of the State two outstanding current characteristics of nationalism soon manifested themselves. Its economic aspect was given greater stress than its cultural and juridic aspects. No longer confined to the abstractions of a few intellectuals it was brought down to the masses in its dynamic and politically charged form.

5. *State intervention.* Statism and middle sector political leadership have become closely linked. The middle sectors early in their bid for political recognition rejected the laissez-faire doctrines of the nineteenth century. As a substitute they offered planned societies. When their recommendations were popularized, the middle sectors rode to new political heights.

Social welfare and industrialization have been the first concerns of the state interventionists. Under the sponsorship of the middle groups the states by 1940 had taken over many of the responsibilities for the welfare of the distressed elements formerly delegated to private and semipublic institutions. The duties of the State in providing educational facilities, medical care, food, and housing for the working groups were written in minute detail into the laws of several of the republics. Also, "in fulfillment of the State's social functions" the governments of Argentina, Brazil, and Mexico took over the direction of the labor movement. As a result the laborer was encouraged to view any benefits he received as coming from the State and to conclude that his well-being and that of his fellow workers lay in political action rather than in direct negotiations with management. With their welfare written into law, laborers ordinarily have preferred to ally themselves with the groups in power, reasoning that only through support of those who administer the laws could they hope to attain what by law is theirs.

State intervention in the economic sphere has been justified on the basis of three socioeconomic tenets upheld by the middle sectors: (1) Industry cannot survive without protection from outside competition, and only the State can provide this protection. (2) Since the accrual of domestic private capital is slow, the State, with its ability to accumulate capital relatively rapidly through taxation and foreign loans, must intercede in the industrial sphere in order to maintain the highest possible rate of development, at the same time that it reduces the share of private foreign capital in the economy. (3) Solicitude for the working groups requires that the State exercise some control over prices of necessaries.

6. *Political parties.* After World War I, important elements within the urban middle sectors began to substitute the organized political party for the family as the focus of political thinking. When this transformation is completed, a whole era—politic, social, and economic—will have passed.

For over three centuries after the initial phase of the conquest ended and the stabilization of the social order began (about 1580), the family—or, more properly speaking, the extended family, kin group, or clan—was traditionally a social, economic, and political institution. The status of each member within the family and his relationship to every other member were rigidly defined. After winning independence (1810–1825), the patriarchal heads of families often became political bosses wielding control over sprawling domains. Political leadership ordinarily passed from father to eldest son.

But the family as a political entity probably never operated as effectively in the cities as it did in the country. In this century it has been progressively less successful as new social and economic forces have undermined the interdependence of the members. The mobility offered by modern means of transportation has encouraged the younger generation to make associations outside the family. Cinemas, clubs, public parks and beaches, and social activities sponsored by the schools increasingly compete with the family for the leisure time of its members. Women have won new freedoms and have taken on new obligations. In ever growing numbers they leave the home to engage in education, business, and the professions, and return with the information that permits them to reach political decisions independently of the male members of the household.

The appearance of large and impersonal businesses has tended to reduce the role of the head of the family in finding employment for the various members of his immediate and extended family. The large corporate enterprises, which are becoming ever more common and which often offer the greatest opportunities for advancement, are inclined to consider individual qualifications more than family credentials. A similar condition is developing in government, which also has become more impersonal as it has become more complex. In the process, nepotism has gradually given ground to civil service systems and professional bureaucracies. The independence which has come with obtaining and holding positions on the basis of merit has helped to sunder allegiances to the family as a political unit. There has been a strong tendency to transfer allegiances to political parties, which provide a common ground for those who have similar objectives based on educational and occupational interests and on social relationships outside the home.

During the decades that the middle sectors have shared power or controlled political decisions in the five republics, the influence of their several components has fluctuated significantly. The pattern of these shifts of relative influence emerges most clearly when the political trends of the five republics are viewed in the long range. Viewed episodically, the trends dissolve into mere political maneuverings in search of short-range solutions, and the main currents of middle sector thinking lose their distinct outlines.

Until World War I, the members of the liberal professions constituted a numerically large segment of the middle sectors in each of the republics. As a group they were learned, and learning conferred considerable prestige. They held a near-monopoly on the formulation of political theory, and, to the extent that the middle sectors participated in practical politics, they were the most active component as well. In recent decades, the influence of the professions on middle sector thought has declined, partly as a result of their loss of relative numerical importance, partly because of their very success: indeed, as the middle sectors as a whole gained in political stature, the rewards of practical politics increased and groups other than the liberal professions began to compete for them.

The role of the Catholic clergy in politics has also been in a general decline in recent decades. This would seem to be true despite the evident part that the Catholic Church played in the overthrow of Juan Domingo Perón in Argentina in 1955, of Gustavo Rojas Pinilla in Colombia in 1957 and of Marcos Pérez Jiménez in Venezuela in 1958. The decline has been more the result of the changing functions of the clergy than of its composition.

The middle sectors continue as always to provide an important part of the Catholic clergy. But the place of the Church in society has been modified and in the process its activities have been circumscribed. This development has been particularly apparent in the urban centers. The urban elements are less inclined than formerly to look to the Church for leadership in those "extra-spiritual" areas on which it traditionally depended for much of its prestige and influence. The State has taken over many of the welfare functions previously performed by the Church. Public elementary, secondary schools, and institutions of higher learning have reduced its share in the field of education. It has lost its semimonopoly on learning in the smaller cities and towns as persons educated and professionally trained at secular institutions have filtered outside the centers of heaviest population. Mass communications have also lessened the dependence upon the clergy outside the large cities. To a considerable degree the popular groups have substituted the motion picture, radio and television, public recreation, and the diversions offered by the labor unions for the holy days and feast days that for four centuries were the accepted source of release from the humdrum activities of everyday life.

As the Church's temporal responsibilities have been circumscribed, the ministering to the spiritual needs of the people has taken up a larger share of its activity, and the opportunities have been reduced for the clergyman to be an individual personality dispensing personal ideas and expressing personal convictions on nonspiritual issues. Consequently clergymen normally are not today politically influential in any of the five republics except inasmuch as they reflect the thoughts of the Church hierarchy, whose thinking may or may not conform to that of the politically dominant segments within the middle sectors. When the political policies of the hierarchy are acceptable to the middle sectors, as they appear to be more and more often, they are disseminated more by Catholic lay organizations than by the clergy.

While the influence of the professional groups and the clergy declined, teachers acquired added political prestige with the public recognition of the importance of universal education. Where schools have been used for the propagation of political ideologies among the masses, the teachers have become essential parts of the political machinery. In recent years, as elementary school teachers have become better trained, they have been accorded middle sector standing in growing numbers. Teaching staffs in high schools and institutions of higher learning—groups traditionally included in the middle sectors—have expanded.

The bureaucrats too have proliferated and their influence has grown accordingly. As the responsibilities of government expanded, the bureaucrats carried out new functions and assumed many of those previously performed by privite citizens.

Given the great number of imponderables involved, it would perhaps be impossible to establish whether the political influence of the officer corps has increased or decreased since World War I. There is some indication that the proportion of officers engaging in politics has declined in recent decades. In the author's opinion, however, there is no doubt that at least since 1930 the social and economic orientation of the politically active officers has been away from that of the old ruling groups and toward that of the civilian middle sectors. The new position of the officers stems primarily from three circumstances: (1) The various branches of the military have become more professionalized and, consequently, less attractive to the old elite groups. But since they continue to offer security at reasonably high salaries, they open up opportunities to men from the middle sectors. (2) As the civilian middle sectors have improved their political status vis-à-vis the elites, military officers have inclined to retain their social contacts with the middle sectors rather than to associate with the elites, as they did in the past. (3) The economic policies of the middle sectors, emphasizing industrialization, conform to those held by the armed forces. Under the widening impact of nationalism, both the civilian and the military elements have tended increasingly to equate industrial growth with national progress. Officers, thanks to their training in organization, have found employment as directors of State-controlled economic enterprises, and the armed forces look forward to domestic production of war matériel. Thus, despite differences in their approach to politics, the military and the civilian components of the middle sectors tend to agree on their broad social and economic objectives.

The swift rise of the commercial and industrial segments has profoundly affected the composition of the middle groups since the end of World War I. The acceptance of industrialization as national policy in each of the republics made the owners of industrial and commercial enterprises a highly effective force both as a constructive and as a veto group. Commercial and industrial leaders today exercise the most powerful influence on middle sector politics. The scientists, technicians, and managers, benefiting as they do from industrial development, have in general identified themselves politically with their employers. The growing role of the industrial and commercial leaders as decision-makers on the national level is a major theme of this study.

So seemingly spontaneous was the political emergence of the middle sectors after 1920 that one is inclined, however momentarily, to disregard the nineteenth-century antecedents of the development. To do so would leave untold vital chapters in the political metamorphosis of these groups, for the foundations from which they sprang into the spotlight after World War I were firmly embedded in the past century. The following two chapters establish those nineteenth-century experiences of the middle sectors which help most to explain their political, social, and economic conduct in this century.

2 *Revolution and Reaction*

1810 TO 1850

The first half of the nineteenth century was a period of remarkable achievement followed by social and economic paralysis and political frustration for the middle sectors. At the beginning of the century intellectuals took the lead in shaping the forces that had set in motion the struggles that eventually emancipated the colonials from the tutelage of Spain and Portugal. Thereafter, during nearly a generation of often bitter warfare in the Spanish colonies, spokesmen from the middle groups articulated the philosophical and juridical justifications for rebellion against legitimacy and the crown and in favor of independence. Once independence was obtained and in some instances before, the middle groups were everywhere forced to surrender leadership to elites composed of the landed aristocracy, the hierarchy of the Catholic Church, and the officer corps of the armed forces. Politically, elite rule, which went unchallenged until the 1850's, was highly personal; economically, it was strongly oriented toward agriculture. The resulting political and economic atmosphere was stifling to the middle groups.

The representatives of the middle sectors who gave political direction to the revolutions were students of the Enlightenment. A few were self-taught. Some were trained in colonial universities. Others had received their instruction in Europe. As students of the Enlightenment, reacting violently against the suppression of personal liberties under the authoritarianism of the mother countries and the Church, they proposed to create an independent Ibero-America in which reason would rule from the throne long occupied by authority and tradition.

The intellectuals had little more than a theoretical understanding of what they proposed to achieve. They had been so effectively excluded from participation in government by Spain and Portugal, in collaboration with the Catholic Church, that nearly all their knowledge of the art of government and politics was academic. Consequently, in their new position of power their actions were determined more often by ideological convictions than by political experience. From the French Revolution and the independence movement of the thirteen English colonies they sought formulas to fit local circumstances. They called conventions. They elected representatives. They wrote abstract systems of laws based upon natural law. They amended those laws and they repealed them. They dissolved governments. They created new governments. In their enthusiasm for personal liberty they exhibited an attraction for words and phrases that bespoke a rationality which they identified with freedom.

The theories of the intellectual leaders soon had to face reality. War might destroy in the colonies the visible power of the mother countries; war could not destroy their invisible power. War might cast off the foreign yoke; it could not cast off the domestic yoke. War might emancipate the body; it could not liberate the mind. The heavy burden of prejudices and customs, of a colonial mentality, and of latent social disorganization that the colonials took with them into battle could not be relieved overnight. Monopoly, restrictions, and privilege remained. Different civilizations and stages of culture continued to co-exist. The lower groups were a "melancholy sea of illiterates." They had no sense of their stake in progress and good government. Only the cultured elements had any real and permanent standards and traditions, and they were blind to the possible evils that those standards and traditions might bring to societies suddenly left to their own resources after being held together for centuries by distant European governments. Nearly every member of every privileged group wished law to be enforced but he wished no less that an exception should be made in his own individual case.

Because the constitution-makers and politicians failed to harmonize theory and practice, and the responsible elements of society refused to couple liberty with law, anarchy arose. Before independence was everywhere secure, anguished cries were raised against the disorder of liberal idealism. Voices of reaction demanded a return to the orderliness and stability of the colonial era. Thus was drawn one of the basic issues around which political warfare swirled for nearly a century. One side contended that liberty—with its corollary, the narrow delimitation of executive power and the rights of the individual—was all important. The other side held that efficient administration and the stability of the State—even if these required the exaltation of executive power—should be the paramount political objectives. One group preferred disintegration to tyranny, the other tyranny to disintegration.* The intensity of the contest generated such political instability that on the occasions when representatives of "Liberty" did attain power their leaders were often forced to disregard democratic forms. It was as if liberty had been invoked in order to impose tyranny.

By the time independence had been achieved those who placed a higher value on public order than on individual liberty had asserted their political hegemony. Within two decades the colonials had made a full political circle. Starting with the concrete authoritarianism of Spain and Portugal and the Catholic Church they had passed to abstract liberalism, only to return to authoritarianism. The difference was that by 1825 authoritarians born in America had replaced those sent from Spain and Portugal; except in Brazil, which remained an empire until 1889, authoritarianism was wielded in the name of republicanism.

Authoritarian rule soon stripped the middle sectors of the advantages that the chaos of war had afforded them. Nowhere did they feel the return to authoritarianism more than in the political area.

In order to neutralize the politically unpredictable—and

* Lionel Cecil Jane, *Liberty and Despotism in Spanish America* (London, 1929), p. 16.

therefore dangerous—urban middle sectors, the elites had recourse to the military, which had been nurtured to maturity during the wars of independence. The victory of the elites thus was one of violence. As success through violence engendered more violence, the general replaced the scholar. Armies became the final arbiters of political matters—sometimes at the urgings of civilians, sometimes on the initiative of ambitious officers who frequently were politicians dressed in military uniforms. Revolution thus bred revolutions throughout Latin America. In turn, providing opportunities for steady promotions for officers and meeting military payrolls became prominent political requirements.*

Elevating force to a political fundamental was particularly costly to the middle sectors, who had almost no rapport with the leadership of the armed forces. Military intervention in civilian matters—i.e., the substitution of government by decree for government by law—violated the republican precepts of middle sector ideology. Military government also meant substituting force for reason, for, like the landed aristocracy and the elite of the Church, the Army officers, who either were from the landed elites or had associated themselves with them, were quick to oppose the least stirrings of the politically undependable social groups.

In a political climate of force, all that remained of representative government were its outward manifestations. The juridic concept of representative democracy was not repudiated but it was ignored. Facts prevailed against the constitutions—sometimes against their letter, usually against their spirit.†

---

* The unceasing pressure upon governmental officials to keep ambitious military officers satisfied is graphically illustrated by Jorge Basadre, a leading contemporary Peruvian historian. Writing of his own country as it was a century ago he observes that "Article 147 of the constitution of 1839 states that there shall be no more than one grand marshal, three generals of the divisions and six brigadier generals. . . . Article 121 of the constitution of 1856 states that there shall be no more than two generals of divisions and four brigadier generals. . . . Nevertheless in 1859 the Army Register showed six grand marshals, six generals of the division and twenty-two brigadier generals." Basadre, *La iniciación de la república* (Lima, 1929) pp. 94–95.

† James Bryce, *South America* (London, 1926), p. 539.

Only a limited and insecure place for the democratic electoral process remained. Bullets replaced ballots. Issues were settled by breaking heads rather than by counting them. Those who achieved power tended to monopolize it, and their monopoly could in practice be ended only by the bloody remedy of revolution.

The party system, upon which the middle sectors have relied so heavily in recent decades, fared poorly in the quarter century after 1825.* Political leaders were often caudillos, the "violent men of destiny" who aspired to the place left by the *conquistadores.* They broke all the bonds of national and social order. Their individualism could not be constrained by a political party based on ideologies. They spoke directly for intriguers and adventurers, not for groups as impersonal as an organized political party. There was no campaigning and there was little speech-writing for a party organization to direct. Electoral platforms were prepared to satisfy a formality and not a necessity. In the words of the Argentine sociologist, Carlos Bunge, the caudillos were "rulers by the will of men without will." To have depended upon a political party would have implied the sharing of power with men of some will. The caudillos, therefore, made the parties, the parties did not make them. Party leaders were selected by the caudillo and were personally responsible to him. Their fortunes rested upon his success.

The development of a party system also suffered from the fact that in the political order laid down by the elites the executive power tended to be the only power in government. The legislative and judicial branches, in which the middle sectors might have served as representatives of the caudillos, were rubber stamps for the president. The members were little more than agents who wrote decrees and judicial rulings and gave a certain subtlety to the rude intentions of political chieftains. Parliamentary debate was the privilege of the agents of the chief executive. The voice of the opposition was not supposed to be heard. Opposition parties thus had little incentive to exist

---

* Only in Chile prior to 1850 was party machinery ordinarily instrumental in the choice of high public officials.

since there were no public forums where they might keep their ideas before the voters.

The middle sectors were unable to take advantage of the differences that arose among the ruling elements. The elites were agreed on the major economic issues. The Church was encouraged to continue as the interpreter of the social value system. Consequently, the issues that drove the elites into different camps were essentially political ones: centralism *vs.* federalism; executive *vs.* legislative and judicial power; civilian control *vs.* militarism; the relationship of Church and State. The disputes over those issues often led to political disorderliness and to fratricidal wars that left material devastation and moral degradation in their wake. The disputes were, however, of such a nature that the contending groups could fight for political advantage without involving the great mass of the population, except as it served their purposes. Hence, the struggles never created a power vacuum into which the lower or middle sectors of society could rush. Also, once the issues were defined, all other differences receded into insignificance, with the result that little room was left for new parties to prosper.

The political victory of the elites over the middle sectors by 1825 also portended an economic victory for the countryside over the cities, which during the wars of independence had experienced an upsurge of commercial activities. At the same time that the political concepts and tactics of the elites spelled a political eclipse for the middle sectors, the rural emphasis in the economic area forestalled the commercial and industrial development of the cities where the influence of these groups was most pronounced. Just as the elite domination reflected past experiences, so the agrarian emphasis projected colonial economy.

Throughout the eighteenth century the tendency was for agriculture to improve its position in the economy in relation to mining. Mineral production at no time figured prominently in Argentina and Uruguay. In Brazil mineral production reached great heights between 1690 and 1765 but declined rapidly thereafter, and agriculture clearly reasserted itself during the half-century preceding independence from Portugal. Chile, although its mining output rose during the eighteenth century, remained overwhelmingly an agricultural colony and in the last years of the century land values rose rapidly. Even in Mexico, where mining production expanded steadily throughout the eighteenth century, the total income from agriculture at the end of the colonial period exceeded that from mining by 25 to 50 per cent annually.

Independence did not alter the trend. Indeed, it underscored and encouraged it. Many mines suffered from neglect during the war years, and the political instability that accompanied independence discouraged foreign investment in the extractive industries. Agriculture and cattle breeding in four of the five republics—Mexico was the exception—had to carry the burdens of keeping the new governments afloat and of earning the foreign exchange required for purchases abroad. Thus any growth of international trade tended further to accentuate the importance of land. Besides these reasons for a rural emphasis in the economic policies of the republics there were others of major consequence. Land withstood the ravages of civil war and was thus an attractive investment in an era of tumult. Also, it offered a hedge against the cheap-money policies that the new republics in general pursued. Land had the mark of permanence and made its owners symbols of stability in societies that in some respects verged on the chaotic.

The two cornerstones of agriculture were the latifundia system and exemption from land taxes. Both served to discourage the development of middle sectors. The latifundia system of large holdings extensively worked was introduced into Spanish and Portuguese America in the sixteenth century and was given new significance by the elite leadership of the young republics. Great acreages, which the states inherited from the Spanish and Portuguese crowns, now passed into the hands of a favored few. At the same time the Catholic Church, the greatest landholder of all, not only successfully met every effort to destroy its temporal power by divesting it of its land but actually added to its holdings throughout the period to 1850. The latifundia owners and the Church meanwhile used their political influence to see that tax policies did not provide for direct imposts upon land.

Freed from direct taxation, land could be left idle while being held for investment purposes. Thus while the latifundia system kept land out of the hands of the potential middle sector farmer, the tax structure invited long-range investment in rural properties rather than in urban enterprises, which would have given vitality to the urban economic middle sectors.

Cities played a distinctly secondary role in the economic system maintained by the elites. The rural estates were largely self-sufficient. They provided nearly everything required by the laborers in the way of food—including alcoholic beverages —shelter, and clothing. The demands of the owners for consumer and luxury items were simple. When they did buy commercially produced goods, however, they preferred articles produced abroad, often because of the prestige of imported goods, thus further reducing the opportunities for domestic industries to take root, other than a few devoted to the processing of agricultural products.

The coastal ports linked the interiors to markets across the seas. International trade gave rise to a few commercial houses in the major coastal cities, but, despite the importance of foreign markets to the new republics, the actual exchange of goods was small prior to 1850, and such trade was usually carried on by foreigners rather than nationals.

Nationalism, to which the middle sectors appealed successfully in later periods, had but a small place in the political milieu between 1825 and 1850. There were efforts such as Chile's to build a merchant marine through various preference arrangements and to reserve a place in the commercial community for nationals. Caudillos, such as Juan Manuel de Rosas in Argentina and Antonio López de Santa Anna in Mexico, often manufactured threats to the national sovereignty from foreign powers in order to distract attention from unfavorable developments at home. But these manifestations were sporadic. Nowhere was there what might be called a sustained nationalism as part of a national policy.

The forces that had shaped the early destiny of the republics were basically antinationalistic. The religion of the people theoretically transcended all political and geographical barriers. Their education stressed humanism and sought universal types. The republics did not have long and illustrious military backgrounds which could be used to arouse pride in common accomplishments. Nor did they have hereditary enemies on their borders against which hatred could be focused.* Unlike Germany, for example, where race consciousness contributed strongly to the growth of nationalism, race was little used by the leadership of the five republics to exploit a prejudice for personal or group advantage. At no time was there the cry, heard in Italy in the time of Mazzini and in France under Napoleon III, that political and ethnological boundaries be made to correspond. On the contrary, the intellectuals in speaking of cultural unity employed such antinationalistic terms as the paradoxical "continental nationalism."

Too, the allegiances of the leaders obstructed the growth of nationalism. From their European ancestors the makers of national decisions had inherited a deeply emotional involvement in their towns and provinces rather than in the State, to them a remote and impersonal thing. The implications of this inheritance were accentuated by geographical conditions and undeveloped communications systems, that discouraged the exchange of ideas even within the individual states. Thus Argentina for a half-century struggled to find a basis for nationhood while the interior provinces fought Buenos Aires for local honor and pride as well as economic advantage. During the 1825–50 period Brazil experienced provincial flareups that threatened the unity of the empire. In Mexico the common man outside his *patria chica* (little homeland) was a stranger in a puzzling world, and the leaders of the province of Yucatán in the 1830's and again in the 1840's explored the possibilities of secession from Mexico and union with the United States.

In this system in which the elites reserved to themselves decisive power and assumed exclusive responsibility for basic

* There are those who would consider the United States a hereditary enemy of Mexico, and the Dominicans have traditionally looked upon Haiti as a menace to their national culture.

decisions, the middle sectors nevertheless had roles to play and tasks to perform. They were teachers and bureaucrats, lawyers, notaries, newspaper men, publishers, and artists. These functions tended to identify them with the elites and to dissociate them from the laboring groups. This meant that the middle sectors had little contact with or understanding of the workingmen upon whom any broadened political base would have to depend.

Either as civilian instructors or as teachers of religious orders an influential segment of the middle sectors was associated with the elites through the schools. Education was reserved for the very select few from middle and upper sector homes from which it was expected the future leaders would be drawn. By 1842, in an estimated population of one million, Chile—the acknowledged educational leader in Latin America —had only twelve thousand matriculated students in primary and secondary schools of all types. However, the very selectiveness of the system made every pupil a potential champion of the existing order or a possible leader shaping new social, economic, and political ideas.*

The middle sectors coveted the bureaucratic posts. Those who received appointments became in effect the employees of the elite elements by and for whom the governments were run. Positions in government were not plentiful, because the elites believed that the least government was the best government. To them the closer the State came to limiting itself strictly to the protection of private property and individual rights by maintaining internal order and successfully carrying on relations with foreign powers the better. Once organized, governments so narrowly conceived could operate with a limited personnel to carry out the routine functions, leaving the middle groups slight opportunity to influence the development of society. Although nepotism and favoritism flourished, govern-

* It should be noted that many young men from "better" homes received much of their academic training in Europe, particularly in France, where they were often introduced to more revolutionary thought than they would have received at home.

ment positions carried some prestige,* and in a society in which salaried positions were at a premium for those with academic skills paid relatively high salaries. With a steady income, the writer, sculptor, or musician could indulge his artistic preferences. In the scramble to obtain and to retain their positions, the bureaucrats became acutely sensitive to changes on the political horizons, and once they spotted a rising political personality, many of them unhesitatingly rushed to associate themselves with him. This lack of strong ideological attachments made it possible for the average bureaucrat to transfer his allegiance from one side to another, and helps to account for the speed with which those who seized power were able to consolidate their positions.

The other skills and services of the middle sectors cemented the relationship with the elites that education and government had established. Lawyers, notaries, and doctors sold their services to them because they were the only ones of any wealth. Within their ranks were an important share of those who had the means to buy books and journals and were sufficiently literate to read them. Newspaper advertisements were directed to them since they for the most part constituted the buying public. Elite-controlled governments commonly subsidized newspapers, and official notices appearing in newspapers were a

---

* An example of the extremes to which nepotism was at times carried is related in a letter of May 16, 1885, from Peru written by S. L. Phelps to Secretary of State Thomas Bayard. "The ministry of government made vacant some time since by the resignation of Aliago being now filled by the appointment of Joaquín Iglesias, a brother of the President, who is made chief of the cabinet, and therefore successor to the presidency in case of accident to the President. The President, Vice President, and the General in Chief of the Army are three brothers." See, *Foreign Relations of the United States 1885,* pp. 599–600. The Mexican despot, Porfirio Díaz, came near to outdoing all contemporaries, if he did not actually do so, in passing out public offices to his cronies and friends. The accounts of his placing army associates in high office are legion. Not so well known but good evidence of the extent to which favoritism in Mexico was carried during the Díaz regime is the fact that in 1886, of the 227 deputies in the national House of Representatives, 72 were from Díaz' home state of Oaxaca. See Francisco Bulnes, *El verdadero Díaz y la revolución,* (Mexico, 1920), pp. 181–82.

primary source of income to the publishers. Because there was almost no market for secular painting, artists without private incomes were forced to seek patronage of the elite elements or to turn out conventional religious art that could be sold to the churches or to "rich and devout ladies."

Had the elites been able to maintain their rigid social order, the middle sectors would have remained relegated to their secondary role. Their numbers would not have increased in proportion to the other sectors of society. Their resources would have remained fixed. Their functions would not have permitted the free play of imagination that later gave them political advantage. They would have had no one to turn to because the people of color, debased and obedient to the point of servility, vegetated on the outskirts of national life as cultural hybrids, economic nonentities, and political ciphers.

But the elites were unable to maintain the degree of rigidity they sought. They had come to power as the result of changes they could not forestall. The leavening that produced the change arrived from Europe and the United States. Liberty, equality, fraternity, reason, and representative, constitutional government were the catchwords. The flow of ideas came in ever increasing quantities after the hold of Spain and Portugal was relaxed. France became a cultural prop, Great Britain an economic prop, and Great Britain and the United States political props, at a time when the people of those countries were undergoing major transformations. New ideas and old ones clothed in new terms from north Europe and the United States struck the inchoate Latin American states with an impact not entirely evident until the latter part of the century. Meanwhile, as a degree of orderliness supplanted anarchy first in Chile in the 1840's, then in Brazil in the 1850's, and later in Argentina, Mexico, and Uruguay, the republics attracted foreigners and foreign capital. The combination of new ideas, new blood, and new capital from abroad set in motion a pattern of development that began slowly, and then rapidly enhanced the political position of the middle sectors.

3 *The Politics of Progress*

1850 TO 1915

At mid-century Argentina, Brazil, Chile, Mexico, and Uruguay were approaching crossroads on their way to becoming modern states. For a quarter of a century the conviction had persisted that the problems raised by independence could be resolved if only workable political systems were developed. Vast quantities of physical and mental effort had been thrown into the search for political solutions. Huge amounts of property had been destroyed as groups uncompromisingly supported either arbitrary or rational politics as the quickest means of attaining human liberties through constitutionalism, which all responsible elements acknowledged to be the ultimate goal. But regardless of the victors, the states seemed constantly to teeter dangerously on the brink of disaster.

Little by little, those responsible realized that achieving political objectives depended upon developing other areas of national life. The day and age dictated that the answer would be found in the economic sphere, for the leading powers of the world were those most advanced commercially and industrially. Within a short time in the Latin American nations, economic solutions were elevated above political ones as offering the panacea for the ills confronting and confounding them. Economic development became an obsession. It dominated the era from 1850 to World War I as completely as political development had dominated the antecedent period.

With national policies geared to economic progress, the achievements of the 1850–1915 period were spectacular, given the burden of economic retardation the republics had inherited from the colonial era. Enormous acreages were put to the plow for the first time in Argentina, Brazil, and Uruguay. In Argentina, for example, land under cultivation increased from 373 square miles in 1865 to 95,000 square miles in 1915, and from one-eighth of an acre per capita to seven and seven-tenths acres. The republic was transformed from a net importer of cereals into one of the world's great bread baskets. The State of São Paulo, Brazil, became an agricultural giant with the greatest concentration of coffee trees to be found anywhere in the world. In 1909 alone, São Paulo exported seventeen million bags, or approximately one million tons, of coffee.

Transportation and communications were pushed with vigor. National governments subsidized foreign and domestically controlled steamship lines in order to give the republics more adequate contacts with Europe and the United States. Before the end of the century hundreds of vessels flying English, French, Italian, German, and United States flags were assigned to Latin American routes. Argentina and Brazil were the principal attractions. They were the leading traders of the area as well as the goals of a great majority of the immigrant passengers. Chile developed a respectable merchant fleet of its own. River boats and ocean liners plied the Amazon and Plata river systems. Old ports were renovated and new ones were constructed.

The lack of railroads was a primary concern of public officials. The first public carrier lines were completed by the 1850's. By 1915 the five republics were served by about 60,000 miles of lines. Argentina had approximately 22,000 miles of track, most of it traversing the rich and rapidly developing pampas. Uruguay was well served by 1,600 miles of line, as was Chile with 5,000 miles. Mexico and Brazil each had approximately 16,000 miles of track in operation.

Thousands of miles of telegraph lines were strung between the major cities. A cable was laid between Brazil and Portugal in the early 1870's. By 1875 London quotations on minerals and foreign currencies were being received daily by the Commercial Exchange of Valparaiso via the cable and the Trans-Andean Telegraph. A combination submarine-and-terrestrial system gave the United States contact with Brazil, Uruguay, and Argentina by way of Chile, the West Coast of South America, the Isthmus of Tehuantepec, the Caribbean, and Brownsville, Texas.

The principal cities were modernized. Gas began to replace whale oil for public lighting in the 1850's, and in the 1890's electricity in turn began to supplant gas. Water and sewer systems were laid. Public transportation was launched in many cities. At first, horse-drawn coaches were employed. By the late 1850's they were being replaced by horse-drawn streetcars. By the turn of the century electric trolleys began to appear in the more important centers. Before 1910 Buenos Aires had in operation an excellent cross-town subway, which still provides the best public municipal transportation in all Latin America if not in the Hemisphere.

Mining was revived. Gold production increased in Brazil after being in the doldrums for the better part of a century. Chile's nitrate fields seized from Bolivia and Peru were made into a major national asset. Mexico increased its ore processing and began to produce industrial minerals on a large scale. By 1910 its coal production had attained peaks not again reached prior to 1940. Mexico became the world's third largest producer of petroleum by 1911 and was exporting crude at the annual rate of 25,000,000 barrels before World War I.

New manufacturing industries were introduced and old ones were expanded and modernized. By World War I the republics had become nearly self-sufficient in the production of coarse textiles. The shoe industry grew significantly in Argentina and Brazil. As early as 1850 Chile had raised wheat flour production to a point where it was exporting to California and Australia, where miners were placing heavy strains on the available food supplies. Meat processing became big business in Argentina and Uruguay before World War I. In Brazil and Argentina, chemical and drug industries were initiated. Manufacturing was clearly on its way out of the home and into the factory. Power and fuel, however, were in chronic short supply then as they are today in each of the five republics.

Banking and finance became a major and vital sector of the

economies. The shift from subsistence farming to commercial agriculture and scientific livestock breeding often required capital in amounts beyond the capacity of the landowners to raise, except through banks. Landowners confident of their future prosperity borrowed against expected sales in order to build city dwellings and to send their families to Europe. This was the era in which absentee landlordism became prevalent in Argentina, Brazil, Chile, and Uruguay. Banks were deeply involved in the promotion of international trade. They made short-term loans that were often essential to founding commercial and industrial operations. Insurance companies chartered in a half-dozen or more foreign countries were engaged in their phase of the economy before the end of the century.

Economic development could not have taken place at the rate it did without large-scale assistance from the outside. Domestic investment capital was not available in quantity. Those with funds to invest favored farms over factories. Technical skills were at a premium. Only Chile and Mexico had efficient unskilled labor in sufficient quantities to meet the demands imposed by expanding economic activities. Foreigners willingly filled many of the gaps in the economic structure. Capital poured into the republics, mainly from Great Britain, but considerable amounts entered from France and Germany. During the last quarter of the century the United States began to invest heavily in Mexican minerals and railroads. Canadian capital found its way to Mexico and Brazil before World War I. Engineers and technicians by the hundreds, mainly from Great Britain and the United States, followed foreign capital into the republics. They filled a huge void at a time when the humanistic studies held sway in the academic world and studies in the physical or natural sciences were widely viewed as signs of intellectual mediocrity.

What had been only a trickle of immigrants in the 1850's became a torrent by the end of the century. The deluge continued until the outbreak of World War I. Argentina, the principal recipient, with a total population of 1,200,000 in 1852, had a net immigration of over 2,600,000 by 1914, the vast majority from Italy and Spain. A census of that year showed the

Argentine population to be 30 per cent foreign born. Large numbers went to Brazil from Southern Europe following the abolition of slavery in 1888 and the fall of the Empire in 1889. Over 200,000 immigrants entered the republic in 1891 ; 167,000 in 1895; and 190,000 in 1913. While tens and hundreds of thousands of immigrants were finding their way to Argentina and Brazil, thousands were being received by Chile and Urugray. In Uruguay, with a population of less than 150,000 in 1852, however, the impact was no less significant than in Argentina and Brazil. Mexico with a reasonably adequate labor supply and a primitive agricultural system was not attractive to the immigrant laborer or farmer.

The immigrants generally came with the intention of making their homes in the rural areas. Many thousands actually realized their expectations. The Argentine pampas were filling with them. The lake region of Chile was opened by German immigrants who began arriving in the late 1840's. In Brazil the state of Rio Grande do Sul owed its development to Germans and Italians. The terms of employment and tenancy offered by the landholders, however, often proved unsatisfactory, and the immigrant was far less inclined than were the Indians and mestizos to accept them. Literally thousands of the discontented newcomers made their way to the cities where foreign capital and foreign technicians were having their greatest effect upon the republics.

This economic transformation played into the hands of the urban middle groups. They gained a greater voice in public affairs and their values gained wider acceptance as the republics sought first to satisfy the requirements for and then to derive the greatest benefits from economic progress. As new elements within and without the middle groups asserted themselves, the middle sectors' political maneuverability was substantially broadened.

The most important development within the middle groups themselves was the rapid addition of the commercial and industrial elements. Although certain phases of commerce and industry were nearly pre-empted by foreigners, there was room for nationals to share directly in their growth. Domestically owned factories sprang up, sometimes as individual ventures, sometimes as partnership or family-owned operations. The domestically owned corporation was, however, almost nonexistent prior to the 1920's. Nationals were conspicuous in banking and international trade, which expanded significantly as exports rose 235 per cent and imports 95 per cent in the era between 1897 and 1915. Mexico's total foreign trade increased from fifty million pesos in 1872 to almost five hundred million in 1910. Nationals controlled an important share of the wholesale and retail trade, which grew appreciably in response to the demands of the parvenus for semidurables and luxury goods and of the hard-pressed emergent industrial laboring elements of the cities for the necessities. Also, foreign concerns, although they often brought top personnel with them, offered employment for nationals at some levels which appealed to those who depended upon their academic skills for a livelihood. Thus bureaucrats in industry and commerce took their place beside the bureaucrats in government.

In addition to giving the middle sectors greater numerical strength, the commercial and industrial segments added new and dynamic economic interests to the essentially political and philosophical interests of those members whose approach was basically intellectual. They gave the middle segments a more direct and more vital stake in the wealth and income of the republics. As representatives of the "new" economic thinking, and with the weight of public opinion behind them, the middle elements of commerce and industry were in a position to wield considerable influence upon national policy.

Education for the masses, which the middle sectors traditionally have supported as requisite for cultural and political maturity, received strong impetus from the emphasis upon economic development. Education ceased to be a luxury and became a necessity when commerce and industry flagged for want of trained personnel. Once it was accepted as a necessity, it increasingly became a public responsibility. Public elementary and secondary education complemented rather than supplanted private education. This was largely owing to the general quality of public elementary and secondary education, which remained below that of private education. Consequently, something of a caste system grew up. Those with limited financial resources ordinarily enrolled in public schools. Those with greater wealth attended private institutions. The two groups, however, converged at the university level, where the offerings of the public institutions often surpassed in quality those of the private schools. There were even some notable exceptions in regard to the public secondary schools. In Chile many wealthy rural families sent their children to the provincial high schools (*colegios*) ; and for more than a century the Instituto Nacional, founded in 1813, was the training ground for a large body of outstanding citizens and public servants. In Brazil, the Colégio Pedro II, a public secondary school founded in 1837 in Rio de Janeiro, attracted students from the most influential families.

Prior to World War I Argentina, Chile, and Uruguay had made serious efforts to create a more alert and responsible citizenry through public education. Under schoolteacher-President Domingo Faustino Sarmiento and his successor in the executive chair, Nicolás Avellaneda, public education in Argentina attained the position of leadership in Latin America which it has never relinquished. Argentine education at all levels advanced rapidly. The demands for trained personnel outran the supply, and immigrants insisted upon schools for their children. Matriculation in Argentine normal schools increased from less than 1,300 to over 7,200 between 1890 and 1912. Between 1890 and 1915 the enrollment in the national secondary schools rose from approximately 3,300 to 11,100. The student body of the University of Buenos Aires, unquestionably the outstanding educational institution in the republic at the time, grew from approximately 900 to 4,600 between 1890 and 1915. The enrollment in the public and private elementary schools rose from an estimated 300,000 to 780,000 between 1890 and 1912.

Chile failed to maintain the fast pace it had set during the 1840's but it still ranked along with Argentina in the prewar period as a leader in the field of public instruction. Matriculation in the public elementary schools jumped from 95,000 to

240,000 between 1891 and 1909. The enrollment in the public secondary schools grew from 5,000 in 1885 to 18,700 in 1910. University enrollment increased from 1,000 in 1886 to 2,400 in 1908.

The roots of Uruguay's good—some would say excellent—present educational system date back to the 1860's and to José Pedro Varela. Prior to that time the republic had been an educational wasteland where theories were spun and plans legislated but none was given a fair opportunity to be tested. In 1850, fewer than one per hundred inhabitants attended schools of any type. Varela was a friend of Sarmiento's, and, like him, studied educational methods abroad. He placed his emphasis upon elementary instruction and established the principle of free, obligatory, and secular control upon which Uruguayan education at all levels rests today.

While education was making noteworthy strides in Argentina, Chile, and Uruguay, it lagged in Brazil and regressed in Mexico. In Brazil, during the last years of the empire, slavery rather than education commanded the attention of the leadership. In the new and highly federalized republic, which emerged from the ruins of the empire, education was made primarily the responsibility of the states and municipalities. Only the coffee-producing areas and, to a lesser extent, the state of Rio Grande do Sul, where the foreign influence was strong, had both the revenue and the will to support reasonably adequate educational programs. To the extent that the coffee-controlled national government did participate in education, it tended to disburse funds in those states already possessing the greatest educational capabilities. In Mexico the dictator Porfirio Díaz and his *científico* advisers—believing in the preeminence of a narrow, scientifically trained elite assisted when necessary by foreign consultants—gave no more than token support to public education at any level.

Advances in education were reflected in the growth of the newspaper and publishing fields. As literacy filtered down to the working elements newspaper circulation grew. Foreign language newspapers were published to satisfy the needs of the immigrant groups. The demand for textbooks,* which stemmed from the expansion of public education, was likewise a boon to the publishing trade. The growth of the middle income groups enlarged the market for popular literary works.

During the years that the intellectuals were leading the drive for public support of education they were becoming increasingly concerned over the real meaning of the economic transformation in terms of national sovereignty, national culture, and national well-being. Their concern, however, was not sufficiently acute to lead to a coordinated group effort until World War I, when the collective effect of individuals working independently produced a considerably greater consciousness of nationality and raised nationalism in its various aspects to the point where it could be converted into a political ideology.

Juridic or political nationalism, which had been exploited on a limited scale by the caudillos, was kept alive throughout the prewar period and ended on a strong note. The search for mineral wealth in mountainous areas formerly regarded as no man's lands, coupled with the influx of immigrants, who at the time appeared to be creating population pressures, made the states conscious of their ill-defined boundaries. When internal conditions permitted, the republics, with an eye to the future and to satisfy a growing pride in the nation-state, pushed claims against their neighbors.

Chile took the lead. At peace with itself after the 1830's and enjoying an unusual degree of unity, it sought to extend its borders with Argentina, Bolivia, and Peru when those republics were suffering from internal dissension. The Tacna-Arica question which grew out of the War of the Pacific (1879–83) kept the nationalists in Chile and Peru on edge from the mid-1880's to the 1920's.

After Argentina attained stability in the 1880's it turned to its unsettled territorial disputes. It had resolved all major differences with its immediate neighbors by 1915, but then, as

* It is probably true that prior to World War I textbooks, other than those in history and geography, beyond the elementary level ordinarily continued to come from either Spain or France.

now, the Falkland Islands—held by Great Britain and claimed by Argentina—offered opportunities for periodic nationalistic outbursts.

A growing nationalism in the wake of the overthrow of the empire and accompanying the coffee boom drove Brazil to assert and, in general, to sustain claims to territories disputed with all its neighbors except Uruguay. Brazil's major territorial acquisition during the period was Acre, which comprises 152,589 square kilometers and was obtained from Bolivia at a time when that republic was unable to offer significant military opposition.

In Mexico there was a rising tide of indignation against the sale of national territory (as Santa Anna had done in the case of the Gadsden Purchase) and against the surrender of sovereignty over national territory (as Benito Juárez apparently had in mind in the late 1850's when he offered the United States control over a strip of land across the Isthmus of Tehuantepec in return for financial assistance in his struggle against the old order).

By the end of the century, as the republics succeeded to a large extent in establishing the principle of arbitration as a substitute for war in settling their territorial disputes, juridic nationalism momentarily lost much of its appeal. It was quickly revived, however, after the Spanish-American War, when the emergence of the United States as the unquestioned Colossus in the hemisphere posed a challenge to the sovereignty of the several states. The role of the United States in the independence of Panama, the Platt Amendment, Theodore Roosevelt's Big-Stick diplomacy, and the continued unilateral interpretation of the Monroe Doctrine provided more than sufficient ammunition to keep aroused those who feared for the sovereignty of their homelands.

Cultural nationalism was stimulated by the inpouring of foreigners, who appeared to threaten the foundations upon which society rested. The intellectuals found a number of developments which disturbed them. A few foresaw the danger of immigrants, notably Germans, isolating themselves and producing cultural cysts. Some—Sarmiento was probably the outstanding one—insisted that naturalization laws should be tightened to make the newcomers more conscious of the privileges and responsibilities that accompanied citizenship. Some cried out against the abuse and degradation of the national labor force by foreign managers and overseers who did not know and were not interested in learning local customs. A few intellectuals objected to the importation of highly paid foreign consultants in fields in which it was contended that nationals had sufficient competence. The Argentine Congress debated, without agreement, whether or not foreign professors lacking a true pride in and appreciation of the nation's heroes were qualified to instruct the youth of the republic. The great Uruguayan statesman José Batlle y Ordóñez in 1878 founded the journal *El espíritu nuevo* whose mission was the "total emancipation of the American spirit from the tutelage of the Old World."*

By 1900, however, the big guns of those who were disturbed over the encroachments on the traditional culture patterns were aimed at the foreign investors and technicians. Whereas a few decades earlier the foreigner had been welcomed as the precursor of aggressive materialism, now the intellectuals increasingly caricatured him as the harbinger of cultural retrogression and as a usurper of the national heritage. The United States in particular drew fire. A strong United States, extending and consolidating its influence in the Caribbean and represented by persons who refused to live and do business under the rules and laws applied to nationals, was much less attractive than the one fighting for human rights that the intellectuals of mid-century had held up as a model to be copied. The new view was that material accomplishment seemed to be the only measure of success the United States understood. The twentieth-century intellectuals contended that such a conception produced values that were in many respects the antithesis of those goals the Latin American peoples should strive for. Until after World War I their primary objective was to warn the youth of the limitations of the way of life the people of the United States were pursuing. Paul Groussac, the French-

* Russell H. Fitzgibbon, *Uruguay: Portrait of a Democracy* (New Brunswick, N.J., 1954), p. 126.

born Argentine hispanophile, warned of the "Yankee spirit" within a "shapeless Calibanesque body," which would substitute force for reason, egotism for generosity, quantity for quality, and would confuse the historical process with material development. Others invited young people to contrast the "individual brilliance" of their peers with the "stupid conformity" that dominated their North American counterparts. When the middle sectors later began to bid for political leadership they, too, offered themselves as the defenders of autochthonous moral and spiritual values against the inroads of "Yankee materialism."

What might be termed economic nationalism remained in its swaddling clothes prior to World War I.* The implications of the alienation of natural resources were not appreciated; the general attitude of all articulate groups was that natural resources were inexhaustible, a view not unlike that once prevalent in the United States.

The complexities of foreign investment were poorly understood; a sufficient body of evidence to gauge its advantages and disadvantages had not been formulated. Granting long-term concessions with monopolistic features was seen as the only way to attract vitally needed foreign capital into the public utilities field. In any conflict of interest between the agricultural and the rising industrial sectors, the rural interest in support of free trade ordinarily prevailed. Tariffs consequently tended to be imposed to raise fiscal revenues rather than to protect infant domestic industry. Despite their inability to comprehend fully the meaning of the coming of the foreigners and foreign capital, the middle sectors eventually built up evidence that associated the old elites with the foreigner in a "vast conspiracy" to prevent the immature republics from achieving their greatest potentials.

The economic expansion had multiple effects upon the political life of the republics. The middle sectors in general profited from the evolution. Before the foreign investor and technician and the immigrant were willing to risk their re-

---

* Uruguay, where economic nationalism was pronounced before 1915, offered the major exception. See Chapter 4.

sources in the republics they wanted guarantees that they would be entering reasonably stable areas. Consequently each state had to put its national house in order. As political theorists, the intellectuals found the philosophic justification for the shift from anarchy to order in the positivist teachings of Auguste Comte, which were enjoying limited popularity in Europe at the time. As modified by the intellectuals to obviate some of the more fundamental objections to it, positivism formed the basis for the predominant political philosophy in Mexico throughout most of the "honest tyranny" of Porfirio Díaz (1876–1910) as it did in Brazil from the overthrow of Pedro II in 1889, at least until the beginning of World War I. The words *Ordem e Progresso* (Order and Progress) on the flag of the new Brazilian Republic bore witness to the influence of positivism upon the leadership that replaced the Emperor and the nobility. In Argentina, Chile, and Uruguay the impact of positivism was strongly felt in governmental and intellectual circles before 1890.

Order meant law. In four of the five states the law was administered in such a way as to permit the middle sectors a growing voice in public affairs. In Argentina, Chile, and Uruguay political parties made some headway at the expense of personalists and narrow oligarchies. In Chile the gains were substantial. The electorate was enlarged in the three republics as more and more people were able to meet the qualifications for the suffrage. In Brazil, where law and order was maintained through the Emperor's judicial exercise of the moderative power accorded him by the constitution, responsible party government did not prosper. The Emperor's refusal to place serious restraints upon personal liberties, however, gave the middle sectors at least as great a degree of freedom of expression as they enjoyed anywhere in Latin America. Only in Mexico, where Díaz held despotic sway for over three decades, did the order requisite to progress reduce rather than enhance the role of the middle sectors in public affairs.

Economic development brought nearer into balance the distribution of wealth, income, and population between the rural areas and the urban centers, where the middle sectors were concentrated. In each of the republics, the cities felt the effects of the injection of new life into the national economy. The non-agricultural segments of the economies received the bulk of the foreign investment and skills. In Chile and Mexico mineral production expanded much more rapidly than agricultural production. In Argentina, Brazil, and Uruguay food processing and manufacturing was concentrated in a few important urban centers. The new and relatively high-salaried managerial group associated with transportation, communications, and finance was essentially urban. The expansion of governmental bureaucracies concomitant with economic development and demographic growth increased the contribution of the administrative centers to the gross national income. International trade, which, as indicated earlier, grew appreciably during the decades immediately preceding the outbreak of war, was primarily an urban activity, as was the expansion of internal commerce.

The demographic shift was in many respects more pronounced than the shift of wealth and income. Everywhere the cities began to feel the growing pains from which they continue to suffer. Montevideo nearly trebled its population between 1887 and 1914. Buenos Aires took only twenty-two years, between 1895 and 1914, to treble its population. Córdoba doubled its population in the same span of years, and Bahía Blanca spurted from 9,000 to 62,000. In Brazil, between 1890 and 1910, the population of Rio de Janeiro increased from 523,000 to 900,000 and that of São Paulo increased from 65,000 to about 350,000. Porto Alegre in the extreme south grew from 52,000 to 130,000. The population of Santiago, Chile, in 1890 was 250,000 and 333,000 in 1907. During those years Concepción, located at the southern end of Chile's great Central Valley, more than doubled in population, increasing in size from 24,000 to 55,000. The population of Mexico City rose from 333,000 to 470,000, and that of Monterrey, which was in the throes of an industrial boom, rose from 42,000 to 81,000. Dozens of other cities, in varying degrees, had the same experience.

The total effect of urbanization was more apparent in Argentina, Chile, and Uruguay than in Brazil and Mexico. Over 43 per cent of all Chileans were living in cities by 1907. Argentina claimed to be 53 per cent urban by 1914. Uruguay, primarily because of Montevideo, was over 35 per cent urban. Brazil despite such population concentrations as Rio de Janeiro and São Paulo remained overwhelmingly rural with probably 85 per cent of its population living on farms or in farm villages. A similar situation persisted in Mexico where a vast majority of the population remained on the haciendas and in Indian villages.

The economic transformation gave birth to the urban laboring groups who, once they won their political spurs, provided the popular support for the amalgams that carried the middle sector leadership to power. It was the workingman who forced the cities beyond their old confines. Many were Indians and mestizos who came from farms and villages by way of the railroads and riverboats that technology had brought. Having broken their bonds with the *patróns* and the local political chieftains, they were on their own for the first time. They were without leaders. They were backward but in their new environment they were considerably more articulate than they had been as farm hands. They were also more easily aroused, and their indignation could be sustained. Many of them sent their children to elementary schools. A number of the workers themselves acquired sufficient skill in reading and writing to claim the voting privilege. Nationals from the rural areas were joined in the cities by newcomers from Europe who had grown up with anarcho-syndicalism in southern Europe, and who gave the early labor movement a strongly anarcho-syndicalist tinge, which called for the use of force rather than collective bargaining in employer-employee relations.

The militancy of the rising industrial labor force was at first disturbing to the responsible elements of society. The middle sectors and elite alike dealt harshly with them. Thus, in Chile the representatives of the middle sectors in government sanctioned the brutal breaking of the dock workers' and nitrate miners' strikes between 1903 and 1907. When the middle sectors struck out on their own and began to provide the urban laborers with direction, however, their intractability was converted into a political asset. Everywhere the industrial workers contributed significantly to the initial victories of the middle sector leadership.

The growth of industry and international trade strengthened the bonds of the leading cities with Europe and the United States. Increased contacts meant that the cities were subjected to ideas coming from the modern and industrialized nations. The groups from commerce and industry were encouraged to look abroad for their economic guideposts; those charged with interpreting the culture of the republics were made acutely aware of the backwardness of their homelands. Their sensitiveness to the outside bound them together and gave them a progressive mentality that contrasted sharply with that of the old ruling elements who clung rather more closely to their Iberian-Catholic backgrounds. The lessons learned from Western Europe and the United States thus not only served as a political catalyst for the middle sectors but helped to crystallize their aspirations.

By the end of the nineteenth century, in each of the republics the ingredients needed for taking another step in their political evolution were being brought together—rapidly in some, more slowly in others. Their Spanish and Portuguese pasts, without disappearing, were being diluted as they proceeded in relatively orderly fashion toward their goals of becoming modern states. Brazil abolished slavery and monarchism, both of which had become anachronistic in the hemisphere. Education ceased to be solely a cultural adornment and became an economic asset. The immigrant pumped new blood and vitality into the economic and social structure. In each of the republics railroads, steamships, telegraphs, and cables knitted more closely the people to the markets. This produced, in turn, a more truly national political life. Cities grew up and aspired to political hegemony. An industrial proletariat, which would in time outstrip rural labor, was knocking at the door of political life.

By 1915 the middle sectors had acquired most of their basic characteristics, although certain of those characteristics would be de-emphasized and others would be accentuated in time.

The importance of the Catholic clergy as a component began to subside as secular elements usurped a substantial share of the Church's role in temporal matters. The military gave evidence of entering more fully into the political calculations of the middle sectors, not so much because of any greater readiness to interfere in civilian matters as because of its increasing middle sector social background and economic orientation. The commercial and industrial components assumed significant proportions and influence. With the rise of modern commerce and industry, the expansion of public education, and the growth of government the salaried middle sectors took their place firmly beside the self-employed professionals and the proprietors of the business community. Public education had already begun to open the way for members of the working groups to move up the social ladder.

The characteristic that they lacked then, but have now, was a well-founded background of political leadership. They had grown up beside the elites. They had not replaced them. In Argentina, Brazil, and Uruguay the influence of the landed gentry was as great as it had been a half-century earlier. The elites still possessed privileges they would not willingly surrender. They still felt warranted in employing force or fraud or both in order to retain power. Although they recognized that there was inherent in the economic transformation a more important role for the middle sectors, they viewed the increased influence of the middle groups as the delegation of responsibility, not as the surrender of it. As a rule the elites made the decisions and the middle sectors carried them out. Thus the middle sectors entered the twentieth century with a minimum of experience in actual formulation of policy.

But a lack of experience in decision-making did not deter them. They had grown economically strong. They had a vital interest in the issues brought to the surface by the transition from neo-feudal agriculture to semi-industrial capitalism. When the anxieties, frustrations, and discontents of emergent groups invited new political arrangements, the leaders of the middle sectors seized the opportunity to place themselves at the head of the new political amalgams, whose popular bases lay in the lower levels of the social pyramid and more particularly in the urban industrial working groups.

Insisting that economic policies of the past five or six decades had failed to provide a "full national life" because they had been conceived in a vacuum, the new middle sector leadership promised not only economic progress but social democracy. To the political and moral abstractions for which their leadership had fought during the period of independence they added the demand that a greater share of the material and cultural benefits that twentieth-century technology made possible be made available to the constituents who voted their pocketbooks. They insisted that the economic problem be made the fundamental political problem and that social guarantees be added to individual guarantees. A new Latin America was indeed coming into existence.

The new amalgams asserted themselves at different times in each of the five republics—their first clear-cut victory on the national level coming in Uruguay in the period between 1905 and 1915. From the first they associated themselves with commerce and industry, from whose continued expansion and the broadening of the social and economic responsibilities of the State and the consequent growth of bureaucracy they have prospered. In varying degrees their leadership has endeavored to consolidate the commercial and industrial elements at the expense of the workers' components, and it has sought to utilize national personnel and skills in order to displace foreign technicians. That same leadership has been plagued with the difficulty of reconciling its wish to move rapidly into industrial capitalism with its strong attraction to values and institutions that grew up to serve semi-feudal agricultural societies. Time and again their twentieth-century radicalism has been tempered by moderation—if not reaction—in line with their nineteenth-century antecedents and by their dedication on the whole to capitalism and the free enterprise system, as will be shown in the detailed analysis of Uruguay, Chile, Argentina, Mexico, and Brazil, which follow.

4 *Uruguay*

POLITICAL UTOPIA

Uruguay has the longest history of uninterrupted urban middle sector leadership of any state in Latin America. José Batlle y Ordóñez, who was elevated to the presidency in 1903, brought to that high office many of the objectives and ideals that came to be associated with the Uruguayan middle sectors. By the time that Batlle had completed his second term in 1915 the middle sectors had firmly established their political predominance. Throughout the half century that the middle sectors have controlled policy-making they have depended heavily upon the urban working groups for electoral strength. The urban orientation both of the leadership and of those within the middle elements and the working groups, who have provided the leaders with popular support, has been reflected clearly in the daring national projects that in this century have made Uruguay a busy laboratory for political, social, and economic experimentation. A sufficient number of the experiments have passed from the laboratory stage to that of practical application to win the little republic a wide and probably well-deserved reputation as being the most progressive and democratic nation of Latin America.

Not only happenstance, but also a set of conditions peculiar to Uruguay, determined the early rise to power of its middle sectors and their distinctly radical orientation. And if anything has distinguished them from their counterparts in the other republics, it has been their greater readiness to modify traditions and cast aside the established economic and political practices. Thus, to generalize about the middle groups in

Latin America on the basis of the experiences and attitudes of the Uruguayan elements would be dangerous, except on the highest level of generalization.

A relatively weak Catholic Church must be given priority among the several circumstances credited with having assisted the early rise of the middle groups in Uruguay. Probably in no other country of Latin America in the early twentieth century was the influence, prestige, and wealth of the Church less significant, a condition that largely deprived the old order of one of its primary supports. A number of factors contributed to that status of the Church. The *Banda Oriental,* as Uruguay was known in the Spanish period, was not effectively occupied until the early eighteenth century, after the Church had lost much of the crusading fervor that had made it such a substantial and lasting part of the culture in the areas conquered during the sixteenth century—as in Mexico, for example.

There were no large numbers of Indians in Uruguay who could be subjected to the proselytizing of the Church. In other regions of the continent its most effective work often was among the Indians and it ordinarily exercised greater influence over that element of the population than any other. The limited number of Indians in Uruguay proved a serious deterrent to the growth and prestige of Catholicism in that area. Also, until near the end of the nineteenth century, Uruguay was little more than a religious appendage of Argentina—the first diocese, that of Montevideo, not being created until 1878. After being freed from Argentine suzerainty, the Uruguayans did not possess sufficient wealth to construct the costly cathedrals that in many areas of Latin America served as ever visual evidence of the Church's ubiquity. Finally, except for Montevideo, and in marked contrast with the situation in Mexico and Peru, there were no important cities in which the Church could sink the roots that elsewhere produced healthy economic and political shoots.

The military—another member of the elite trilogy—was also weak in Uruguay. Hemmed in between Brazil and Argentina, Uruguay owed its creation largely to the fact that it served as a buffer between the two "giants," and to a considerable extent it was always able to depend upon the mutual animosities of its larger neighbors to guarantee its borders. This favorable situation did not prevent the emergence of a military establishment in Uruguay in the nineteenth century but it did discourage the growth of an army and navy comparable in size and cost to those that many other of the smaller republics felt forced to maintain. By 1890 what little civilian respect the armed forces might have commanded as an agency of law and order had been dissipated by the propensity of its leadership for using high military office as a steppingstone to political power. The almost constant struggles among the military chieftains to see which one would control the nation had brought the armed forces into such disrepute that they were compelled, as the century drew to a close, to surrender their political leadership to civilians. Once the military gave ground its political influence deteriorated rapidly to the point where it ceased to play a positive role in its own behalf. In the 1930's and 1940's it was used by constituted authorities to achieve political ends; in no case, however, did military action impair the basic rights of individuals.

A weak Catholic Church and a military in disrepute were in a sense the negative factors that served to assist the middle sectors in their bid for power. There were also positive developments, of which three are particularly noteworthy: the modernization of the economy, the appreciable influx of immigrants from Europe with somewhat different political interests and objectives than the creole elements, and the rapid growth of Montevideo as compared to the rest of the republic.

In the quarter of a century preceding the choice of Batlle as president, Uruguay underwent major economic changes. The economic transformation experienced by the little republic (with an area of approximately 72,000 square miles, it is only slightly larger than the state of Washington) paralleled but did not keep pace with Argentina's. In the 1870's the livestock producers of Uruguay began to take steps to improve their competitive position in the growing market of the industrial and commercial centers of Western Europe. Livestock associations were formed. Fences were built. Blooded stock was imported. Herds were enlarged. And, in the 1890's a series of developments over which Uruguay had no control operated to its advantage: the Boer War, the droughts in Australia, and the cessation of the live-animal trade with Europe owing to an outbreak of *aftosa* (foot-and-mouth disease) in Argentina contributed to an increased demand for Uruguay's principal export commodities, and led directly to the founding of Uruguay's first *frigorífico* in 1904. With the institution of the chilled-meat industry, the industrial sector of the economy received an important impetus.

At the same time that Uruguay was modernizing its livestock industry, it was also increasing its output of wheat and as an exporter of that commodity came to rank second to Argentina among the republics of Latin America.

Expanded livestock and agricultural production created the need for and provided the means of financing improved transportation. The railroad age was just reaching Latin America when Uruguay's interest in improved transportation was aroused, and it turned to the new mode of travel as the answer to its transportation problem. The republic's undulating plains made railroad construction feasible and, at the same time, less costly than in any other nation of Latin America except Argentina. By 1895, mileage had reached 1,075. By 1911, the railroad system had been completed substantially in its present form—1,874 miles in 1948—and by Latin American standards the form was remarkably satisfactory. The little country had the most mileage in relation to area of any state in Latin America.

Building fences reduced the labor requirements of the cattle and sheep ranches. Laying tracks drastically cut down the man-hours needed to move livestock and agricultural products from farm to port. The two together combined to drive many of the gauchos of the northern provinces out of their jobs. Most of the gauchos who did not leave for Argentina or the state of Rio Grande do Sul in southern Brazil sought employment in Montevideo.

The displaced gauchos were not alone in making their way to Montevideo. Newcomers from Europe were flowing into the city in relatively large numbers. By 1889, there were 100,000 foreigners in Montevideo and 114,000 nationals. In 1900, when Montevideo had reached a population of 270,000, the foreign element still comprised over one-third of the total population, and first-generation Uruguayans constituted an appreciable part of the remaining two-thirds. The foreigners in Montevideo represented a major share of the four thousand immigrants who annually came to Uruguay between 1879 and 1903 and contributed to making the republic's population, along with that of Argentina's, the most predominantly European in Latin America.

The newcomers, as a group, did well financially. They possessed more than half the "declared national wealth" by the end of the last decade of the nineteenth century, and controlled a large part of the commerce and industry. The immigrants had shown a strong preference for business. The sons of immigrants often sought careers that offered greater social prestige and dedicated themselves to learning as the surest road to the recognition they cherished. Possessing academic degrees, they could compete successfully with the creole element in law, medicine, secondary and university teaching, publishing, and the government bureaucracy. Because they recognized the value of education to their offspring, the immigrants were strong supporters of public education. Nor were they supporters in name only, since their economic position meant that they bore a large share of the tax burden needed to finance it.

Montevideo had already won a reputation for being the world's largest capital in proportion to the population of the country when Batlle assumed the presidency in 1903. The census of 1900 showed the capital to contain 30 per cent of Uruguay's total population of 900,000, and this in a country overwhelmingly agricultural! The city had already earned its name "the Suction Pump," a characterization which it has retained to the present day. Not only had it established its pulling power in so far as the gauchos and immigrants from Europe were concerned but it had proved its capacity to attract and hold a large share of the nation's wealth.

Since Uruguay's was a highly centralized government and

because nearly all public expenditures were made by the central government, wealth poured into the capital in the form of public revenues. Because Montevideo dominated the republic's internal and international commerce as thoroughly as it did the national government, wealth reached the capital in the form of commercial profits. Railroads funneled into the city. Ocean-going vessels ordinarily made Montevideo their only Uruguayan port of call. Part of the wealth was sucked into the "pump" when landholding aristocrats, although they distrusted political control from the city, maintained homes in the fast-growing metropolis because of its unquestioned advantages.

To the extent that comforts and conveniences and the means of arousing intellectual curiosity were available in the nation, they were found in by far the greatest quantities in the capital. Montevideo contained the only high schools in the country. It was the seat of the one recognized institution of higher learning. It contained the only libraries and museums that commanded more than local attention. So complete was Montevideo's cultural monopoly in 1900 that it can be said without undue exaggeration that learning ended abruptly at the limits of the city. Nor did any other urban center of the republic seemingly have even a remote chance of someday challenging the capital. Paysandú, the second city in size, with a population of less than 16,000, was devoted to serving the basic material requirements of its own inhabitants and those of the surrounding agricultural area.

All of these developments, which contributed significantly to the political rise of the middle sectors, might have lain fallow had there not been a powerful catalyst. The catalyst was provided in the form of José Batlle y Ordóñez. Twice as president of the republic and for nearly three decades the strongest personality in the majority wing of the dominant Colorado Party, Batlle shaped the nation's destiny. Whether he is viewed as an able and farsighted statesman or as a political opportunist, the fact remains that during more than a quarter of a century of public life he was responsible for a vast majority of the directives that further guaranteed the political control of the nation by the urban-oriented middle sector leadership. His successors have carried on in much the same vein.

Once in office Batlle moved as quickly as political realities permitted to build the "modern" Uruguay he envisaged. He began by exploiting those conditions that had favored his own rise to the presidency. The armed forces were among the first to feel the impact of his reform movement. He had to rely upon the army during his first year in office, but that only served to convince him further that the military should be dispossessed of the power to resolve political differences. After the threat of armed revolt had subsided he took steps designed to guarantee the subordination of the army to the will of civilian forces. His policies, carried on by his successors, had achieved their goal by 1920. By the end of World War I the armed forces had been so reduced in size and prestige that they no longer decisively influenced political developments. Since then the military has not been a major political factor. In no other republic of Latin America, it is generally accepted, have the armed forces been more apolitical in the past quarter century.

Before achieving the presidency Batlle had waged a prolonged campaign against the Catholic Church in his newspaper *El Día.* As Chief of State he readily took advantage of the opportunities to minimize the influence of the Church. His measures against it set a pattern of anticlericalism that has persisted to the present day and has left the Catholic establishment in Uruguay in as debilitated a position as it is anywhere in Latin America. As early as 1905 a divorce law was introduced into the legislature and passed in 1907 in the face of strong public objection by the Catholic clergy. A law of 1909 prohibited teaching religion in public schools. The State has added requirements to the curricula at both the elementary and secondary levels to the point where Church-sponsored schools have very little time for religious instruction. The Constitution of 1917, which was written under the watchful eye of Batlle and was something of a tribute to him, clearly separated the Church and State. Russell Fitzgibbon, writing in 1954, indicated the effectiveness of the official campaign against the Catholic Church when he pointed out that its clerical personnel amounted to one archbishop, two bishops, and about 250 secular priests or approximately one priest per 10,000 in supposedly Catholic Uruguay. In Spain the ratio was at the time approximately twelve times as favorable for the Church.*

While the military and Church were being contained, the Colorado Party with Batlle in control was moving ahead in several areas where growth contributed to the numerical expansion and greater influence of the middle sectors. Education was one such field of development. The Colorado Party, which has controlled Uruguay continuously since the 1860's, early committed the country to an advanced public education system capable of providing the trained personnel necessary for the sound expansion of business and government. Coeducation was introduced and steps were taken to assure girls the same educational opportunities as boys at a time when in most nations of Latin America pleas for better educational facilities for girls ordinarily fell on deaf ears. The State simultaneously worked to educate employers and the public at large to accept women in certain positions formerly reserved exclusively for men. Public education was made free, and an elaborate State-supported scholarship program was evolved which theoretically guaranteed that no youth would be deprived of an education at any level because of financial need. A large share of the national revenues were allocated each year to public education. In 1954 over 19 per cent of the national budget—the largest single item —was assigned to education. The central government's continued interest in education is today reflected in Uruguay's favorable literacy rate and the quality of the graduates from its institutions of higher learning. Approximately 85 per cent of the population is literate, a record equalled only by Argentina among the Latin American republics. Uruguay's success in training scientists and technicians was indicated by the representatives of the International Bank for Reconstruction and Development who visited Uruguay in 1948 and again in 1950.

* Russell Fitzgibbon, *Uruguay,* pp. 230–44.

Their report stated that "the Republic possesses an alert and intelligent population with free access to general and technical education. The level of technical abilities is consequently high, and the capacity exists to organize and administer industrial and other productive processes—a valuable natural asset which partly offsets the absence of physical industrial resources."*

The recognition given education has made the teaching profession attractive. The State, as a result, has been able to demand a comparatively high degree of academic training from the instructional staff in public schools. The prestige of education in general, combined with the relatively high academic qualifications of instructors, has afforded teachers at all levels the opportunity to be accepted as middle sector. Increased literacy has given rise to a growing reading public and in turn to an expansion of the publishing industry, which in Uruguay, as elsewhere in Latin America, is generally controlled and operated by individuals belonging to the middle sectors. Uruguay's estimated newspaper circulation per 1,000 inhabitants stood at 238 in 1952, the highest in Latin America.

Commerce and industry were still in their embryonic stage, despite their recent achievements, when Batlle became president. The large rural estates were essentially self-contained. Only a small percentage of the urban population was in the market for anything but the absolute necessities. Municipal public services were largely limited to Montevideo. There was no mining industry of consequence. The manufacturing industries were devoted almost wholly to the processing of agricultural products and, as noted earlier, a significant share of the capital investment in them was of foreign origin.

Batlle was determined to enlarge the commercial and industrial sectors and to reduce the "insidious influence" of foreign control over them. The program that he initiated and sponsored for a quarter of a century was two-pronged: (1) he instituted measures, including protective tariffs, tax exemptions, and freedom from duties on certain essential imported

---

* International Bank for Reconstruction and Development, *Studies in Economic Development, No. 2, Uruguay,* mimeographed (Washington, 1951), p. 20.

equipment; and (2) he increased credit facilities to make investment by nationals more attractive. Of the two, the latter proved by far the more significant. In no other republic of Latin America has the government by direct participation in the financing and management of commerce and industry so decisively affected the course of a nation's economic development.

As begun by Batlle and later refined, public ownership and operation of utilities and various industrial, commercial, and financial enterprises not only effected a notable economic expansion but before 1910 brought foreign investment in Uruguay to a near standstill. A state electric and telephone company organized in 1912 by 1948 owned and operated all electric power services in the country. The State began its program to nationalize the railroads during World War I, and by 1949 it owned and operated all but one common carrier—and that line was domestically owned. A national port administration created in 1915 has exercised a monopoly over the services of the Port of Montevideo since 1932. It also manages other Uruguayan ports and has operated ocean-shipping services. A national insurance bank founded in 1911 had extended its activities by 1926 to the point where a formal monopoly could be decreed for all insurance risks other than those of life, fire, and marine. Since 1926 a national law has prohibited the formation of any new private insurance company of any type to underwrite risks in competition with the national insurance bank. In 1928 the State entered the meat-packing industry. Since Batlle's death, the State has controlled and operated monopolies or near monopolies in milk production and distribution, in the fishing industry, in imports and sale of coal, in petroleum refining, alcohol distillation, iron and steel production, and in the supplying of cement for public works.

In response to such encouragement, industry and commerce grew rapidly in the first three decades of the century. By the mid-1920's over 50 per cent of the gross national product was derived from the manufacturing and processing industries. To industry and commerce fell the brunt of supplying jobs for those newly entering the labor pool. Meanwhile the rural economy lagged. The livestock industry, upon which the republic was largely dependent for its foreign exchange earnings, showed only a slight expansion after 1900. To the extent that agriculture expanded, its growth was primarily in response to the increasing requirements of Montevideo. Developments within agriculture failed to create a substantial demand for labor and in 1930 only six thousand more people were employed in livestock and agriculture than in the 1913–16 period, when the figure stood at 92,000.

The State's vigorous participation in the economic field and its promotion of education, commerce, and industry have had a snowballing effect in creating a popular following for the Colorado Party. Four socioeconomic groups have seemed to profit most from the policies laid down by the Colorados. Large segments of the membership of three of the four—the commercial and industrial elements; the industrial labor groups; and the intellectual and professional elements, including the bureaucrats—have been associated with the Colorado Party throughout this century. The members of these groups provided much of the theoretical underpinning and popular strength that made it possible for the Colorado Party first to contain the opposition National Party and then to pursue its radical program in the name of the Uruguayan nation. The fourth group—the dirt farmers of the southern provinces—grew up largely in response to the demands for foodstuff by the members of the first three groups who traditionally have concentrated in Montevideo, which in the mid-1950's contained at least 35 per cent of the nation's total population.

The Colorado's ties with the commercial and industrial elements date to the founding of the Party in the 1830's. From the first the Party's personalized leadership stood in public opposition to any arrangement that might hurt the business community of Montevideo and benefit Buenos Aires across the Plata estuary. Later in the nineteenth century when the recently arrived immigrants from Europe began to reinforce the economy of the capital city, the Colorados successfully sought working arrangements with them. By the close of the century the political opposition was disparagingly referring to the Colorados as the "Party of the foreigners." From their being the "Party of the foreigners" the Colorados became the Party of the sons of foreigners who were active, articulate Uruguayans.

The new commercial and industrial element was also attracted to the Colorados because of considerations other than the nineteenth-century antecedents of the Party. The Party's success in dominating the government during the preceding decades suggested that in it was to be found the greatest hope of permanently suppressing the political turmoil, which the business community viewed as the most serious threat to its future prosperity. And when the struggle for internal orderliness was still in the indecisive stage, the Colorados, under constant prodding from Batlle, discovered that another "threat" to the welfare of the business interests was the foreign investor. In an abrupt about-face from its solicitous attitude toward foreign investors, which had characterized nineteenth-century thinking, these were now portrayed as "vampires and bloodsuckers who swell their pockets at our expense" and make Uruguay "a captive in the hands of foreign enterprise."*

Thus at a time when the governments of Mexico, Argentina, Brazil, and Chile were in some cases alienating their subsoil, and were in other cases awarding to foreigners long-term concessions of a monopolistic nature, Batlle was launching what soon grew into a vigorous nationalistic doctrine directed against the foreign businessman. This antiforeignism combined with the conviction that domestic private enterprise lacked the capacity to replace foreign capital led to State intervention in the economy. Subsequently the preference for State enterprises has stemmed more from the failure of private initiative to make the expected contribution to output and services and less from any strong belief in fundamental social theories. A privately controlled domestic industry, however, grew up behind the protective walls erected by the State, and beside the State-controlled enterprises. This private industrial component of the economy developed under "hothouse" conditions and has re-

* Quoted in Simon G. Hanson, *Utopia in Uruguay: Chapters in the Economic History of Uruguay* (New York, 1938), p. 184.

mained sheltered from free competition from abroad. The entrepreneurial element has thus been induced to remain politically loyal to or at least tolerant of the Colorado leaders who, experience indicates, can be trusted to display a strong disposition to keep national industry in the hands of nationals. In the eyes of the middle income groups, this policy of protection sponsored by the Colorado Party has more than offset the restrictions imposed by it on private initiative. Likewise the protection against outside competition has been sufficiently attractive to those in commerce and industry to discourage them from breaking with the Colorados, despite the Party's close and prolonged affiliation with the industrial working elements.

Batlle had laid the foundations for the Party's alliance with urban labor before he assumed the presidency. In the mid-1890's his newspaper *El Día* had strongly supported labor's right to strike, and Batlle thereafter remained on friendly terms with the industrial working element, which numbered approximately 40,000 by 1903. When he became president he encouraged labor to organize. This was the first step in a long series that made the working conditions and privileges of the Uruguayan laborer among the most favorable to be found anywhere in the world. The republic became the first Latin American country to adopt an eight-hour day; it instituted minimum wage legislation in 1928. Women were accorded the same privileges in their jobs as men. Elaborate legislation was written to protect the worker in his job and to establish the terms under which he might be separated from his employment. In the late 1920's when many of the Latin American states were opposing labor organization and others were maintaining close surveillance over union activities, the Uruguayan labor movement was enjoying near absolute independence from government control, which it has continued to enjoy.

That favorable status was reached in two stages. In the first, foreign enterprises were the principal employers of industrial manpower, and decisions favorable to the working groups were primarily at the expense of the foreign operatives who did not have a direct voice in the government. By supporting the laboring groups in their contention that they were being

unduly exploited by foreigners, the State won strong adherents
to the nationalistic doctrines that at the same time it was offering to the rising commercial and industrial elements.

In the second stage, the State replaced the foreign investors
as the principal purchaser of industrial manpower and as such
it came to set the standards of employer-employee relations.
Its economic preeminence and the dependence of private capital
upon its protection gave it a considerable degree of freedom in
determining labor's welfare. The State was generous. Private
investors in commerce and industry had no choice but to be
generous also in view of the fact that alternatively they would
have had to associate themselves politically with the Blanco
Party, whose orientation was rural and agricultural, not urban
and industrial.

The intellectuals' support of the Colorado Party antedated
the Batlle era. Throughout most of the nineteenth century the
Party, like the intellectuals, stood for change based upon the
experiences of Western Europe, particularly France and England. Like the members of the Civic Union in Argentina,* the
intellectuals in Uruguay viewed the landholders as reactionary.
And when Batlle launched his nationalistic campaign directed
primarily to the commercial and industrial elements and the
urban working groups, he struck at the heart of a problem that
was becoming of increasing concern to the intellectuals. Many
intellectuals had already become aroused over the impact of
foreign-induced economic change upon Uruguayan culture.
Just at the time that the urban leadership of the Colorados was
consolidating its power position, the nation's outstanding
writer, José Rodó, was warning the rising generation that
Uruguay's cultural heritage was at stake. Acknowledging the
benefits to be gained from technological development and mass
production, Rodó pointed out that "the material prosperity of
the United States was as immense as its incapacity to satisfy
even a mediocre view of human destiny." Thus the youth of
Uruguay, and by extension all the youth of Latin America,
should avoid being seduced into surrendering their cultural

* See Chapter 6.

superiority for the material gains offered by the United States' way of life. It was a warning that before 1930 was echoed repeatedly and often in a most virulent form by nationalists from one end of Latin America to the other.

In this century, the Colorado Party's advocacy of a "vital" State that requires a sprawling bureaucracy to exercise close and direct influence over the life of nearly every citizen has helped to keep the intellectuals in the fold. The steady growth of the bureaucracy has provided an unusually favorable outlet for middle sector skills. In 1900 the number on the government payroll stood at 20,000. The bureaucrats were charged with carrying out the ordinary administrative functions of government. By 1930 a 300 per cent increase in government expenditure had made possible a proportional increment in personnel. At that time, in a total population of two million, approximately 60,000 were employed by the government, including those in the industrial enterprises the State had taken over or developed. Bureaucrats were not only carrying out administrative responsibilities, they were advising in health and welfare agencies, selling insurance, distributing electric power, and determining who might and might not retail basic commodities. By 1947 over 61,000 positions were included in the national budget. This figure included teachers, police, and military personnel in addition to the classified services but did not include those employed by the autonomous entities set up to run the State's "industrial empire." Russell Fitzgibbon accepted the figure 145,691 as the number of government employees of all kinds in 1953.* This represented 5.82 per cent of the population of the country and meant that probably no less than one in every five Uruguayan families was at that time at least in part directly dependent for its living on public funds.

The dirt farmers of the southern provinces who have supported the Colorados have had good reason for doing so. The Party has actively solicited the approval of this particular farm element. Public funds in various forms have been showered on the area to the neglect of the livestock-producing regions that

* Fitzgibbon, *Uruguay*, p. 165.

earn such a substantial share of the nation's foreign exchange.
The dirt-farming areas have been provided with a good system of roads, which makes possible the rapid and low-cost
movement of agricultural produce to Montevideo, practically
its sole market. The economy of the southern provinces has
become so closely tied to Montevideo, in fact, that it may be considered as part of the capital's economic complex. The government has fostered the development of mechanization to the
point where, within the Latin America area, Uruguay by the
mid-1950's ranked second to oil-rich Venezuela in the number
of tractors per unit of area harvested. Agronomists have been
provided at national expense to counsel the farmers on developments in their field. Credit facilities have been made available.
Farm commodities have been subsidized from time to time to
guarantee the producers a reasonable return and the people of
Montevideo a price they can pay. For example, the dairy industry for several years has depended upon State subsidization
of its products. To the extent that educational, health, and welfare services have been provided in the rural areas the southern
provinces have been favored over the livestock-producing regions.

Contributing to the consolidation of urban middle sector
leadership as exemplified by the dominant elements within the
Colorado Party are the extraordinary concentration of population, wealth, and government in the single city of Montevideo;
the wide and continuous appeal to nationalism; the aggressive
public intervention in the social and economic fields; and the
unusual degree of internal peace and political stability that
Uruguay has enjoyed in the past half-century. At least two
additional considerations of a somewhat different nature must
be taken into account in explaining the unique political experience of the Uruguayan middle sectors. The first is the extent
to which its leadership has used compromise as a political tactic.
The second is the success the middle sector leadership has enjoyed in winning the confidence of the individual through giving him greater personal dignity.

Early in the century the Colorado Party's willingness to

settle for something less than the whole was probably fundamental in ending the civil strife that had plagued the nation
throughout most of the nineteenth century. When Batlle assumed the presidency he found it necessary to use force in
quelling an uprising led by members of the opposition National
Party. But Batlle permitted the suppression of the Nationals
to cease before the prestige of the leaders had been seriously
impaired and the economy of the republic further weakened.
Also, as part of the settlement, the Colorados gave the National
Party tacit control over five provinces in which their influence
was recognized as being predominant and, apparently, made
a cash payment to the revolutionary leaders for laying down
their arms. The Nationals have controlled the five provinces
politically ever since and only recently have significant inroads
on their suzerainty been made by the central government. By
compromise, Batlle had bought time against the day when the
influence and wealth of the urban-oriented elements would be
sufficient to discourage the rural groups from resorting to force
in efforts to negate the popular will.

The spirit of compromise that has pervaded Uruguayan
politics was manifested in other developments that vitally concerned the Nationals. Neither Batlle the reformer nor his
successors, who have been somewhat less reform-minded, saw
fit to arouse the landholding aristocracy by seriously considering reapportioning the lands held in latifundia. Also, the Colorados have studiously avoided taxing land directly, which would
seriously agitate the landholding element. The Colorado-con-
trolled governments prudently did not insist upon applying the
progressive social and economic reform measures in the domain
of the livestock magnates. Since World War II, however, there
has been a serious attempt to give the rural workers in the livestock-producing areas some of the benefits of labor legislation
that won Uruguay an international reputation, although even
today the successful enforcement of labor law is largely limited
to the area in and immediately surrounding Montevideo.

The plural executive with which Uruguay has experimented
since 1917 has also evolved into an institution for political com-

promise.* Providing for the distribution of the responsibilities assigned to the executive branch of government, it was first advocated by Batlle as a means of reducing the opportunities of a potential strong man to usurp power. As approved by a plebiscite in 1951, after having undergone many vicissitudes, the plural executive guaranteed the principal minority party representation on the national council charged with carrying out the functions of the executive branch of the government. Although the arrangement at all times leaves the control of the council in the hands of the dominant party, it guarantees the Nationals, who have formed the principal opposition throughout this century, a forum from which they can keep their views before the public while at the same time they serve as a check on the conduct of the majority membership. The writing into the national constitution of a provision for minority representation in the legislative branch of government is an added example of political compromise by the middle sector leadership.

Much of the reservoir of good will that the urban middle sector leadership has built up has resulted from a widespread conviction that the national leaders have been seriously concerned with the interest of the individual. At the same time that "reforms" of a collective nature have been carried out the feelings and dignity of the individual have been carefully weighted. Nowhere in Latin America, in this century, has the individual's freedom to express himself been more jealously guarded. The adherence of the political parties to the decision of the people as expressed at the polls has given the individual an unusual degree of assurance that by voting he is actively participating in government, an assurance that has served to make him a politically conscious individual. In turn the individual's rising level of political maturity has steadily increased the pressure upon the parties to act responsibly—an environment favorable to the continued leadership of the middle sectors.

As pointed out at the beginning of this chapter, the urban middle sector leadership has been in control in Uruguay for

* The plural executive has also been referred to as the bifurcated executive, the multiple executive, and the collegiate executive.

a longer period of time than anywhere else in Latin America. In concluding, it can be said that the prospects of the middle sectors' continuing to direct the political life of the republic seem to be good without being favorable in all respects.

The military still seemingly offers little threat to the middle sector political leadership. The Uruguayan armed forces have been apolitical for many years. There is little to suggest that the officer corps will develop or will be permitted to develop political ambitions in the years immediately ahead.

It appears unlikely that the present power group will suffer any major loss of support through an attack upon its traditional anticlerical position. Catholicism does not appear to be making the headway that will permit it to become a decisive political factor.

Montevideo, where middle sector support traditionally has been concentrated, now contains well over one-third of the total population of the republic, and its share of the total population has increased since World War II.

There is little to indicate that the present leadership will alienate its support by significantly reducing the number of individuals upon the public payrolls. Neither will it permit the wages and salaries and benefits of government employees to fall noticeably below those in private enterprise. Thus the huge Uruguayan bureaucracy, including those employed in State-controlled economic activities, will, it appears, continue to be reasonably contented and challenged, and consequently will continue to furnish the present middle sector leadership with both ideological and electoral support.

The fast-growing laboring element in manufacturing, commerce, and the service industries traditionally has looked to the middle sectors for political leadership. There is little to suggest that labor will in the foreseeable future provide political leadership from its own ranks that would be acceptable to a large number from those sectors of society that control the wealth.

The middle sector leadership can look forward to continued support from the agricultural south. The dirt farmers owe their present strong position in the economy to help from the middle groups in power at Montevideo. Their future is closely tied to the welfare of the urban groups that have steadily expanded as a result of the middle sector policies.

Nowhere else in Latin America has the middle sector leadership more firmly established itself as a reasonably impartial arbiter of social and economic differences. Public confidence in its intentions has built up a feeling of trust that will not be quickly dissipated by any opposition element.

If there is a weakness that might conceivably contribute to the political disadvantage of the middle sector leadership, it would appear to be in the nation's economy. The policies of the Party that has controlled decision-making on the national level for a half-century have not produced a sound economy. The steadily rising cost to the nation of the welfare programs has in recent years accentuated certain economic weaknesses. The present leadership has permitted production for export to lag to the point where in the past decade Uruguay has often been faced with a disequilibrium in the balance of payments. On the other hand, certain parts of the nation's industry have been permitted to expand beyond the needs of the domestic market, while in other areas the growth has failed to keep pace with the requirements. The effects of the highly nationalistic policies that make the republic unattractive to private foreign investment are being more pronouncedly reflected in the nonagricultural areas where the rate of development has been declining.

The mounting burden of the social welfare programs has led to deficit-spending year after year. A weakening of the national currency has been a major by-product of unbalanced budgeting. As the financing of the welfare programs places further demands upon the nation's resources—as it must if the programs continue as they are presently operated—the danger that the already precarious state of the country's economy will worsen is a possibility publicly acknowledged by both its politicians and its scholars. Should the economy deteriorate seriously and a spiralling inflation result, discontent and frustration over failure to achieve private and public objectives might place heavy strains upon existing political arrangements. In such a circumstance, and in view of the social and economic indoctrination to which the popular masses have been submitted, the wage-earning groups might well become receptive to demagogic appeals of an ardently nationalistic nature, appeals that offer further State intervention as a national panacea. Such a development would tax the republic's cordial relations with the United States, thereby compounding the nation's problems, since the United States government would appear to offer the best prospect of assisting Uruguay out of any economic difficulty in which it might find itself.

5 *Chile*

THE MIDDLE SECTORS POLITICALLY
ENTRENCHED

In Chile the urban middle sectors have achieved major political success. They first played a decisive role on the national political scene in 1920 when they directed the campaign that lifted Arturo Alessandri Palma to the presidency. Middle sector influence in government was considerable between 1920 and 1938, an era made noteworthy by a military dictatorship from 1924 to 1931 and by a control of the executive branch by a Center-Right coalition that became progressively rightist between 1932 and 1938. From 1938 to 1952 the middle sector leadership, with few restraints, ran the republic by controlling the Radical Party. Middle sector elements who, in despair and frustration, deserted the Radical Party and took their labor following with them probably provided the "extra" votes that made ex-dictator Carlos Ibáñez del Campo president in 1952. Despite the extremism expressed during the campaign by the candidate and his entourage, once in office, Ibáñez avoided a frontal attack upon either the basic problems or the established institutions and relationships—social, economic, and political. He ran a government that continued the trend toward the development of industry and commerce. Thus in its major aspects the Ibáñez program bore the imprint of the thinking of a large segment of the middle sectors. The election of Ibáñez, consequently, may be considered as their victory despite the fact that the Radical Party suffered a resounding defeat.

The split within the Party's ranks in 1952 was consistent with the political conduct of the Chilean middle elements.

Since striding decisively onto the political stage in 1920, they have displayed anything but monolithic tendencies. Their political preferences, like those of the middle sectors in the other four republics, have ranged from Marxist socialism to the corporate state. The majority, however, like their contemporaries in Argentina, Brazil, Mexico, and to a lesser extent in Uruguay, have been social, economic, and political moderates. Like the others, too, they have not been averse to blending progressive social and economic objectives with considerable quantities of political opportunism.

Since the middle sectors, even if united, would have always lacked the numerical strength to provide the popular vote required to control the nation, leaders from their ranks have had to seek support outside of their own socioeconomic groups. Sometimes they have relied most heavily upon the wage earners, who prefer more radical approaches to complex problems. On other occasions they have solicited the support of the propertied element, who advocate a more cautious approach to progressivism. This dependence upon approval from outside their own groups goes far to explain the lack of consistency exhibited by the Chilean urban middle sectors, who are themselves weighted in favor of the salaried or dependent elements but contain large numbers of property owners. It also partly explains the eventual reconciliation of the radical approaches to immediate problems with the accepted values of the more culturally stable and economically affluent elements.

The differences and antagonisms existing between the workers and the capitalists have not by themselves determined the political role of the middle sectors. The explanation of their successes and failures goes deeper. Most of the conditions and circumstances that helped to shape their political thinking are the same as those found in other republics in which the middle groups are politically conspicuous. Most of them, however, have had a Chilean tinge. Some of them have come near to being distinctly Chilean. All of them, including the rise of a substantial urban industrial economy and concomitantly a vocal industrial proletariat, were a part of the Chilean milieu by the end of World War I.

The Catholic Church, whose activities have always been important to the middle sector leadership, has for several decades occupied an unusual place in the country's politics. The Constitution of 1833 made the Roman Catholic Church the State Church. The defense of Catholicism was a primary objective of those who ruled during the "Autocratic Republic" from 1831 to 1861. Then the Church came under persistent attack during the "Liberal Republic" from 1861 to 1891. By the end of that period many of its prerogatives had been swept aside in favor of civilian authority. Civil marriage, civil registration of births and deaths, and the establishment of public cemeteries had destroyed the Church's former monopoly in those fields.

The legal status of the Church remained essentially unchanged during the era of "Parliamentary Government" from 1892 to 1925, but the general atmosphere changed. In accordance with the encyclicals of Pope Leo XIII—the most famous of which, *Rerum novarum* (1891), set forth the basis for relations between capital and labor—certain strongly Catholic elements with the approval of the Church began to dissociate themselves from the more reactionary segments within the Conservative Party. This more liberal element advocated a reexamination of the social structure in light of the trend away from feudal agriculture and toward industrial capitalism. At the same time the anticlerical elements continued their propaganda in favor of a complete break between Church and State. Their demands were written into the Constitution of 1925. The Church thus entered a new era.

The political direction that it would take once freed of its ties with the State was indicated during the debates over the separation. Unlike the Churchmen in certain of the other republics where they gave ground with the greatest reluctance and oftentimes only after an unsuccessful resort to force, the Chilean ecclesiastical authorities cooperated with the civil authorities in reaching the terms under which the separation was consummated. The civil authorities on their part contributed to a peaceful break by guaranteeing the Church a state subsidy for five years while it adjusted to its new "independent" status.

Since the separation of the Church and State, the Chilean Catholic Church has shown a generally enlightened attitude, which has been reflected in the political life of the republic. Catholic lay organizations, such as Acción Católica, and political parties, such as the Falange Nacional de Chile—now known as the Christian Democratic Party—have advanced programs that are distinguishable from those of the anticlerical center parties only in their emphasis upon the need for a more "Christian approach" to social problems. Meanwhile, the Church hierarchy has refused to take an aggressive position on political issues other than those involving communism and Marxian atheistic doctrines. Instead, it has sought to provide a moral fiber in political life that the political parties themselves have not supplied. Thus the Chilean Catholic Church and its more politically conscious lay membership, far from continuing to lend prestige to the position of the traditional Right as they did throughout the nineteenth century, have actually helped to isolate that element and to move the entire political base toward the moderately progressive Center, where the middle sectors have thrived.

In general the behavior of the Chilean military has been favorable to the growth of the middle sector political leadership. Since 1831, only in the years between 1924 and 1932 did the Chilean armed forces engage in politics on their own account. For nearly a century prior to 1924 the army and navy assumed a cooperative role in the forceful settlements of differences brought about by the strife of civilian groups. In fulfillment of this policy in 1851 and again in 1891, years of turmoil in Chile, the armed forces returned to their assigned tasks and ceased to be preoccupied with exercising control of government after peace was restored. Since 1932 the armed forces have not openly interfered with government by civilians. Over the years no military establishment in Latin America has built up a better record of noninterference in political matters. For the period since 1920, it would probably have to

bow to the Uruguayan military and share second-place honors
with the Costa Rican armed forces.

During the years from 1924 to 1932, when the military did
direct the destinies of the republic, the conduct of the leadership
reflected the important role of the middle elements both in
the military itself and in the socioeconomic development of
the nation. At least by the end of the War of the Pacific
(1883) and perhaps before, the Chilean army had lost its attraction for the elites, and cadets came to be drawn almost
exclusively from middle sector homes. After the revolt of
1891, a similar development took place in the navy, which
traditionally had been preferred over the army by the sons of
Chile's ruling clique. In the 1890's, as both the army and the
navy became increasingly professionalized, they lost any remaining appeal that they had held for the elites. As a consequence, young officers of middle sector background moved
readily into positions of responsibility. The effects of this
phenomenon were apparent by 1900. By 1925 the junior officers from middle sector families had become senior officers.
Meanwhile, the overthrow of the old elites by the civilian
middle sectors in the 1920 presidential election portended the
declining political influence of the traditional ruling elements.
It was not necessarily surprising, consequently, that the military directorate headed by Colonel and later General Carlos
Ibáñez sought to pursue a course which appealed to the economic aspirations of the urban middle groups and working
elements more than it did to those elements whose interests
were essentially rural.

Ibáñez arbitrarily implemented a considerable part of the
social program that Alessandri, "the people's president," had
been unable to set in motion because of the Conservative opposition in the senate. Ibáñez borrowed heavily from the
United States until that source of funds dried up following
the disruption of international trade after 1929. The funds
were employed, among other purposes, for public works and
school construction in an effort to alleviate unemployment
consequent to Chile's loss of a large part of the world's nitrate
market to synthetic producers.

Civilian middle sector elements in general approved the Ibáñez welfare program and benefited from it. Intellectuals joined the ranks of the bureaucracy as directors of official boards and corporate bodies created to promote and regulate the essential aspects of the economic life. The teaching corps expanded. The middle groups of commerce came in for their share of gain as the economy responded to the spurious prosperity generated by foreign borrowing. At the same time the Dictator supported the request of the industrialists by raising tariffs and establishing subsidies.

When the university students and the professional elements, notably doctors, lawyers, and teachers spearheaded the strike in 1931 that forced Ibáñez to abdicate, their outcries were primarily against his political methods. He had, in effect, disregarded the electoral process and had ruled as an authoritarian. Many within the middle groups believed that the Chileans had outgrown that stage in their political development. The governments that followed, however, did not undo what the military had initiated in the social and economic fields. Rather, they built on it.

One of the most important of the factors that have favorably affected the political fortunes of the middle sectors was the early development of and the continued respect for the party system and party accountability in government. Both were firmly established by 1920 when the middle groups made their bid for control. Parties had come to derive their force from the doctrines they propounded rather than from the candidates they offered the electorate. In turn the candidate was ordinarily no stronger than his party. Thus, there was relatively little room in Chilean politics for the personalism that prevailed, as it had since independence, in most of the remainder of Latin America.

The party system has had a continuous existence in Chile since 1831. At that time a narrow oligarchy, comprised primarily of landholders of the northern part of the Central Valley, resolved its differences and chose the leaders rather than allowing the leaders to impose themselves upon the country, as was occurring, for example, in Mexico, Argentina, and Uruguay.

Before the political monopoly of the oligarchs was seriously challenged in 1861, the orderly transfer of public office had been more firmly established in Chile than elsewhere outside of Brazil, which was peculiar in that it was ruled by an emperor. The next stage in the development of the party system was the acceptance of the principle that the opposition was entitled to a voice in government. This did not necessarily mean honest elections, but it did mean that the opposition might be seated and heard when it could overcome the control of the electoral machinery by the party in power. Elsewhere in Latin America it was not unusual for the victorious groups to claim 95 to 99 or even 100 per cent of the popular vote and all the seats in the legislature as well as the presidency. In Chile, after 1870, at least three parties were regularly represented in congress. This gave the minority parties a reason for existing between elections, and hence the continuity that was missing in those republics where parties ordinarily disintegrated following the defeat of the particular caudillo and his hand-picked candidates for minor offices, in whose name the party had been founded.

The principle of party accountability was appreciably strengthened during the era of parliamentary government. The multiparty system toward which the republic had been advancing since 1861 flowered. Government was by coalition. To the leaders of the parties went the privilege of filling the cabinet posts and the other high government positions in return for their congressional support. At the same time the powers of the executive branch were weakened vis-à-vis the legislature. This meant that the president's ability to shield party deserters was lessened.

The party system and the principle of party accountability gained added stature after 1932, once the articulate citizenry had experienced military rule and became convinced that they did not approve of it. As a consequence, the electoral process continued to gain in prestige and the electorate was encouraged to take a more active part in elections.

Throughout the development of the party system the Radical Party was viewed as the political organ of the middle sectors. It is still so considered. Although, as noted earlier, members of the middle groups find their way into all political camps, including the two extremes, their convictions and aspirations are most closely portrayed by the Radical Party. In fact the Party's political experience and doctrinal development to 1952 so closely paralleled the expansion of the middle sectors and their shifting political philosophies that the two may be examined together.

The Radical Party came into being in 1862 as a reaction against oligarchic rule. The Party drew support from a number of sources, including the dissidents from the elite groups who often were at one and the same time large landholders of the south and members of the Masonic order, and who resented both the political domination of the propertied class of the region around Santiago and its strong clericalism. The Party also attracted an important share of the politically conscious teachers, bureaucrats, and merchants, elements that were necessarily limited in number at the time. Schools had only begun to dip into the lower social groups for students; accordingly the teaching staff was small. The duties assigned to the State could be fulfilled by a handful of officials. Less than 25 per cent of the population lived in settlements of one thousand or over. The remainder of the population, for the most part, existed outside normal business channels. Nonetheless, the teachers, bureaucrats, and merchants were a valuable asset to the Party because of their intellectual resources and because their numbers were concentrated in and around the three leading cities: Santiago, Valparaíso, and Concepción. They contributed significantly to the election of Radicals to congress in the 1860's and to lifting the Party to national prominence in the early 1870's.

In 1873 the Party directorate was invited to participate in a liberal coalition formed by President Federico Errázuriz Zañartu and dedicated to clerical reform and progress along neopositivist lines. In 1885, the Radicals were instrumental in removing the income restrictions as a condition for exercising the voting privilege required by the Constitution of 1833. Radical support of a broadened political base, implicit in lowering the suffrage requirements, was justified on at least two grounds. It was in line with the nineteenth-century liberal philosophy of the Party, as it was with dominant elements within the middle sectors everywhere in Latin America. The Party stood to reap more of the added harvest of votes than either the Liberals or Conservatives since the industrial working groups would be the most likely to qualify under the relaxed stipulation, and the Radicals came the nearest to representing the objectives of the working groups.

The social elements from which the Party ideological leadership came expanded appreciably following Chile's winning of the highly valuable nitrate area as a result of its military victory over the combined forces of Bolivia and Peru between 1879–83. Revenues from nitrates relieved the threat of direct taxation of the monied elements and made possible a sizable public-works program during the 1880's. Commerce expanded rapidly. Firmer foundations for industrial development were laid. Foreign capital was attracted by the new-found prosperity. The urban movement was hastened. Santiago, the capital, in particular exhibited the ability to draw the restless from the countryside. The census of 1907 showed Santiago to contain approximately 12 per cent of the total population of the nation.

The Radicals entered fully into the political scramble that came when Chile's "praetorian peace" gave way to the rough and tumble of parliamentary government in the 1890's. Politics became the chief pursuit of the middle elements. The conduct of the Radical Party leadership did not differ substantially from that of the other parties. The members, many of whom had become newly rich from commerce, industry, and mining, used their wealth to buy votes, just as did those who represented the traditional parties. Politics became a contest for privilege and high office in which the Radicals fought by the same rules as the other contestants.

No vital issues separated the Radicals from the other principal parties during most of the era of parliamentary government. Despite the fact that the Party had come to represent the emerging working elements and to include immigrants in its ranks, the attitude of its leadership toward agriculture was much the same as that of the Conservative and Liberal leadership.

The late nineteenth- and early twentieth-century position of the Radical Party is in large part accounted for by the conditions peculiar to Chile's agricultural economy. The nation had a very limited amount of arable land, and the farming frontier had disappeared before the close of the colonial period. Consequently, by the end of the nineteenth century some large landholders were investing their profits in urban enterprises and sending their sons to the cities to direct the new family holdings. Thus, the rural aristocracy had an interest in commerce and industry not generally found elsewhere in Latin America, and in turn the managerial element had closer ties with the land than was ordinarily the case. An added consideration was the fact that many immigrants successful in business had married into the landed aristocracy.

Reflecting the Party's ties with both agriculture and commerce and industry, the Radicals supported the cheap-money policies that generally prevailed after 1890. Currency depreciation became the chief instrument by which real wages were kept down in both rural and urban areas. Real wages declined 10 per cent between 1913 and 1923.

The Radicals were, until near the end of the parliamentary era, individualists *par excellence*. As the spokesmen for individualists, the Party leaders were doctrinaire liberals in their politics and laissez-faire adherents in their economics. This was in sharp contrast, it should be noted, with the social convictions held by the dominant element within the Party by the 1930's.

While the parties, with little regard for the popular masses, had sought whatever advantage they could gain from a rehashing of the traditional issues, the nitrate boom and developments resulting from World War I had produced the changes in Chile's social and economic structure that had invited political exploitation. Wartime demands for the nation's nitrates and copper had reached unprecedented heights. Prosperity in mining had been reflected in the increased purchasing power of the people. New manufacturing establishments had been created, and production in old ones had been stepped up to alleviate the wartime shortages in finished goods ordinarily obtained from abroad. The growth of mining, manufacturing, and commerce in turn had led to an enlarged industrial proletariat. It also had heightened the expansion of cities at the expense of the country-side. The census of 1920 showed the population of the nation to be 45 per cent urban. Santiago contained over 500,000 inhabitants or approximately two out of every fifteen Chileans.

The problems arising from the social and economic transformation had been left to multiply. There had been no reapportionment of congressional representation to provide for the demographic changes that were taking place. Electoral liberty had progressively tended to mean "liberty to indulge in fraud and bribery." Vote buying had become so widespread that many workers in their political ignorance considered the right to sell votes a privilege which went with the suffrage. Landholders had sworn to the literacy of their *inquilinos* and had marched them to the polls to vote as they had been told. Cost-of-living indices had risen faster than wages. The living conditions of the urban workers had remained among the worst in the Western world. The *conventillos* of Santiago, where the workers lived promiscuously in cramped and unsanitary quarters, had attracted world-wide attention without arousing to action those who controlled the country. Chile's infant mortality rate had become the highest among the nations of the Western World. The only effective instrument the workers possessed to call attention to their plight was the strike, and they struck 293 times between 1911 and 1920.

The discontent of the working groups was sharpened by the reports they received through their leaders of developments in Europe. They knew that as a result of war the latent weaknesses of European society had come into their full expression. New ideas had wrought havoc with the entire social fabric. Monarchies had fallen. New states had risen and had organized armies to seize coveted territory as one means of satisfying their growing nationalism. Within the working groups there had developed a revolutionary spirit that could no longer go unheeded. Prime Minister Lloyd George had announced that England must become "a country fit for heroes to live in." Recognition of the social question had been written into the Treaty of Versailles. The stirrings of the European workers were felt almost immediately in the Western Hemisphere. The Mexican Constitution of 1917, in a very real sense, had anticipated the new feeling. It found expression in Chile as early as 1918.

Nineteen eighteen was an election year in Chile. Control of the Lower House of Congress was at stake. Discontent was abroad in the land. The abuses perpetrated against the working groups were being felt by an ever enlarging number of persons belonging to the middle sectors. Many trying to get a start in business had felt the effects of inflation and high interest rates. Real wages and fixed incomes had deteriorated, including those of State employees. In addition, the intellectuals grew more and more sensitive to the fact that the gap separating them from the elites was widening as wealth increasingly competed with learning as a prestige item. It was to capture the vote of the urban workers and the low-income components of the middle sectors, who held a common distrust of those who had controlled politics, that the Liberal Alliance was formed.

The guiding spirit of the Liberal Alliance of 1918 came from the progressive wing of the Liberal Party and the Radical Party. The objectives of the leaders varied. A few were dedicated reformers. Some sensed that the moment had arrived when it was politically expedient to institute reform measures. Others desired simply to win office by getting out more votes than the landed aristocrats and their allies could muster. They had little concern for or faith in the working group.

The Liberal Alliance won a striking victory at the polls and captured control of the Lower House, which was organized under Arturo Alessandri's directorship. Those who had sought only an electoral victory—events established that they were primarily from the Liberal Party—soon broke with the Alliance and joined with the Right in voting Alessandri's ministry out of office. But the 1918 election was a landmark in Chile's political development.

The Radical Party still retained within its ranks powerful liberal elements dedicated to individualism, but in accordance with its pre-election promises it remained associated with the emerging working elements and the depressed salaried groups belonging to the lower middle sectors. This decision involved, as suggested earlier, a doctrinal shift away from the extreme individualist position the party had held and toward the social oriented position that became the hallmark of the Party after 1932. Also, for the first time in Chilean history, the Liberal Alliance had forced politics out of the "smoke-filled room" and into the streets. The Alliance had given the working groups a hope for the future.

The 1918 victory started the middle sector leadership on its way to political preeminence. The success of the Alliance in electing Alessandri to the presidency in 1920 gave the new leadership the offensive. The old ruling element, however, was still in a position to offer a tenacious opposition through its ability, until 1938, to exploit the apportionment of seats in the Senate in favor of the agrarian interests. With its heels firmly implanted in the nineteenth century, the "traditional rightist bloc" prepared to obstruct the rate of change. The political drama between 1920 and 1938, consequently, focused on the dogged struggle of the traditional ruling element against the "inevitable," while the middle sectors were acquiring a more distinct political personality and the workers were becoming more politically sophisticated.

The best maneuvers of the reactionary forces could not divert the new political amalgam that grew out of the Liberal Alliance from the direction in which it was headed. Electoral defeats for the traditional groups in 1918, 1920, and again in 1924 were followed by the promulgation of the Constitution of 1925, which bore repeated evidence that Chile was breaking with its past. The Church and State were separated. A strong executive was established at the price of a weakened legislative branch, in which the old ruling groups were strongest. The new charter paved the way for direct taxation, a defeat for the propertied elements. From those points of departure the constitution-makers went on to include provisions for some of the

most advanced labor and welfare legislation to be found anywhere in the world at that time. Finally, the document, in giving the State considerably broadened powers to intervene in the
social and economic fields, was an added manifestation of the
drift of the middle groups away from their former extreme
laissez-faire position.

The middle sectors profited from the new environment. By
1938, when the republic had again regained its political com-
posure under civilian leadership and had recovered from the
worst blows dealt it by the depression, the middle components
had moved ahead on a wide front. Educational facilities had
been increased by 50 per cent since 1920. Enrollment in elementary schools had nearly doubled. There were 25,000 students attending classes at the high school level. There was a
corresponding expansion of the teaching corps. Too, teachers
were better trained and commanded more respect. The University of Chile had been made autonomous and was a strong-
hold of intellectualism in the country.

Numerically, the bureaucracy had soared to record heights
after suffering cutbacks when fiscal revenues dropped as a
result of the depression. In 1924, the white-collar workers had
won the legislation that helped protect their jobs against foreign competition by providing that at least 75 per cent of all
white-collar employees in each enterprise be of Chilean nationality. In the 1930's the percentage of foreigners that could be
employed was reduced to fifteen, and measures had been taken
to assure Chilean workers a proportionate share of money paid
out for salaries. All, however, was not favorable for those who
lived by their intellectual skills. Bureaucrats and white-collar
workers alike were poorly paid. Many of them held to their
positions for the prestige derived therefrom rather than for
monetary considerations.*

Commerce and industry showed remarkable growth in the
years before the depression struck, and displayed strong re-

---

* P. T. Ellsworth in his volume *Chile: An Economy in Transition*
(New York, 1945) found that 84 per cent of the *empleados* (white-collar
workers) received only the equivalent of thirty-six dollars U.S. per
month in 1936.

cuperative powers thereafter. Much of their success prior to the depression may be attributed to the solicitous attention of the State and, as mentioned previously, to the public-works program promoted by Ibáñez. In 1927, a provision was made to pay bounties to ships of the Chilean merchant marine carrying nitrates abroad. In 1928, a series of decree laws provided for aid to industry and commerce. A plan designed to encourage the use of domestic coal was written into law. Duties on petroleum were raised to induce domestic exploration. Subsidies were provided to establish industries considered essential to the national welfare. Also in 1928, the first move toward a definitely protective viewpoint came about when the prosperity engendered by large foreign loans stimulated the development of local industry, which gave rise to a strong interest group that began to demand tariff protection. The impact of public spending upon the economy can be imagined when it is appreciated that the per capita consumption of iron and steel—one gauge of economic development—in the 1925–29 period averaged approximately 83 pounds against 64½ pounds in 1947–51. In 1930, the per capita consumption of iron and steel reached an all-time high of over 126 pounds.

The manufacturing industries suffered less than the other branches of the economy from the collapse of world markets and the drying-up of foreign loans, which destroyed all semblance of equilibrium in Chile's balance of payments after 1929. Industrial production was sustained at a relatively high level throughout 1930. The low point of 65 (1927–29 equals 100) was reached in August of 1931. A year later industrial production stood at 110, where it remained more or less steadily until 1933. Thereafter the trend was upward, reflecting, in particular, the improved conditions in mining and building. By 1937 the industrial index stood at 154. Between 1928 and 1940 investment in industry augmented 150 per cent.

In regard to the promotion of the industrial and commercial sectors between 1930 and 1938 there was little to choose between the military, the Socialists, and the Center-Right governments that came in rapid succession. Industry had a high priority in each administration. The measures instituted by one regime were expanded by the next, provided it remained in power long enough to initiate a program. Despite the politicans' claims to the contrary, real wages were kept down throughout the period to facilitate the accumulation of investment capital. Tax remissions were provided to encourage building. Domestic industry was stimulated by increased customs duties, import licenses, and exchange controls. Together the measures spelled out an official willingness to experiment in financial matters, which set Chile apart from its neighbors.

In the 1932-38 period the wage earners and the salaried groups upon whom the middle sector political leadership depended were experiencing, in general, unfavorable times. They lived a precarious existence. Like the salaried middle groups, the urban workers grew numerically without appreciably improving their economic status. At one time during the depression, one-third of all industrial and commercial laborers were out of work. Although the employment picture improved rapidly after 1934, when economic recovery provided job opportunities, wages in all but special circumstances barely kept pace with or actually lagged behind costs-of-living increases. The Association of Chilean Architects in 1934 found that one-third of all Chileans were inadequately housed.

The total effect of the workers' economic status was to drive them to seek extreme solutions to their problems. The Chilean Communists, who had been improving their position in labor ranks since the early 1920's, exploited the discontent of the urban workers to gain control of the largest union in Chile. In the presidential election of 1938, the Communists, from their entrenched position in the labor movement, were able to lead the workers into the Popular Front, which seemed to offer the freshest approach to the problems troubling the workers and the poorer paid white-collar employees.

The Popular Front was composed of the main body of the Radical Party and the parties to the left of the Radical's basically centrist position. It brought together for political action such heterogeneous groups as, on the one hand, southern landholders, industrialists, merchants, and intellectuals, and, on the other, workers among whom were those who advocated the

overthrow of government by force. The objectives of large segments of the middle groups had become steadily more difficult
to reconcile with the traditional political patterns. The middle
sectors and the workers alike were threatened with isolation
and defeat if they went their own ways.

The social and economic aspirations of the components comprising the Radical Party and the working groups were similar
at several points. Each group within the Front recognized the
need for greater attention to public education. All felt the need
for a political approach that would lift morale by giving promise
of a better future. All were convinced that the nation must de-
emphasize agriculture and mining in favor of industry. Except
for a few, primarily in the Radical Party, all believed in the
need for a more equitable distribution of the national income.
As socioeconomic groups, all had come to rely in varying degrees on the State; the bureaucrats for jobs and prestige; the
workers for the right to organize and to strike and for public
welfare benefits; and the businessmen for various aids—quotas,
exchange controls, credits. In short, the middle sectors had
firmly committed themselves to broad governmental control
over social and economic matters, a position toward which they
had been heading since 1918. In effect, they had accepted the
State as the arbiter of social and economic differences.

Antiforeignism was another factor providing the diverse
socioeconomic elements with grounds for common action. Isolated intellectuals had long warned of the dangers to Chilean
culture of the materialism of foreigners who came to Chile.
They had also made known their resentment of what they considered the refusal of foreigners to accept Chileans as equals.
Laborers and white-collar employees for some time had fought
to limit the number of immigrant workers and foreign technicians and managers competing for positions in the nonagricultural sector of the economy. The Communists had helped
keep the issue alive by persistently holding the foreigner responsible for all or most of the economic ills that beset the non-
propertied groups. Meanwhile, during the depression years
the domestic industrialists discovered that they could profit
from the agitation against foreign economic control. By 1938

they had fused their antiforeignism with their support of State intervention in the economy and had come up with the appealing thesis that, considering Chile's stage of development, only direct government action could effectively reduce the importance of foreign economic interests. It should be pointed out, however, that antiforeignism in Chile throughout the 1930's was of a mild nature as compared, for example, to the xenophobic type manifest in Mexico at the same time.

Pedro Aguirre Cerda, a member of the Radical Party, was named as the standard bearer of the Popular Front and won the presidency in 1938. Of a total of 440,000 votes cast he received less than four thousand more than the Conservative candidate. Aguirre Cerda garnered most of his votes in the north where the Communists brought out the labor vote, and in the three major urban concentrations, Santiago, Valparaiso, and Concepción. It was the ability of the southern landholders to hand him more than 50 per cent of the votes in some farm states, however, that gave him his margin of victory.

Aguirre Cerda was an *hacendado* as well as the Dean of the University of Chile School of Commerce when he was named as a candidate by the Popular Front. He thus appealed to the regard for property and the respect for learning held by Chilean upper and middle sectors. He was also a reformer, moved by the abuses he felt had been inflicted upon the depressed elements. As long as he was president—he died in office in 1941— he sought to promote social reform and reconcile it with his prosperous middle sector background.

Soon after assuming control of the government Aguirre Cerda began to implement the Popular Front program. Wage earners were supported by the government in their efforts to win raises. Nonunion industrial labor and government employees were encouraged to organize to protect their interests. Individual liberties were honored.* The popular masses were urged to become more politically conscious. Steps were taken

* It should be pointed out that this was not exceptional in Chile. But during Alessandri's second administration (1932–38) many felt that liberties were trampled upon, and there was agitation against him because of his treatment of the political opposition.

toward giving women the suffrage.* A new concern for social problems resulted in a significant expansion of educational facilities and health and welfare programs. At the same time industry, given strong backing from the State, added considerably to the national income. The *Corporación de Fomento,* or the Development Corporation, was created to funnel public capital into those basic areas of the economy that were unattractive to private investors and to provide private enterprise with relatively low interest-bearing loans. Funds from the Export-Import Bank helped to capitalize the *Fomento* and gave prestige to the Aguirre Cerda government. The President's program helped the Center-Left capture 62 per cent of the vote in the congressional elections of 1941.

Juan Antonio Ríos succeeded Aguirre Cerda as chief executive. The new president, a wealthy businessman of Concepción, was, like Aguirre Cerda, a member of the Radical Party, but he possessed little of the reformer's zeal that had won for his predecessor a popular following. As a candidate Ríos repudiated Aguirre Cerda when he let it be known that he would neither solicit nor welcome Communist votes. In Chilean political parlance this was, in effect, an offer to trade the extreme Left vote for added backing from the Catholic-oriented Social Christian elements. Ríos' bid was accepted. The Popular Front was shortlived.

Ríos' campaign statements had carried an implicit promise to moderate Aguirre Cerda's reform program but to retain the State-interventionist philosophy that had gained wide acceptance in the 1930's. He had hardly assumed office when it became apparent that he was determined to correct some of the "mistakes" of his predecessor, who had been "duped" by the Communists. Ríos' attitude offers a good example of the strong compulsion within the middle sectors to seek firmer ground after they have felt compelled to make a fundamental departure from normal conditions. As a result of a number of circumstances directly related to World War II, Ríos was able, with

* Women participated in a presidential election for the first time in 1952.

a minimum of friction, to shift the ideological base of his government in favor of the industrial community at the expense of the
remaining socioeconomic groups.

He began his move with an appeal for unity in the face of
the growing threat to the nation that resulted from the war.
Patriotism, he insisted, required that the airing of differences be
postponed until after the emergency. The impact of this call
to unity was all the greater because the Communist Party
(which numbered perhaps no more than ten thousand but had
a large following) found itself in a position where it was forced
to give credence to the President's position, despite its thorough
dislike for him. When the Nazi forces invaded the USSR the
Communist leadership, without a warning to its rank and file,
had made a propaganda about-face. Thus, by the time that Ríos
assumed the presidency the Communists had dropped their
class-warfare campaign and their attacks upon the United
States in favor of unity in the struggle against fascism. This
shift tended to complete the isolation, which began with Ríos'
election, of those workers seeking primarily to improve their
economic status. They quickly lost to the administration the initiative they had enjoyed for a brief time under Aguirre Cerda.

A strong demand at favorable prices for Chilean copper and
nitrate further eased Ríos' efforts to run a moderate administration. Employment throughout his term was maintained at a
high level. Workers received regular pay envelopes. The nation, in lieu of receiving capital goods on demand, built up exchange balances to finance an anticipated wave of industrial development after the war ended. Under such conditions it was
difficult to keep the working groups conscious of their long-term
objectives.

The industrial area, meanwhile, profited from the war. As
the more industrialized nations directly involved in the conflict girded themselves to take the offensive they could not
satisfy the requirements of their regular customers abroad for
consumer goods and semidurables. Chile, along with many
other nations, was forced to rely to a considerable extent upon
its own resources. Although conditions abroad dictated that increased production must come from speed-ups in established

enterprises, the Ríos government went out of its way to assist industry. High profits were permitted to those who invested their savings in industry. The failure to carry out effective price-control measures tended to favor industry. The administration also used its influence to acquire from abroad equipment and raw materials in short supply. Finally, the administration invested directly in industry and made loans available to private investors. In 1945, the last full year of the Ríos administration, public investment constituted over 40 per cent of the total gross investment in the economy.

When Ríos died in office in 1946, it was evident that his policies had satisfied only the industrial element among those to whom the Radical Party looked for electoral support. Little had been done to appease those concerned with the nation's economic independence, since foreigners, particularly citizens of the United States and the United States government, still figured prominently in major plans for future economic development. Chilean dependence upon the export of exhaustible natural resources was greater than when Ríos assumed office. The continued prevalence of fraud and corruption in government offered little encouragement to those who had supported Ríos in the expectation that he would strengthen the moral fiber of public officials. No significant steps had been taken toward correcting the landholding system, which still permitted a major share of arable lands to be controlled by a handful of families. The bureaucracy had expanded, as had the teaching corps, but the salaries of the middle sector elements remained low and for the first time women from middle sector homes sought outside employment on a considerable scale.

Gabriel González Videla, who succeeded Ríos in the presidency, was the third Radical during the period covered in this volume to hold that high office. During González Videla's term of office the middle sectors grew numerically and those in industry and commerce, in particular, increased appreciably their role in the economy and their influence in the government. The working groups, including the salaried elements within the middle sectors, however, steadily withdrew their support from the Party, and in the 1952 presidential election the Radical candidate ran no better than third in a field of four.

The choice of González Videla as their candidate was an obvious effort on the part of the Radical leaders to rehabilitate themselves with the working elements that Ríos had alienated. González Videla, a self-made man and a prominent lawyer, had early associated himself with the Left Wing of the Party. In the Party's presidential convention in 1942 the working groups had indicated their preference for him over Ríos. In the intervening years he had done nothing to discredit himself with the depressed groups. In his successful campaign for the presidency he appealed to the Communists for support, and the Communist Party responded by instructing its followers to vote for him.

The new President soon proved a disappointment to his popular following. He began his term of office with Communists in his cabinet, but within a matter of months he removed them from his government and aligned himself with the business community. His decision was apparently prompted by two circumstances that could not be reconciled with a Left-Wing prolabor government. He seemingly became convinced that Chile had to industrialize at all costs. He also, it would appear, became satisfied that Chile's welfare depended upon close and friendly relations with the United States.

His decision to throw his weight behind industry and commerce involved a certain calculated political risk. Industry had proved a disappointment on two scores. When the Radicals began promoting industrialization in the 1930's, they had argued that within a short time it not only would cease to absorb capital but would provide the new investment capital needed to have a continually expanding economy. Industry had not lived up to their expectations in this regard. When González Videla came to office industry was absorbing capital at an ever increasing rate and throughout his term of office it continued to depend upon new capital. Also, the Radicals had predicted that industry would provide a high level of employment for those entering the nation's labor pool, which was enlarging at the rate of approximately 50,000 a year. As it turned out, however, industry on an average was able to take on only a few thousand a year. In 1949, industrial employment was actually below the 1947 level. Industry's failure to fulfill its promises caused many to question whether or not the present generation of workers, living at near-subsistence standards, should be further sacrificed in the interest of future generations, who supposedly would be the ones to benefit from industrial development.

The cold war and the consequent efforts of the United States to reduce Communist influence in the Hemisphere apparently was highly instrumental in bringing about González Videla's break with the Communists. The United States was the principal market for Chilean copper and in fact the only one in the free world that could absorb Chile's huge output, which in this period ran in the neighborhood of 350,000 tons per year. Also, González Videla hoped for loans from the United States to rehabilitate the nation's railroads, to expand its hydroelectric power, and to construct an iron and steel plant at Huachipato, near Concepción. The latter project was a pet of the nationalists despite the fact that its successful completion was contingent upon sizable assistance from the United States in the form of loans and skills. González Videla decided that cooperation with the United States would be worth the price that such a step would cost in terms of good will among the working groups, especially among those under Communist influence. And the United States did maintain a favorable attitude toward Chile. In addition to providing a limited amount of credit, Washington stockpiled Chilean copper, which helped to maintain the price for that commodity.

As a result of policies the González Videla administration pursued, the fixed-income and small-business elements within the middle sectors paid dearly in terms of material well-being and confidence with which to face the future. They showed their resentment by deserting the Radical Party in the 1952 presidential election. Nonetheless, the policies carried out by the administration were in every major aspect well within the framework of the thinking that conditioned middle sector political conduct since World War I.

The passage in 1948, and the subsequent enforcement of, the Defense of Democracy Law, which made the Communist Party illegal, was considered by many members of the middle sectors as an infringement upon personal and political liberties. The record of the administration, however, in respecting the rights of individuals and the decisions made at the polls was widely conceded to be among the best in Latin America.

The regime diligently intervened in the social and economic fields in line with middle sector twentieth-century concepts of the role of government in the increasingly complex modern state. To carry out the multifarious responsibilities heaped upon the central government, the bureaucracy was expanded to where it contained 5 per cent of the actively employed in the nation, 7 per cent of the nonagricultural labor force, and 18 per cent of all persons employed in services. Between 1945 and 1950, the share of current government expenditures going to general administration (largely for salaries) rose from 35 to 37 per cent.

The González Videla government maintained a friendly attitude toward the printing and publishing industries. The administration promoted public education, a cornerstone of middle sector doctrine dating well back into the nineteenth century. Chile's literacy rate stood at 75 per cent, placing the republic behind only Argentina, Costa Rica, and Uruguay in that respect. The administration reduced the percentage of expenditure going to the defense agencies from 27 to 26 per cent between 1948 and 1950, an approved middle sector procedure. Discreet relations with the Catholic Church were maintained.

The government increasingly became the guardian of industry. Under the administration's guidance and assistance, the industrial index rose from 135 (1937 equals 100) in 1945 to approximately 165 in 1950. The number of persons employed in industry and services exceeded the number in agriculture by 1952.

Urbanization continued apace. Preliminary tabulations of

the census of 1952 showed the republic to be 59.9 per cent urban. Greater Santiago, with a population of over 1,300,000 out of a total population of 6,200,000, contained two of every nine people in the republic. In the presidential election of 1952, the department of Santiago was responsible for over 29 per cent of all votes cast, the province of Santiago over 33.3 per cent. Under middle sector guidance Chile had indeed moved a long way from its rural-agriculture antecedents. Santiago's dominance had not become as complete as that of Montevideo in Uruguay, but it had grown to a point where its sway could be overcome only by a concerted effort by the remainder of the country.

Carlos Ibàñez, an erstwhile dictator in the late 1920's and early 1930's, succeeded González Videla in the presidency in 1952. An independent without the organizational support of any major party, he personalized to many the repudiation of discredited political machines. During his campaign he sketched out a nebulous catchall program built around the theme that the only thing wrong with Chile was the selfishness and lack of determination of the men who had been running it. He offered something to each of the frustrated elements within Chilean society. To attract the economically depressed, including the salaried elements that were suffering from the effects of a spiraling inflation, he demanded a more equitable distribution of the national income. He made "Bigger Loaves of Bread" the symbol of a better future for wage earners. To the propertied elements he offered a reexamination of the economy with a view toward integrating agriculture, mining, and industry. He crossed socioeconomic lines by appeals to national pride and the national sovereignty. Thus, he called for a new look at foreign investment. He promised to repeal the recently ratified Military Assistance Pact between Chile and the United States if it was established that it infringed on Chile's sovereignty. He assured his followers that Chile would pursue an independent course in international organizations. He insisted that Chile was in no way bound to sell its exportable strategic materials to the West, if the Iron Curtain countries offered higher prices.

A serious deterioration in the economy and party politics

and at times the President's erratic and authoritarian conduct prevented the Ibáñez administration from successfully resolving any of the problems he identified during the campaign. The workingman's loaf of bread became smaller not larger. The nationalists were not appeased. Far from being a threat to foreign capital, as was predicted, the Ibáñez administration created an investment climate that attracted private foreign capital in relatively large amounts. Chile cooperated in restricting the sale of strategic materials to the Iron Curtain countries, although it could probably be established that considerable Chilean copper did reach the USSR and its satellites. Ibáñez was not able to integrate the economy.

To the extent that Ibáñez was free to follow his own dictates he leaned in the direction of the more economically and socially conservative elements of the middle sectors. In general he resisted the extreme methods advocated by the more intolerant of his followers. He did not meddle with the economic and social structure. He preferred to overhaul rather than to overthrow. He sought to shore up rather than to expand industry. He left the problem of land redistribution to his successors, with the result that 75 per cent of Chile's arable land remains in the hands of 5 per cent of the landed proprietors. The administration indicated a willingness to see private capital, including, in some instances, private foreign capital, supplant the State in certain industrial and commercial ventures. In short, the Ibáñez regime, brought to power by discontented elements from many walks of life, did little constructively to serve any socioeconomic group. It succeeded, however, in preserving the foundations upon which future middle sector leaders justify their claims to the right to rule the nation. The Radical Party, not the middle sector leadership, lost the election of 1952.

Chile faces a precarious future. A number of highly favorable developments over the past four decades will, it appears, in large part be offset by the serious decline in public morale and the extremely grave economic situation. The nation apparently has settled its major religious differences. Its military establishment for the past twenty-five years has been content to see civilians responsible for the conduct of government. Chile has a strong party system and a tradition of settling political disputes at the polls. In its efforts to resolve its problems it has on its credit side a record of representative government unsurpassed in Latin America. It has a growing and politically entrenched middle sector leadership, which, barring the setting aside of democratic processes, will continue to play an important and basically moderating and progressive role in politics, although it may on occasion find it politically expedient to advocate and temporarily pursue extreme measures.

Chile has a good record of relations with the United States, whence outside assistance seemingly must come, if it comes at all, in sufficient quantities to affect appreciably the nation's economic health. The fact that government-to-government loans have tended to replace private loans reduces the possibilities of tensions and thus makes continued satisfactory relations more probable than might ordinarily be expected, considering the large United States investment in Chilean minerals. The Chileans have not displayed as yet what might be called a virulent type of nationalism. This fact has helped them to maintain workable arrangements with the leading powers of the Western bloc.

Counterbalancing the country's assets and perhaps weighting the scales against a favorable development in the foreseeable future are the following conditions:

Public morale is low as a result of the growing conviction, dating from around 1945, that the political parties are sacrificing the nation in their own interests and that a vast majority of the politicians are corrupt. The levels of living of large segments of the population have been deteriorating for several years. A large component of the public has lost faith in the ability of the political machines to provide the type of action needed to give the promise of a better future. The Communists, taking advantage of the personal liberties that Chile guarantees, have kept the discontented elements in a constant state of agitation at a dangerously high price to the national welfare.

The advantages of an independent labor movement, which Chile has had for nearly three decades, have been in large part negated by the fact that its labor leaders have given the rank and file little training in their responsibilities to society as a whole.

The nation is not rich in agricultural lands. Its landholding system discourages maximum exploitation of available land. Its technical resources are in extremely short supply.

Chile is faced with serious economic maladjustment. The failure of agricultural production to keep up with population has been noted. Not discussed above but of considerable consequence, given the present stage of Chile's economic development, is the unduly large number of persons engaged in the service industries—i.e., in nonproductive activities. In 1950 they constituted over 37 per cent of Chile's total labor force, as compared with less than 35 per cent in agriculture and mining combined.

The nation has no untapped sectors of its economy capable of providing the impetus to further immediate basic development. Landowners lack the capital to modernize their operations. Industry still absorbs capital faster than it produces it.

The failure to create a viable economy—a probability, barring considerable aid from the outside—will invite political instability and efforts to find short-term solutions. The middle sectors have in the past profited politically from such a climate. Formerly their opposition came from the Right, and the middle sectors allied with labor. Should the opposition in the foreseeable future come from the Left and should the working groups seek to provide leadership from their own ranks several possibilities would remain from which the middle sectors could hope to retain control of the nation. The democratic process could be suspended by the military. Such a step would appear to have greater political than economic and social implications. The military leadership is almost solidly of middle sector background and there is little reason to assume that it holds to other than middle group social and economic values. Any likely alternative to the suspension of the democratic process would appear to be a Social Christian Alliance. An effective labor leadership in the foreseeable future would in all probability have to be under Communist direction. Such a situation would invite a pro-Catholic, anti-Marxist, Social Christian Alliance, with good prospects of splitting the working forces. The leadership of such an alliance would presumably come from the urban middle sectors.

6 *Argentina*

ON THE POLITICAL DEFENSIVE

The political experience of the urban middle sectors in Argentina has been vastly different from that of their counterparts in Uruguay and Chile. The Argentine groups have not in this century enjoyed the steady growth of influence in the political field that the Uruguayan and Chilean middle sectors have. And unlike the Uruguayan and Chilean middle sectors whose prospects for continued leadership appear promising, the Argentine groups, since the overthrow of Juan Domingo Perón in September 1955, have been engaged in a dangerous and still indecisive struggle with military and labor elements in an effort to regain the political preeminence they lost as early as 1930. That such should be the case in one of the most technologically advanced, urbanized, racially homogeneous, and literate republics with an early record of positive middle sector participation in public affairs is somewhat surprising but also in large part understandable when viewed historically.

In so far as the political role of the Argentine middle sectors is concerned, the historical past falls into three rather clearly defined periods. The first period preceded the election, in 1916, of Hipólito Irigoyen, whose elevation to the presidency marked the beginning of fourteen years of middle sector leadership on the national level. The second period corresponded to that fourteen-year era, which terminated with Irigoyen's overthrow, in 1930, by the military in alliance with the conservative oligarchy.* The third period extends from

* At the time, Irigoyen was in his second term. Between his first and second terms the presidency was held by the antipersonalist Radical, Marcelo T. de Alvear (1922–1928).

1930 to the present; an era characterized by efforts on the part of the middle sectors to evolve a program that would permit them again to dominate the Argentine government. It is within the framework of these three periods that the political role of the Argentine middle sectors is discussed.

During the half-century prior to the election of Irigoyen the histories of the Argentine nation and the Argentine middle groups were, broadly speaking, not unlike those of Uruguay and Chile. In every major area of human relations the predominant philosophy in each of the republics was essentially the same—democratic and representative government, laissez-faire economics, Catholic religion, and cultural dependence upon Europe. In all three countries the members of the privileged groups were highly individualistic. To the extent that developments were conditioned by local circumstances the differences seemed, in general, to favor the Argentine middle elements.

At the turn of the century, the status of the Catholic Church in Argentina was similar to its position in Chile, and to its position in Uruguary prior to the advent of José Batlle y Ordóñez. The Argentine Constitution of 1853, which was still in force, had set the pattern. That document provided for the support of the Catholic Church by the Argentine government but it also recognized freedom of worship. In the 1880's the anticlerical elements had forced the passage of legislation that prohibited religious instruction in public schools. The Church had not been particularly active in politics, and there had never been a clerical party such as was found, for example, in Mexico or even in Chile where the Conservative Party was said to be more Catholic than the Church.

The record of the Argentine armed forces in staying out of civilian matters was better than that of Uruguay's prior to 1910 and compared favorably with Chile's. They had not engaged in politics on their own account since 1852, when they were instrumental in the overthrow of the tyrant, Juan Manuel de Rosas. Thereafter they remained aligned with the ruling oligarchy, and in 1890 and again in 1905 they efficiently suppressed uprisings of the "untried new groups" against the established authority. But when Irigoyen was elected, the armed forces accepted the shift of power from the elites to the new groups without serious incident. At that time there was good reason to believe that the military had become professional and would henceforth devote itself to those functions assigned it by the Constitution.

Relative to its neighbors, Argentina had enjoyed an abundance of the benefits resulting from the influx from abroad of investment capital, technological know-how and skilled labor. The nation had by far the most highly developed land and water transportation system to be found anywhere in Latin America, which had given its people considerable mobility and numerous contacts with Europe, from which new ideas were flowing to all parts of the world. It had also contributed to the development of a truly national economy. With the aid of foreign capital, the firm foundations of a commercial and industrial economy had been laid. The republic, with 50 per cent of its people already living in cities, was the most urbanized in Latin America. It had received more than its share of immigrants, who had played a major role in making the pampas one of the richest agricultural areas in the world. The impact of the immigrant upon fast-growing Buenos Aires, whose population in 1890 was 50 per cent foreign born, was equally apparent.

Argentina had also usurped Chile's leadership in education. The republic's claim to cultural superiority in Latin America could not be challenged. The generation of the eighteen nineties (*La Noventa*), which included such names as Alejandro Korn, Carlos Bunge, Lucas Ayarragaray, and José Ingenieros, comprised the greatest single collection of scholarship and ability ever assembled in Latin America up to that time. The graphic arts were more highly developed than anywhere else in Latin America.

The celebration of the centenary of the winning of independence, observed in 1910, had given encouragement to the growth of an ardent patriotism without producing an ardent nationalism. Argentine patriotism was predicated primarily upon future potential rather than upon past achievement. Although there were isolated outbursts against the foreigner, the

majority opinion was that the foreigner would and should continue to play a significant role in building the new Argentina.
There was little wonder that such was the case. If Argentina
had a distinct national characteristic in 1916 it was that it contained a higher proportion of new blood than any country in the
Western World, including the United States. The honor rolls
of public figures and scholars and artists were peppered with
Italian, French, German, Irish, and English family names. In
the economic area there was little of the antiforeignism that in
Uruguay had led to a national policy designed to eliminate the
foreigner from direct participation in the economic life of the
republic.

Xenophobia, however, had already entered into the nation's
thinking on foreign policy, and the United States was the bête
noire. Argentina foresaw itself as the leader of a South American bloc, and a strong United States, dominating a Western
Hemisphere union of nations, stood between Argentina and
that goal. By 1916 the narrow area of agreement in foreign
policy between the two republics foreshadowed the strained
relations that have become normal in this century. The United
States recognition of British claims to the hotly disputed Falkland Islands added to the leadership's sensitiveness.

The preparation of the Argentine middle sectors for political leadership compared favorably with that of their counterparts in Uruguay and Chile. In the 1860's and 1870's the
Argentine middle elements had exercised a pronounced influence upon the administrations headed by Bartolomé Mitre,
Domingo Faustino Sarmiento, and Nicolás Avellaneda. Each
of those regimes, as noted in Chapter 3, encouraged education
and cultural development; probably the two foremost newspapers of Latin America, *La Prensa* (1869) and *La Nación*
1870), were founded during the presidency of Sarmiento. The
three executives also promoted immigration and technological
development, both strong planks in the middle sectors' political
ideology. Finally, each of the presidents lent his support to the
growth of representative government. Thus, the Argentine
middle sectors gained valuable experience in policy-making at

about the same time as the Chilean middle groups, and earlier than the Uruguayan elements.

The Conservatives, controlled by landed oligarchs, returned to power in 1880 through resorting to extensive electoral coercion. But the groups led by the urban middle sectors were literally growing by the day in numbers and prestige, and within a decade they rose in armed revolt against the fiscal bankruptcy and official malfeasance of the Conservatives as represented by President Juárez Celmán (1886–90). The "Revolt of 1890" was shortlived, as the military remained loyal to the legal government. The uprising, nonetheless, signaled a new era in the republic's political life.

During the new era the urban middle sector–led groups so strengthened their claims to a greater share in the government that the Conservatives were finally compelled to give those claims legal recognition. The Civic Union, which had provided the intellectual ferment for the Revolt of 1890, was established as a political party in 1892. The new party was known officially as the Unión Cívica Radical, but traditionally it has been referred to as the Radical Party or simply as the Radicals. Although it drew support from wide segments of society and had a broad geographic base, it was from the start the party of the middle sectors, particularly those in Buenos Aires. Soon after the founding of the Radical Party, the highly regarded Argentine Socialist Party was established (1894) under the extremely able Juan Justo. It appealed both to the intellectuals, especially the university students, and to the rising industrial workers, who were beginning to organize in unions.

In 1905, largely to call attention to the pressures that were building up in the boiling political cauldron, the Radicals again arose in a revolt that was promptly quashed by the military. But throughout the 1890–1916 period, probably the Radicals' most effective tactics were the political education of the electorate through the press and party organizations and abstention from the polls. Abstention, used widely at times in Latin America to avoid a show of strength, repeatedly called public attention to the frauds that the Conservatives were perpetrating against society. The very fact that the middle sectors were free to make their objections known is highly significant. It suggests above all that the Republic had passed out of the stage of brute force and into one of greater political refinement and finesse. This development was made manifest when the mounting agitation of the Radicals, and to a lesser extent the Socialists, forced the passage of the Reform Bill of 1912. Popularly known as the "Sáenz Peña Law," it was introduced and passed by a Conservative government. The law, for the first time in Argentina, established the secret ballot and provided for broader suffrage and minority representation. It was under the terms of this bill that the middle sector–dominated Radical Party was victorious in the national elections of 1916.

The 1916 elections placed Argentina under the leadership of the middle groups. But control was not firmly in their hands. The Radical Party won narrowly and only with substantial and absolutely essential assistance from the rural elements who supported it because they disliked it less than they disliked the Conservatives.

Middle sector leadership was destined to last fourteen years. No middle sector leadership in Latin America ever came to power under more auspicious circumstances or, once in control, had more with which to work. There was not, for example, an armed revolt such as had confronted Batlle in Uruguay. Also, Irigoyen soon built up the presidential power to the point where it far exceeded that exercised by Alessandri in Chile, who was hamstrung by a malfunctioning parliamentary system. Nor were the Radicals faced with an aroused working element, as were the Mexican and Brazilian middle sectors when they took over control of their governments.

No middle sector element in Latin America ever inherited a more financially sound government. Argentina had already largely recovered from the first shock of economic dislocation following the outbreak of World War I. By the time Irigoyen took office, the nation's products were being urgently sought by the Allies. After the war, Argentina's prospects for future development along modern, progressive lines remained highly favorable in relation to the other four republics. The war had proved an incentive to industrial development more or less to the same degree that it had in the other countries, but in other respects the advantages lay with Argentina. It possessed the most highly integrated railroad system in Latin America and one of the seven best in the world. Its working elements were the healthiest, the best fed, and the most literate in the area. There were, of course, in some of the more backward farming regions hundreds of thousands of workers who were neither healthy and well fed nor literate. Land values rose precipitously after the economic readjustments of the early 1920's. Foreign investment capital and credit were available in plentiful supply. Throughout the decade following the end of the war, there were signs that Argentina was in balance and at peace with itself.

But then the depression struck and the nation was shocked out of its complacency. Overseas markets dried up, and easy credits from abroad disappeared. With them went the supreme confidence in the republic's future that a rising crest of prosperity had produced. For the first time in a decade and a half there was widespread discontent. For the first time the record made by the middle sectors since 1916 was closely scrutinized. The findings revealed that the Radicals had been largely unaffected by what was going on around them. The 1916 platform that had brought victory still provided the guiding spirit of the Party. The Radicals had been successful in carrying out some of the highly commendable goals of that platform, but they had failed to cope successfully with certain other developments that had not been foreseen in 1916.

The 1916 program had called for political democracy, and the Radicals had assiduously promoted representative government and freedom of expression. They had broadened the electoral base. They had maintained an atmosphere of freedom. They had permitted the waging of campaigns and the holding of elections. In most instances they had seen to it that ballots were fairly counted and that the victors were sworn into office. The picture, however, was not entirely favorable. Irigoyen's record of intervening in the political life of the provinces had been surpassed only once, by Justo José de Urquiza (1852–

60). Irigoyen's centralization of authority in the national government had been recognized as posing a threat to democratic government. Patronage had been used to buy political support. Official corruption had not been cured; if anything, it had become more widespread. But these adverse developments should not be permitted to discredit the very solid contributions that the Radicals made to the growth of representative government between 1916 and 1930. For in the latter year no other country in Latin America gave the impression of being as politically mature as Argentina.

As outs the Radicals had supported education. As ins they gave it considerable public backing. The University Reform of 1918, which guaranteed the universities greater autonomy, was a major contribution to Argentine learning and set an example that was emulated in several of the republics during the following decade. Elementary education was viewed as a right by the Radicals; and they gave their strong approval to public education, which was reflected in increased appropriations for the nation's schools and by a steady drop in the illiteracy rate. The population of Buenos Aires became one of the most literate in the world. The children of the more economically affluent families continued, ordinarily, to go to private schools, as the Argentine middle elements, like the middle sectors throughout Latin America, viewed public education as being for the masses. Education under the Radicals placed much greater emphasis upon preparing for the "mechanical age" than did the education of a generation earlier. Education became increasingly semiprofessionalized with the products of the high schools and the other more advanced institutions, such as trade schools and normal schools, being prepared in growing numbers for white-collar and managerial positions. Buenos Aires also achieved recognition as the outstanding publishing center in Latin America. For the first time, books and periodicals manufactured in Argentina began to find their way in sizable numbers to the other Latin American republics.

In so far as the Radicals' political future was concerned, their contribution may be considered largely to have ended with what they did by way of promoting the development of democratic-representative government and education. That was, of course, no small contribution; nonetheless, it must be recognized that it represented primarily the fulfillment of the principles they had held in the nineteenth century rather than a response to the changing conditions of the postwar world.

One of the significant failures of the Party was its inability to galvanize major segments of the middle sectors into a political unit. In fact, the leadership's conduct had had the opposite effect, and by 1930 the middle groups had become increasingly fragmented. There were good social and economic reasons why this was true, and they are discussed below; but politically, the responsibility for diffusing the middle sector political strength would seem to lie primarily with Irigoyen. He had been a member of the Party since its founding and its leader since 1896. Almost from the start he had viewed the Party as a personal vehicle and, as he strengthened his position, he became a personalist in the extreme. Before 1916 his capriciousness had driven the "Santa Fé Agrarians," under Lisandro de la Torre, out of the Party, and they returned only long enough to provide Irigoyen with the votes he needed to unseat the Conservatives in 1916. By 1922 his tyranny as president of the nation and as head of the Party had forced the antipersonalists, made up of the more conservative elements of the Party, into secession. Thenceforth, *Irigoyenistas* and the antipersonalists, who continued to consider themselves Radicals, were at loggerheads. When the antipersonalists won the presidency in 1922, Irigoyen used his influence in Congress to void a large part of the antipersonalist legislative program. When Irigoyen lost his popular support and faced an armed revolt during his second term in the presidency, the antipersonalists refused him their backing.

Traditionally the Radicals had been free traders, and the prosperity that Argentina, particularly in the rural areas, enjoyed during the decade following the war was to them evidence that free trade was working satisfactorily. Consequently they did little to upset the economic system that seemed to be serving Argentina so well but was coming under attack in other countries heavily reliant upon the sale abroad of raw materials. The Radicals had maintained an investment climate that had attracted large sums of foreign capital to transportation, communications, and the public services. They saw to it that trade treaties kept a steady flow of Argentine livestock and agricultural products on their way to Europe. On the other hand, the Radicals had not made a serious effort to break up the vast agricultural establishments, often controlled by absentee owners, on which it was becoming increasingly difficult for a laborer to rise to the level of a tenant farmer or a tenant farmer to the level of a landowner. The Radicals' refusal to make an issue of the status of large rural holdings was in accord with their strong commitments to the private ownership of property. Unlike the Colorados in Uruguay, the Radicals in Argentina with few exceptions kept the State clear of intervention in those spheres of economic activity traditionally reserved for private capital. Throughout their tenure, tariffs continued to be primarily for revenue purposes. The total effect of the Radicals' economic policies was to keep Argentina an underdeveloped country with much of its nonagricultural wealth in foreign hands, its life attuned to international exchanges, its well-being subject to all the vagaries of an international economic system over which it had no control.

The Radicals' record in support of the "neglected" elements of society was checkered. During their fourteen years in office they produced nothing to compare with the progressive and enlightened constitution that Chile had promulgated in 1925. Unlike in Uruguay and Chile, where the State had assumed a "social responsibility," in Argentina the Radicals had been content to leave the welfare of the less fortunate elements in the hands of Catholic charities. The Party could not point to anything concrete that it had contributed by way of permanent gains for organized labor. Following the week-long strike of 1919, which Irigoyen finally broke with the help of the police and the national army, and at a heavy cost in lives, the Radicals at no time demonstrated an abiding faith in the political capabilities of the workingman, although they continued to rely upon the votes of the urban workers to stay in office. They did place in the law books a considerable body of piecemeal legislation in favor of industrial labor. But their labor philosophy was heavily impregnated with paternalism and reflected a profound conviction that the benefits of the nation's prosperity would eventually filter down to the working groups whether there was legislation or not.

Any possibility of labor's profiting from the laws passed by the Radicals was largely nullified by the government's failure to provide for the enforcement of labor legislation, by the government's liberal use of court injunctions to prevent strikes, by the government's use of armed police as strike breakers, and by the government's imprisonment of labor leaders who refused to show their gratitude for favors received. The over-all view of labor's status under the Radicals revealed that the leadership's thinking had not been affected by the Mexican Revolution or the world trade union movement.

The Radicals' failure to respond favorably to the plight of the urban labor forces drove many socially conscious members of the middle sectors into the Socialist Party. By 1930 the Socialists had won over an important part of the laboring element of the city of Buenos Aires. Although Irigoyen retained to the end a large following among the working groups of the city, the inroads made by the Socialists forced him increasingly to rely upon that portion of his political organization centered in the province of Buenos Aires. In the national legislature the Socialists comprised the third middle sector–led element—the antipersonalists and the Santa Fé agrarians being the other two—that opposed the Irigoyenistas and in so doing they dissipated the energies of the middle groups.

Cultural nationalism was largely ignored in Argentina during the Radical era and economic nationalism received only moderate attention. Some laws were passed to protect domestic investors from "foreign trusts," and tariffs were made mildly protective in certain fields. Legislation that established closer control over immigration was passed. The laws to protect industry, however, were not the result of a predetermined policy in favor of industry and they did not offer a serious threat to foreign investors. Argentina continued to be looked upon as a highly favorable area for foreign investment right up to the time that the depression struck. The restrictions on immigration did not seriously curtail the flow of Europeans into the nation, for during the 1920's more immigrants entered the republic than in any decade except the one between 1905 and 1914. The surest sign that a latent economic nationalism did exist was the creation in 1922 of the State Petroleum Monopoly (Yacimientos Petrolíferos Fiscales—YPF),* which gave the State complete control over petroleum resources, and which at present stands as the symbol of Argentina's defiance of foreign economic control of natural resources. On the other hand the Radicals, as indicated earlier, offered no significant threat, as did the Colorados in Uruguay, to foreign investors in the utilities field.

The relative calmness with which the Radicals viewed the danger that foreign capital and foreign enterprises offered to Argentina's economic development did not carry over to the international relations field, in which they continued the highly nationalistic course set by the Conservatives prior to 1916. During the war years Irigoyen steadfastly hewed to Argentina's neutrality line, resisting the recommendations of many influential Argentines as well as the coercion of outside governments designed to force the nation into the European struggle. After the war, Argentina displayed an acute sensitiveness to any infringement upon its sovereign rights. The republic found it impossible actively to participate in the League of Nations for any length of time. The Radicals' concern over the possibility of surrendering certain sovereign rights led them throughout the 1920's to oppose expanding the Pan American Union into the political field or setting up hemispheric security systems. Further, in line with their concern over the defense of sovereign

* The first steps toward the development of state control of the petroleum industry were taken in 1907 and 1908. YPF observed its golden anniversary in late 1957 and early 1958. No constructive action, however, was taken until the 1920's.

rights, Argentina became the leader of the anti-interventionist elements in Latin America, whose efforts were directed toward keeping before the world the issue of United States interference in the Caribbean.

The armed forces, in league with the Conservatives, moved against Irigoyen and were able to take over the government with a minimum of confusion. The Radicals were out and the middle sector leadership of the nation was at an end.

There were a number of factors which conduced to the fall of the middle sectors in 1930. The depression had struck. The toppling of governments had become contagious. There was widespread unrest. Irigoyen had become senile—he was eighty years old—but he still refused to delegate authority. The students at the University of Buenos Aires had lost faith in his ability to lead the nation. As suggested above, Irigoyen's headstrong leadership of the nation and of the Radical Party had destroyed any unity from which the middle sectors might have profited in a period of political unrest. But there were at least three more basic considerations.

The first consideration was that no other nation in Latin America was more dependent than Argentina upon its agricultural resources and in no one of the other leading republics were the economic forces that might have countered the influence of the landed element relatively less developed. Unlike in Chile and Mexico, where minerals provided a large share of fiscal income and foreign exchange, in Argentina the national revenues, in one form or another, came almost solely from agriculture. Unlike in Uruguay, where a domestic industrial element already was exercising a major voice in policy-making, in Argentina the industrial community was politically weak because it was foreign-dominated. The nation's exclusive dependence upon agriculture gave the agrarian element an unusual influence in government, as the program of the Radicals between 1916 and 1930 had in fact acknowledged.

The second basic consideration was that the landed oligarchy's seemingly impregnable position had a profound effect upon the thinking of the military, which took the lead in deposing the middle sector political leadership in 1930. At a time when the military in Uruguay and Chile had mostly associated itself with the urban middle elements, and in Mexico had submitted under duress to revolutionary agrarian leadership, and in Brazil was about to break with the "coffee kings," the officer corps of the armed forces in Argentina remained closely aligned with the landed aristocracy and the beef barons. Nor did their alignment show signs of weakening until the end of the thirties. This arrangement between the military and the landholding elements indicates, although it cannot be established as fact, that unlike in Chile, Mexico, and Uruguay, in Argentina the advantages and prestige that the rich landowners continued to enjoy were sufficiently valued to encourage the officers of the armed forces to aspire to them rather than to the privileges the middle sectors had won. Of at least equal consequence to the middle sectors was the fact that the military had cast off its professional role and had again assumed the position of arbiter of political disputes. Force had once more replaced reason. The very fact that the armed forces could venture such a step suggests that they did not consider the middle sectors to have the vitality to lead the nation in a crusade against militarism.

Finally, the third consideration was that the middle sectors were undoubtedly the victims of Argentina's prosperity. The plight of the articulate sectors of Argentine labor had never been sufficiently serious to threaten a class struggle such as was waged in Mexico, or even to give birth to a sociopolitical movement such as was developed in Chile at the end of World War I. Also, good times, as noted earlier, had served to keep nationalist sentiment subdued. Thus, there had not developed at any time in Argentina in the 1920's the conditions that in Chile and Uruguay had contributed to strengthening the social and economic bonds between the middle sectors and the working groups. When the depression came in 1930 and the Argentine laborers suffered serious economic distress for the first time, the bonds they had formed with the middle sectors were not sufficiently strong to maintain their allegiances in a united front against the military and the Conservative oligarchy. When the working forces withdrew their support the middle sectors were isolated.

The Radical Party was out. The forceful removal from office of Irigoyen ended Argentina's first experience with civilian middle sector leadership on the national level.*

When the military returned the government to the civilians after 1932, the Radicals were replaced by the old landed oligarchy supported by a large segment of the antipersonalist Radicals and a sprinkling of the more nationalistically inclined commercial, industrial, and intellectual elements.† This alliance of Conservatives, antipersonalist Radicals, and Nationalists came to be known as the *Concordancia*. In a surprising resurgence of strength the *Irigoyenista* Radicals in 1931 won a sweeping electoral victory—later to be voided—in the province of Buenos Aires; and the death in 1933 of Irigoyen, the symbol of the Radical Party, generated near mass hysteria in and around Buenos Aires. But these developments, which indicated that the Center-Left wing of the Radical Party was recapturing its popular following, served only to alert those in power to the need of tightening their grip on the nation.

The military and Conservative elements that expelled Irigoyen held power until 1943. The government they directed was run for the agrarian interests. Politically the 1930–43 period was disastrous for the middle sectors. The Conservatives revived practices that recalled the worst features of nineteenth-century political life. Press censorship was resorted to. Critics of the administration were arrested, some were sent into exile. Elections were in some cases nullified, and in others fraud and manipulation of returns were widespread. Intervention in the provinces was freely used to control political developments. Control of the national government was increas-

---

* Augustín P. Justo, who became president in 1932, was an antipersonalist Radical as was Roberto M. Ortiz who assumed the presidency in 1938. Both had joined the Conservative dominated *Concordancia*, and it was the *Concordancia*, through resort to extensive fraud and political corruption, that put them in office. Also, in the period immediately prior to the military's seizure·of power in 1943, the Radicals and Socialists controlled the lower house of Congress. But the fact remains that the Conservatives were actually in control and making the decisions throughout the 1930–43 era.

† The military continued to exercise considerable influence behind the scenes.

ingly centralized in the executive branch. Although the military surrendered the government to civilians, it nonetheless played an active part in decision-making.

The party system suffered a severe setback under the *Concordancia,* which was not so much a party as a "group of determined men." It held power not because of party organization or strength but because of military backing, and the demoralization of the opposition. Even with the support of the military it had to "borrow" candidates from the antipersonalist Radicals in order to make a show of running a representative government. The Radical Party suffered because Irigoyen had not trained an heir to take over his leadership of the organization. This and the fact that the Party was deprived of its patronage cost the leadership much of its disciplinary power. The steadfast refusal of the middle sector–led Socialist Party to sacrifice its basic objectives in return for immediate advantages prevented it from cooperating closely with other Center and Left organizations for extended periods of time. Also, the Socialists' reluctance to use their influence with the labor movement to interfere in the internal affairs of the unions cost them the vote of the workingman who supported groups both to the Right and the Left that favored drastic and direct methods of obtaining his objectives.

The economic policies of the *Concordancia* were somewhat similar to those carried out by the middle sector leadership in Chile and Uruguay during the 1930's. In much the same fashion, the Conservative leadership in Argentina took measures to protect the nation's fiscal position in the face of a deteriorating economic situation. To protect domestic labor, severe restrictions were placed on immigration. As a result, entries dropped from 149,000 in 1929 to 30,000 in 1937. In the latter years 10,000 more persons left Argentina than entered. Controls were established over foreign exchange, prices, agricultural production, credits, and banking. As did Chile and Uruguay, Argentina kept alive previously established State-directed agencies such as YPF and founded new ones. Industry was offered limited protection and credits, which resulted in an appreciable expansion in that sector of the economy. State in-

tervention in economic matters did not prove to be a bitter pill
for the middle sectors, who prided themselves on being individualists, because, as in each of the four other republics, the
buffeting that the depression had given the Argentine business
and agricultural communities had prepared them mentally to
share their burdens with the State.

But there were some significant differences between the
economic approach of the leadership in Chile and Uruguay on
the one hand and in Argentina on the other. The *Concordancia*
moved more deliberately. In sharp contrast with the developments in Uruguay and the objectives of the Corporación de
Fomento in Chile, the *Concordancia* kept the State largely out
of the public-utilities field, which remained primarily in foreign hands. Also, in Argentina the leadership paid close attention to the welfare of agriculture and livestock at the same
time that it promoted industry. Thus the desire to advance industry did not prevent the government from making trade
treaties with Great Britain, which were detrimental to the
growth of Argentine manufacturing, but favorable to those elements producing agricultural commodities and livestock for
export. This meant, in effect, that the *Concordancia,* in its concern for the welfare of the rural sector, brought to an end the
laissez-faire economy without substituting in its place the type
of highly nationalistic doctrines based upon vibrant and domestically owned industry that had replaced laissez faire in
other republics, most notably in Uruguay.

The regime that controlled Argentina between 1930 and
1943 did little or nothing to correct social injustices and inequities. The gap separating the working groups from the
middle and upper social sectors was not narrowed. A few
possessing immense wealth but lacking a well-developed sense
of social responsibility used their influence to prevent the passage of even minimum social-reform legislation. No organized
effort was made to give the working groups or the farm-tenant
element a fuller and more responsible part in society. The industrial labor movement continued to be distrusted as it had
been under the Radicals and, as a consequence, it remained

weak. It had little political influence and its membership probably did not constitute 10 per cent of the urban working force.

The middle sectors as social groups experienced both gains and losses under the Conservative coalition. On the credit side was the fact that the expansion of commerce and industry increased the need for technical and managerial skills. Throughout most of the period there was a steady demand for teachers to provide instruction for the growing population. The State's assumption of a broader economic responsibility resulted in a notably enlarged bureaucracy. Remarking upon the bureaucracy, the Argentine economist, Alejandro Bunge, implied that it was the Conservatives' padding of the bureaucracy that was primarily responsible for the fact that between 1922 and 1939 the cost of government rose 138 per cent while the population was increasing 45 per cent and the gross national product was being augmented by only 41 per cent.*

On the debit side were a loss in self-confidence and a decline in the economic status of the salaried middle sectors. The collapse in 1930 of the political system they were nourishing to maturity was a serious blow to the morale of the middle groups. Given their weak economic position vis-à-vis the landed elite, politics had become the middle sector *raison d'être*. Once their political influence was reduced and the nation's economic policy was again given a strong rural orientation, the historic tendency for the Argentine middle sectors to splinter was accentuated. Their weakened economic position resulted on the one hand because the nation's schools were supplying graduates with the middle sector skills faster than they could be absorbed by the economy, and on the other hand because the ruling elements, in making their political assessments, did not feel required to award the middle groups a greater share of the national income. Since the ruling clique felt approximately the same way toward the working groups, the situation in 1943 was not unlike the one in 1890 when the prosperity of the few

* Alejandro Bunge, *Una neuva Argentina* (Buenos Aires, 1940), p. 404.

camouflaged a sea of discontented elements who included not only the middle sectors and working groups but a growing body of nationalists.

Extremist groups — Nationalists and Communists — increasingly exploited the discontent of the wage-earning elements and the uncertainties provoked by World War II, until, on June 4, 1943, the Argentine army overthrew the civilian government and assumed control of the republic. During the months immediately following the coup it became evident that the military had no intention of returning power to civilian hands. It became equally apparent that decision-making power resided in a highly nationalistic and pro-Axis "colonels' clique," known as the *Grupo de Oficiales Unidos* (GOU). By mid-1944, Juan Domingo Perón established himself as the undisputed leader of the GOU. Perón came from a middle sector background. He had little sympathy for what the landed oligarchy represented politically and economically. Especially did he detest the oligarchy's "subservience" to Great Britain.

A number of the officers belonging to the GOU, including Perón, had served their apprenticeship in the Revolution of 1930, which drove the Radicals from power. Some of them had disapproved of restoring the government to civilian control in 1932, on the ground that the state of the nation required authoritarian rule under the military. Their confidence in military authoritarianism was strengthened during the thirties through numerous contacts with German and Italian officers in Argentina and through serving on missions abroad. Their travels in Europe had also convinced them of the invincibility of the German and Italian armies, a conviction that seemed confirmed by the Axis successes in the early years of World War II.

Perón was elected president in February 1946; he took office in April of that year, and retained control of the nation until September 1955. As far as the political life of the Argentine middle sectors was concerned Perón's dictatorship was an enigma. At no time in his regime did he feel the need of seeking the political support of the middle groups. He held in disdain their political objectives and tactics. He showered attention and public funds upon the armed forces. But his administration also displayed many of the characteristics that have come to be associated with middle sector leadership. He promoted education. He favored industrialization over agriculture. He was highly nationalist throughout most of his regime. He went to extremes in State intervention. The total effect of his program was to encourage urbanization. But most important, he brought the working groups to the surface. The combination of ardent nationalism and aroused workers seeking greater social and economic justice, as distinguished from the political equality that the Radicals had offered, produced for the first time in Argentina a politically charged movement with strong indigenous roots.

Perón's regime was so patently undemocratic that elaboration of the point hardly seems necessary. The dictator methodically destroyed most of what remained of the democratic processes and procedures achieved under the Radicals. The judiciary, which under the Radicals had won national and international respect for integrity, was destroyed as *antiperonista* judges were purged. For extended periods of time the country was declared to be in "a state of internal war" and consequently subject to control under legislation that had the effect of martial law. The press and the radio were gagged. Imprisonment and torture were commonly employed. Political exile was freely resorted to. An elaborate spy system was developed to intimidate the populace. Elections were deceptions. Voting could be held in an ostensible atmosphere of freedom because the terms under which the opposition was permitted to campaign left no doubt as to the final results. In 1951, Perón polled two-thirds of the votes for the presidency. His candidates won every seat in the Senate and all but 14 of the 149 seats in the Chamber of Deputies. But Perón's electoral tactics should not be construed to mean that he did not have popular support. He did. He just could not tolerate organized opposition.

The party system suffered severe blows. Perón built his own political organization, controlled it absolutely, and poured public funds into its support.* At the same time, innumerable

* Technically Perón created two parties, one for men and one for women. Both were rigidly controlled by the dictator.

barriers were thrown up to obstruct the opposition or possible opposition. New parties were required to register their names, doctrines, platforms, and officers, and to wait three years for a ruling on legal recognition, which was left to courts packed with *peronistas*. Coalitions of parties were made unlawful. The government was empowered to dissolve any party whose program appeared to threaten the "social peace." Small regional parties were hamstrung by a law that required parties to present candidates for each election. To the problems created by Perón were added the others that resulted from the differences between the opposition groups regarding the best methods of opposing the dictatorship. From the already badly splintered Radical Party emerged a wing that proposed "to out-Perón Perón" in its bid for the support of the working groups. When Perón was through with the opposition parties they were little more than groups "against which the people could jeer and he could rail."

While with one hand Perón finished off the democratic process, which the *Concordancia* had dealt a crippling blow, and created an impossible environment for the opposition political parties, with the other he heaped favors upon the military. Officers were called upon to fill a large number of cabinet posts and were freely used as interventors in the provinces; they were placed in charge of new industrial plants. The salaries of military personnel were raised. At certain levels the salaries of commissioned officers in the Argentine military were in excess of those received in the United States armed forces. Each of the three armed services was expanded and provided with considerable new equipment. The attention shown the military in the early years of the regime was reflected in public expenditures. In 1945 the military was allotted 37 per cent of all current public expenditure, 32 per cent in 1950, and 23 per cent in 1954.

It is still too early to measure Perón's effect upon education. Certainly, however, he could claim a quantitative victory. More schools were built during his régime than ever before. A larger percentage of school-age children received instruction than at any time previously. Argentina's literacy rate probably improved slightly. For 1945, 1950, and 1954 education was allotted, respectively, 17, 18, and 16 per cent of the funds for current public expenditure. This apportionment compared favorably with the 9, 13, and 8 per cent for the same years in Brazil, but it was low in terms of Chile's 24, 23, and 22 per cent.

There is, however, considerable question about the type and quality of the instruction that the schools imparted under Perón. The central authorities instituted close restrictions on education at all levels. The national government assumed responsibility for providing a large share of the textbooks, thereby appropriating the right of censorship over subject matter. Instructors were required to teach Perón's social and economic doctrine at all grade levels. But we do not know how closely the requirement was observed in the private schools from which, it is highly probable, the next generation of Argentine leaders will come. The universities, in particular, felt the heavy hand of the dictator. Before he was driven from office he had deprived them of the autonomy granted them under the Reform Law of 1918. He had usurped the power to name university rectors (read presidents). The rights, privileges, and responsibilities of the universities were rigidly established by law. A National University Council was named to serve as a liaison between the government and higher education. During Perón's regime, 90 per cent of the teaching personnel of the universities was changed through retirement, discharges, and resignations. Such change could not have failed seriously to harm the quality of university instruction.

Perón turned out to be a much worse economist than many (including this author) believed possible. It is now clear beyond any reasonable doubt that he led the republic to the brink of, if not into, economic disaster. It is equally evident that the nation will be years recovering from the effects of his unsound economic measures. Largely because the profits allowed farmers and livestock producers by the government were strictly limited, production seriously declined. Such development was extremely dangerous in the face of a rapidly expanding population that would have to be fed and an increasing need for foreign exchange which only farm commodities could earn. At

1950 prices agricultural and pastoral production declined by 50 per cent between 1946 and 1952. During the same period, farming became progressively less efficient because of a lack of new equipment and replacement parts.

Although Perón strongly supported industrial development, it fared poorly in terms of growth. For example, manufacturing reached peak production during his era as early as 1948–49. Meanwhile the contribution of general services to the national gross product rose from 50.5 per cent in 1947 to 53.2 per cent in 1954. After 1948 the gap between supply and demand of energy and fuel remained approximately stationary. Throughout the dictator's regime there was steady disinvestment in the transportation sector of the economy. In the case of the railroads decapitalization in rolling stock and equipment amounted to more than 20 per cent between 1948 and 1954. The mileage of highways kept in "good repair" declined. At the end of 1953 the average age of trucks in service was probably over fifteen years.

Real wages reached their peak in 1948, when remuneration of workers absorbed 59.4 per cent of the republic's total income, compared with 46.7 per cent in 1945. Subsequent to 1949 real income declined steadily until 1954, when there was temporary improvement. By the end of 1954 the per capita gross production in all areas of the Argentine economy was barely 3.5 per cent higher than in 1946, and the poor showing was reflected in the earning power of the workers.

Perón was a dedicated state interventionist. Before he was driven from power he had made major inroads on the sphere of activities that the Radicals and Conservatives had retained for private enterprise, and the State had become the owner of or partner in a wide range of industrial and commercial undertakings. With foreign-exchange balances built up during the war, Perón bought the French- and British-owned railroads, thereby giving the nation a complete monopoly over railroad traffic. He purchased the sprawling I.T. & T. holdings in the name of the State. He vastly expanded and modernized the Argentine merchant fleet. State funds were employed to finance and administer domestic and international airlines. The State engaged in a considerable number of manufacturing activities, including meat packing and distribution. The State became almost the sole source of internal credits for industrial expansion. Through the government trading corporation, the Instituto Argentino de Promoción de Intercambio (IAPI), the State was given the final voice regarding all imports and exports. In 1954 public expenditure constituted approximately 23 per cent of the gross national product. The State exercised close control over the labor unions, whose membership rose to a claimed six million under Perón. The State replaced the Catholic charities as the principal welfare agency. The State was represented in the political field by the *peronista* parties, which received financial assistance from the central government.

The last three of the State enterprises mentioned above— the unions, the charities, and the *peronista* political parties— were the agencies through which Perón won and maintained the support of the working elements, which, along with the armed forces, were requisite to his continuance in power. It was through those agencies that the dictator gave a "social content" to the government and gave the workingman a sense of belonging to the nation. The laboring element responded with enthusiastic political fervor but not with economic output. Even in 1951–52, when fringe benefits and spiraling wages on the one hand and declining productivity on the other could no longer be reconciled and when Perón was forced to deny part of the demands of his beloved *descamisados,* all but the old-line union membership remained strongly behind him. And apparently they were still with him when he was expelled from office by the military. Two years later in the election held in July 1957 to choose a constituent assembly, the *peronistas,* who were not permitted to put up candidates, cast approximately one and a half million blank ballots out of a total of approximately eight million.* History will, it seems, have to rank Perón along

* *New York Times,* July 31, August 4, 1957.

with Getulio Vargas of Brazil and Lázaro Cárdenas of Mexico among the twentieth-century Latin American politicians having unusual popular appeal. Each was a master political tactician.

The multiple activities of the State required an outsized number of public servants. By 1951, one-half of Argentina's five million salaried workers were in public administration or working in enterprises controlled by the State. In 1954 those in public administration, excluding defense, education, and public health, numbered 520,000, which was equal to 7 per cent of the total economically active population of approximately 7,600,000. The comparable figures for Brazil—which had about three times as large a population but was considerably less developed—were 306,000 in public administration, or 2 per cent of the total active population.

Perón had outdone his middle sector counterparts in increasing the number of those feeding at the public trough. The higher level bureaucrats were telling Juan Pueblo what he could buy, see, hear, and, they hoped, think. The bureaucrats were, in turn, taking detailed orders from above. They were powerless before Perón's controlled press and radio, which engaged in character assassination—one of the dictator's more sophisticated ways of ruining those who appeared to have pretensions to power. When Perón fled into exile it became apparent that he had completely broken the initiative of the bureaucracy, as it did not play—nor has it yet played—a positive role in the juggling of political forces since September 1955.

The bureaucrats did not fare noticeably worse or better than the other segments of the middle groups. Perón did not aspire to the destruction of the professional elements or of the commercial and industrial middle sectors. Unlike the Communists, he did not look upon the business community as an "unhealthy social organism." But he was determined to destroy those in the liberal professions, in commerce, and in industry who persisted in publicly opposing him. The usefulness to the Argentine nation of thousands upon thousands of persons belonging to the middle sectors was reduced. Despite the best efforts of the dictator, however, many of the pre-Perón elements remained influential to the end of his regime. Also, in a large majority of the cases, some provision was made for successors to carry on in place of the victims of the dictator's wrath. Thus, the number of university professors was reduced only slightly, if at all, as replacements were found for those who refused to instruct under the terms laid down by the dictator, or were driven from their posts by him. For every newspaper editor or radio-station owner who was jailed or driven into exile, another was created, often more than one. As in the field of education, it was the quality, not the quantity, among the liberal professions that suffered.

The effects of the dictator's whims upon the commercial and industrial elements were similar to those upon the liberal professions. For every business or industrial enterprise that was driven to the wall by price fixing, wage boosts, bonuses to the workers, fringe benefits, and forced contributions to Perón's political parties and the Eva Perón Welfare Foundation, another business or industrial enterprise prospered in the hands of a friend of the administration. In fact the Perón regime was in a very real sense favorable to industry and commerce. The growth of the industrial working groups and the bureaucracy, with the resultant increase in purchasing power, vastly enlarged the domestic market. Many businesses responded to the growing demand for their products by expanding beyond the point where family and partnership control remained feasible, and stock was offered to the public in greater quantities than at any previous time. Furthermore, a study of 150 companies listed on the Buenos Aires Stock Exchange showed that their dividends rose from an average of 9.92 per cent in 1940–45 to 17.71 per cent in 1946–49, and even in the depression year 1952 they declined only to 16.7 per cent. Although the latter figure included a considerable proportion of stock dividends to offset inflation, it was still well above the level for the six years immediately preceding Perón's inauguration in 1946.[*]

Although Perón offered himself as the friend of all laboring groups the fact of the matter is that his policies were much

[*] Arthur P. Whitaker, *The United States and Argentina* (Cambridge, Mass., 1954), p. 207.

more favorable to the urban workers than to the rural labor force. One result was a swift movement to the urban centers. Between 1943, the year that the military took over the government and Perón began his rapid ascent to power, and 1947 about 900,000 to 1,000,000 persons, or 20 per cent of the rural population in 1943, are believed to have moved into the urban areas. During the same span of years Greater Buenos Aires (including the capital and seven centers within the urban agglomeration) gained approximately 750,000 inhabitants, all but about 150,000 of the increase resulting from internal migration. Sixty-two per cent of the Argentine population lived in cities of 2,000 or more by 1947, and by 1950 the percentage stood at 66. In the latter year, 48 per cent of the population lived in towns of 20,000 and over. By the end of the Perón regime, Greater Buenos Aires, with 5,617,000 inhabitants, contained over 29 per cent of the total population of the republic. And the total urban population stood at nearly 70 per cent. Argentina's fifteen largest cities could outvote the remainder of the nation.

With the bulk of the dictator's popular forces concentrated in a few cities, Perón, for approximately seven years, or until 1953, and with hardly a letup, plied them with what was probably the most virulent and sustained nationalism ever offered a people of a major Western Hemisphere nation. In the field of juridic or political nationalism, where the Radicals and the *Concordancia* had largely limited themselves to defending Argentina's sovereign rights, Perón took the offensive, which undoubtedly had considerable support in every major segment of society, including the intellectuals. Sympathy for the "underdog colonials" comes almost naturally to nearly all Latin American intellectuals, among whom there remains a residual faith in an eventual universal brotherhood of man, which dates back to the humanist intellectual climate of the nineteenth century.

United States Ambassador Spruille Braden's efforts to discredit the Argentine military and Perón as Fascist-oriented gave the dictator an unusual opportunity to establish himself as the defender of national sovereignty. Braden openly en-

couraged the opposition. After his recall to Washington, he
took the lead in preparing the State Department's "Blue Book
of Argentina." That document, which was published to
"prove" Perón's and the Argentine military's connections with
Nazi-Fascist elements, appeared two weeks before the presidential election in February 1946. Perón seized upon the
document as evidence of United States interference in the internal affairs of Argentina. "Braden or Perón" became his
slogan in the last days of the campaign, and it is conceded by
many that it probably won ballots for Perón, since the Argentine voter traditionally has been acutely sensitive to any en-
croachment upon his nation's sovereign rights.

Once installed in office, Perón became the champion of
national sovereignty in all parts of the Hemisphere. His representatives at international congresses vocally supported the
doctrine that colonial people have the right to self-determina-
tion, especially in the Latin American sphere of influence.
Colonization suggested cultural retardation, and Latin America
was civilized. At the Tenth Inter-American Conference, held
in Caracas in 1954, the Argentines backed proposals "to gratify
the desire of colonial people of the hemisphere for self-govern-
ment." Perón's controlled press and radio, and his spokesmen
for Argentine-organized labor, including the "labor attachés,"
pointed accusing fingers at the United States for keeping the
Puerto Ricans in an "inferior status" while posing as the
apostle of justice in world forums.

Until 1953, Perón vehemently opposed the military assistance pacts that the United States was making on a bilateral
basis with certain of the Latin America republics. He insisted
that they infringed the rights of the nation involved. In remarking upon Mexico's refusal to join in such a pact, Perón
declared that "imperialists would encounter difficulty in finding
cannon fodder in Latin America."

Perón lent his support to those nations—notably Mexico,
Ecuador, Peru, and Chile—that since World War II have
claimed the right individually to establish the linear limits of
national sovereignty over adjacent waters and submerged
lands. Closer to home, he reasserted Argentina's claims to the

Falkland Islands, and made a show of force on occasions when it appeared that Great Britain might be infringing Argentina's claims in Antarctica.

The dictator pursued economic nationalism no less fervently than he did juridic nationalism. He had a fertile field to harvest. The republic was still highly dependent upon outside sources of supply for war material and manufactured goods. It did not produce any heavy machinery. Much of its industrial plant, transportation system, and utilities were in foreign hands. This economic dependence was everywhere evident and could be pinpointed. Because economic nationalism was less abstract, the working groups could understand it more fully than they could juridic nationalism. It was not difficult to convince the worker that domestic-controlled enterprises would strengthen him in his job. At least in its initial stages, the domestic industrialists welcomed Perón's promises of protection against competition from abroad. Thus the foreign investor was made the common enemy.

In his efforts to drive the "foreign imperialist" from Argentina, Perón ran through the entire list of tactics employed by the economic nationalists up to his time. He raised tariffs. He provided credits to domestic investors. His welfare legislation hit the foreign companies particularly hard. He insisted that certain Argentine imports and exports be carried in Argentine bottoms. He bought out foreign investors in Argentina's railroads and in some major utilities. His rubber-stamp legislature passed controls over nondomestic capital which had the effect of making the country a largely barren field for further foreign investment. The Constitution of 1949, which was written at his instigation, contained provisions that made minerals, waterfalls, petroleum, coal, gas, and other national sources of energy the inalienable property of the nation.

As additional evidence of his devotion to Argentine nationalism Perón declared that he would "never" contract a foreign loan. He did, however, as early as 1950, when he accepted a $125,000,000 "commercial credit" from the United States. Thereafter, there were other break-throughs. The climate improved for foreign investors, and the controls over the remittance of profits were eased. Most important, Perón in effect acknowledged that the YPF, the State's petroleum monopoly and the symbol of Argentine economic independence, was incapable of developing the petroleum industry as fast as was needed. He turned to Standard Oil of California. At the time of his fall from power he appeared prepared to go through with the arrangement that had been worked out with that company. But he had preached economic nationalism so convincingly that his handpicked Congress did not trust itself to support him in the face of widespread and vocal public disapprobation. Nor have those who followed him in control of the nation dared to turn to the outside for assistance in overcoming the nation's acute petroleum shortage. Perón had indeed raised nationalism to a basic ideology pregnant with political possibilities. As in several other instances he outdid the middle sector leadership at its own game.

The armed forces had put Perón in office, and ten years later they drove him from office and into exile. Those involved in the overthrow knew when they started that the defeat of Perón, if it came at all, would be a relatively quick and simple matter compared to ending Peronism, which for a decade had fed upon unrest abroad and class hatred and antiforeignism at home. The machinery of government had broken down. The economy had ground to a halt. Argentina's standing abroad was lower than at any time in a century. But the greatest obstacle to recovery would be the profound distrust and suspicion that Perón had engendered in the people.

Two and a half years "after Perón" the situation had not changed notably except that the military on May 1, 1958 had peacefully surrendered power to civilian elements. By that time the prospect of rapid economic recovery had faded. The nation continued to suffer from a lack of domestic sources of fuel and industrial metals. Highly trained technicians were in serious short supply. Land and capital resources were strictly limited. The insistent and often unrealistic demands of several articulate socioeconomic groups for a greater share of the national product reduced the prospects of the newly inaugurated civilian leaders originating and successfully directing a practical program of recovery. The republic was in the grip of a virulent nationalism made strong by popular support ranging from Communist to Fascist on the one hand and from workingman to aristocrat on the other. Nationalism kept the foreign investor wary.

Few inroads had been made against the antagonisms that Perón left in his wake and that continued to obstruct every path that might lead to a successful national effort to cast off the shackles the dictator had imposed. Once freed from Perón's domination, labor split. The long-established and well-paid groups—i.e., railway engineers, firemen, typographers—distrusted the "new" and "irresponsible" industrial working elements who clamored for a greater share of the national income with little thought of how production might be expanded so that their demands might be met. Those within the military who favored surrendering power to civilians had opened deep wounds when they resorted to firing squads. Those wounds were far from healed when civilians took over. Within the middle sectors bitterness toward those whom Perón had raised to high posts in education, mass communications, and the bureaucracy still ran at near fever pitch. Within the business world there was deep resentment against those who had enriched themselves with the blessings of Perón.

If agreement had been reached in any major area by 1958, it was that there could be no turning back of the clock. Many, including large segments of those who had bitterly opposed the dictator, were satisfied that the changes brought about by Perón had had to come. Many were convinced that they were for the better. But even those who viewed the changes as socially and economically regressive acknowledged them to be politically realistic. Perón had succeeded politically because he had sensed what was happening in other underdeveloped countries and had applied what he had understood to Argentina. Many of those who succeeded him borrowed his techniques and appeals, and much of the demagoguery at which he was so expert. "Workers' rights," "social responsibility," "industralization," "state intervention," "nationalism," and "anti-imperialism"—terms that Perón had made commonplace without the voter's understanding their full implications—entered into the calculations of every person who aspired to high public office.

Although in May 1958 Argentina returned to civilian control under the freely elected and scholarly Arturo Frondizi and the intransigent wing of the Radical Party, it remained to be seen whether or not the new regime was capable of creating a viable government. A number of considerations seemed to argue against such a possibility. In the first place there was deep-seated discontent in the armed forces, where the *peronista* issue persisted and many officers disapproved of the decision to return the country to civilian control at such an early date. If the differences within the armed forces should be brought into the open the chances of the government's becoming involved would be good, and its involvement could not fail to have profound consequences in a period of instability such as exists in Argentina.

Also, several developments in the civilian area would appear to militate against the creation of a stable government. Despite two national elections since the overthrow of Perón, the workers brought to the surface by the dictator remained largely an unknown political quantity. No one knew for sure where they fitted into the political picture. Great danger lay in the possibility that some politicians would seriously overestimate the political strength of labor and that others would seriously underestimate it. Given the delicate balance in which Argentina found itself, a significant miscalculation one way or another could produce political conditions that could be resolved only by a group or groups capable of taking a strong stand. Indecision on the part of a civilian government might provide an invitation for the military to return to power.

Profound economic instability likewise tended to discourage confidence in the formation of a viable civilian administration. In the economic area Argentina seemed to need two things above all others: a healthy agricultural economy capable of earning a maximum of foreign exchange and an investment climate capable of attracting large amounts of foreign capital. The attainment of these basic necessities to economic well-being would require long-range planning. But the serious economic position of the workers, whose interests must enter strongly in the estimates of politicians, made their objectives essentially short range. This meant that any long-range effort to strengthen the economy by developing agriculture at the immediate price of a significantly increased cost of living to the workers and the poorly paid middle sectors would likely meet strong resistance. Nationalism, meanwhile, had been maintained at such a high pitch that it was difficult to foresee its being tempered to the point where foreign private investment capital would be given an opportunity to contribute substantially to Argentina's economic resurgence. The branch of the Radical Party that assumed control in May 1958 was firmly committed to policies that were in most respects at least as nationalistic as those pursued by Perón.

Although on balance it appears that over the next five years or so conditions in Argentina will be weighted against the maintenance of a stable democratic-representative government free to dedicate itself to the national welfare, the forces of reason and moderation will not be entirely without weapons. The republic is inherently rich. Even Perón was unable to destroy the pampas, which, despite several decades of soil-mining, remain the finest farm lands in Latin America. Increasing evidence piles up in support of the view that the republic possesses sizable deposits of petroleum and industrial mineral ores. It also probably still possesses the most literate and efficient labor force in Latin America despite the decline in its record of production under Perón and subsequently.

The party in power has a tradition of middle sector leadership, and these groups experienced the advantages of responsible government between 1916 and 1930. Also, the middle sectors are the only civilian groups capable of moderating the differences between labor and capital which are certain to arise during the years immediately ahead. The moderative influence of the middle sector leadership will be enhanced by the fact that it is committed to the promotion of public education and to the protection of the workingman's interest but not to a degree that makes it greatly feared by the industrial and agricultural sectors who may be expected to be called upon to carry a major share of increased public spending.

Perhaps as important as any of the above considerations in any attempt to evaluate the future of civilian government in Argentina has been the emergence of a Catholic and middle sector–led Social Christian movement, which is essentially centrist. For political purposes the movement operates under the name of the Christian Democratic Party. A Catholic party is new to Argentina, where the Church has generally shunned active participation in politics. Such groups, however, have already shown strength in Chile and in Costa Rica. In view of the Church's positive role in bringing about the fall of Perón the Social Christians may expect to command some recognition from the Frondizi following, which is by tradition essentially anticlerical. To the extent that the voice of the Social Christians is heard it should have a moderating influence. Through the movement's relationship to the Catholic Church it could influence the Catholic laboring elements. Also it could provide a rallying point for those who believe politically in representative government and who are economically dedicated to private property and individual enterprise. As a result of its bonds with the Church it has a clear-cut mandate to fight the brand of nationalism propagated by the Communists. Finally, it may provide a "moral prop" in the insecure state of mind in which the Argentine people collectively find themselves.

Should the forces of moderation triumph over those of extremism, and Argentina does succeed in returning to stability under civilian guidance, much of the credit will have to go to the middle sectors. Even though they are currently seriously divided and are in the process of profound change they are the only civilian element which possibly possesses the necessary leadership capabilities.

7 *Mexico*

REORIENTATION OF A REVOLUTION

Decision-making in Mexico has been dominated by the urban middle sectors since the early 1940's. The members of the present leadership were able to assert themselves only after the socioeconomic elements they represent had waged a prolonged and tenacious holding action against the forces of radical agrarianism born of the Revolution of 1910. The middle sectors' conduct between 1917, when the Mexican Constitution now in force was promulgated, and 1940, when the election of Manuel Ávila Camacho paved the way for the urban middle groups' emergence as the primary influence in formulating and administrating national policies, offers unusual examples of their ability to survive in a wide variety of political climates. Similarly, their conduct in office affords constant reaffirmation of their basically conservative tenets. Their impact upon the Revolution both before and after they became a primary political factor goes deeper than mere slogans, symbols, and solutions, for the Revolution has been and continues to be presented to the Mexican people as a movement by and for the popular masses.

The present era is not the first in which the Mexican middle sectors have figured prominently in politics during this century. Discontented intellectuals were primarily responsible for iniating the Revolution of 1910, which toppled the dictatorship of Porfirio Díaz and set in motion the developments that have shaped Mexico's destiny in recent decades.

The intellectuals harbored many grievances against the old

dictator. He had been in control of the nation for over thirty years. He had failed, in general, to promote the developments that would have created opportunities for those who relied upon their intellectual skills. He had permitted education to languish to the point where Mexico was referred to as a cultural desert. He had held a close rein on the press.

The intellectuals' primary charge against Díaz, however, was political. Although he had provided jobs for nearly every member of the middle sectors who would cooperate with his regime, he had reduced the level of appointment and the possibility of advancement to all but a select few. This lack of opportunity to grow stemmed from Díaz' reliance upon the military and upon a group known as the *científicos*.

Díaz was a militarist, and he ruled by force. When he came to power be brought with him a sizable group of friends, many of whom were former comrades-in-arms from the civil wars of the 1850's and the struggles to expel the French-sponsored Maximilian regime from Mexican soil during the 1860's. Díaz appointed some of them to important federal and state posts. Others he ordered elected to high positions. Those who year after year proved loyal to the dictator were permitted to retain their offices. These civil servants, who knew only obedience to their chief, epitomized the role of force in the life of the republic. In Mexico, unlike in Argentina, Chile, and Brazil, militarism was an ingrained part of political life at the time the middle sectors were preparing their bid for power.

Meanwhile, the aging dictator, who was himself a Europeanized-mestizo, lost his earlier affinity for his own social element. Increasingly he surrendered policy-making in all but the political and military fields to the *científicos*, who were mostly creole by extraction and neopositivist by training and ideology. They represented the extreme adulation of Europe and the deprecation of things Mexican.

With high public office monopolized by the dictator's personal favorites and decision-making, particularly in the economic area, delegated to the *científicos*, there was little opportunity in public life for those who did not qualify for one or the other of the two groups. Promising young men who under other circumstances might have looked forward to rising in the government to a point where they could find expression for their political aspirations were either permanently relegated to minor posts or entirely barred from government. In either case, this meant social as well as political ostracism, since government service offered practically the only opportunity for such individuals to earn a livelihood in a manner considered befitting their social status.

By 1910 the political isolation of the generation that had grown to maturity under Díaz had become so complete that the members were faced with either submitting to further humiliation and degradation or seeking to upset the established system by employing force. They chose the latter. With Francisco I. Madero, a socially minded scion of a rich landholding family of the north, as their principal spokesman, and using an election fraud as their immediate justification for taking the law into their own hands, they called upon the nation to rise against the stultifying atmosphere of the *pax porfiriana*. Their slogan, "Effective Suffrage and No Reelection," indicated both their nineteenth-century liberal philosophy and their primary objective. Their demands could be satisfied by a change in government. A revolution to them had become a political necessity.

The intellectuals added an anticlerical bias to their requirements for political reform. Without abrogating the anticlerical provisions of the Constitution of 1857, Díaz had winked at the resurgence of the Catholic Church. By 1900 that institution had recovered much of the prestige it had lost during the civil strife of the 1850's. It was regaining its hold upon education, as the State ignored its responsibilities in that field. It had again acquired extensive property holdings. It was once more exercising considerable influence on the government through Carmen, the wife of the dictator. Thus, as had been the case a half-century earlier, the secular activities of the Church could be attacked without offending many of those who accepted its religious dogmas. Compared to the role of the Catholic Church in Argentina, Brazil, Chile, and Uruguay, that of the Church in Mexico was a major one.

While the discontented intellectuals were still planning their course of action, they won the support of a large segment of the mestizos in the commercial colony, whose stake in the business community and influence in government had been deteriorating steadily for several years. The mestizos had acquired a place in commerce as early as the 1850's. They had been instrumental in the reform movement of that decade and in promoting Benito Juárez first to the leadership of the nonclerical, nonmilitarist elements and then to the presidency of the republic. In turn, the Juárez government dedicated itself to justifying the enlarged political role of the emergent economic element. Subsequently, Díaz drew his major support from the mestizos engaged in commerce and industry. He repaid them by governing in their interests until the 1890's, but when the dictator came under the influence of the *científicos,* at their instigation he turned increasingly to the United States, France, and Great Britain for the financial means and technical skills needed to modernize the country. As the foreigners rapidly took over major segments of the Mexican economy and bought justice in the high courts, the Mexicans in commerce and industry were as thoroughly isolated in the economic field as were the intellectuals in the political field. And when the businessmen made common cause with the intellectuals, they added to the political requirements and the anticlericalism of their allies a demand that "Mexico be returned to the Mexicans." What they wanted was a revolution directed against foreign capital. Thus antiforeignism in Mexico was raised to the level of a political tenet, where it has remained.

But the disgruntled intellectuals and embattled business elements were small in number. The abstract appeals of the intellectuals were understood by few of their countrymen, a considerable share of whom had been so degraded by the three-decade-long tyranny that they lacked the will required to lift themselves from the mire into which they had sunk. Their apathy characterized the early days of the revolt. They seemed incapable of militant action. Then, as the revolt threatened to collapse, the malcontents, in their despair, turned to the landless Indians with vague promises of land reform and to the non-Europeanized mine and factory workers with equally vague promises of social legislation.

The peasants and the workers responded with a determination that first surprised and then startled the middle sector leaders. The anarchic-socialism of the worker and the radical agrarianism of the landless peasant amalgamated to give the Revolution a new base. Only then did the movement catch fire. Numberless bands led by self-appointed *caciques* joined the struggle. The workers and particularly the peasants gave the Revolution meaning by giving it concreteness. They, like the intellectuals, wanted political reform. But bread and land they wanted more. When they entered the conflict, action became antecedent to rationalization. The old regime, unable to offer effective resistance, crumbled with a suddenness that astonished the Western world. Díaz fled into exile with the observation, "Madero has a tiger by the tail, let us see what he does with it."

Madero did indeed have a tiger by the tail. He and his lieutenants had unleashed forces they could not control and few could understand. Military victory had been made possible before a body of doctrine, to which the various revolutionary elements could adhere, had been evolved. Madero, who was made president, instead of enjoying a period of cooperation in erecting a new and stable government on the ruins of the old, was faced with a multiplicity of contradictory plans and programs thrust upon him by those who had had a part in making victory possible. Madero was indecisive. Before he could settle upon a course of action he was assassinated by old Díaz supporters who feared the radicalism of the new revolutionaries. Mexico was immediately plunged into a prolonged and bloody civil conflict.

The conflict began, or so it appeared to the traditionally articulate elements, as another contest of personalities. In its early phases it assumed the characteristics of a power struggle not unlike many that Mexico had previously witnessed. It proved to be vastly different, however. Before it ended, it had spawned a social revolution strongly impregnated with the hopes and aspirations of the hitherto neglected elements of the Mexican population.

Venustiano Carranza, who in the contest of personalities emerged on top, had bought his victory with pledges of agrarian reform and better working conditions for those employed in mines, factories, and commercial establishments. Carranza was an *hacendado* and he had served as a senator under Díaz. He had become the spokesman of those middle sector elements who continued to reject *porfirismo* after the assassination of Madero. He had turned to the agrarians and the workers only after it appeared certain that he could not achieve his political ambitions without their support.

Carranza believed that the workers and the peasants could be manipulated after order returned to the country. But they proved Carranza wrong. After nearly four centuries a power vacuum had finally formed, and the working classes surged in to fill it. They refused to surrender their newly won influence in the political field, which they had entered on a permanent basis. Any lingering doubts as to the workers' ability to keep alive their indignation were removed when the Constitution of 1917 was promulgated.

The Assembly called to write a new constitution convened late in 1916. Carranza and the middle groups he represented were still satisfied that the unrest that had prevented Madero from consolidating his position could be quieted. They would provide the changes demanded by the lower groups not by creating something new but, rather, by returning to the past. Specifically, they would reactivate the liberal Constitution of 1857, which had been written to meet the requirements of the emerging middle elements. There would be limited departures, however, from the 1857 charter. There would have to be some provision for agrarian reform. There would have to be legislation in the interests of the urban working groups. The monuments to political liberalism and economic laissez faire, however, would remain essentially as cast seven decades earlier. Thus the new constitution, if the middle sectors had their way, would be a political document.

The leaders of the middle elements were so manifestly

confident their will would prevail that they permitted the Constituent Assembly to be filled with many political nonentities who had earned a measure of local prestige through their participation in the Revolution. Many of them emerged from obscurity only long enough to help write the Constitution. They were, however, men with a purpose. They withstood the concerted efforts of the middle sector delegates to humiliate and discredit them. The charter they gave the nation, far from being merely the political instrument the middle sectors had foreseen, was a prescription for the social and economic ills from which the republic was suffering.

The Constitution of 1917 was filled with contradictions. It borrowed liberally from the Constitution of 1857 in the areas that the representatives of the middle sectors in the Assembly made their primary concern—democratic representative government, freedom of enterprise and initiative, freedom of the press. But the social and economic demands of the peasants and workers were also amply expressed. The document spelled out in detail the popular demands for land and labor reform. The State was made responsible for social and economic justice and for protecting the popular elements of society from alleged oppression by the Catholic Church and the foreign capitalists. The stipulations that the spokesmen of the lower sectors wrote into the Constitution in effect negated many of those features written in by the representatives of the middle groups.

The popular elements had clearly won a major victory over the urban middle groups. The grievances of the peasantry and the working elements had been written into the law of the land, and the State had been charged with enforcing the law. The social and economic principles of the Revolution had been crystallized. Redistributing the land had been made an ideal of social justice and economic policy. Instead of providing the framework of a classical nineteenth-century liberal "inactive state," as those who had begun the Revolution and who had called the constitutional convention desired, the document provided for an energetic state ready to devote its resources to the aid and rehabilitation of any of its social components that might be in danger or distress.

The Constitution of 1917 also recognized the role that armed force had played in Mexican politics, and in the future might be expected to play. As noted above, armies—sometimes national and at other times private—traditionally had made and unmade governments. To have pretended to legislate such a powerful factor out of politics would have been foolhardy; therefore, armed force would have to be tolerated. It was not until 1929, under President Plutarco Elías Calles, that the military was finally forced to submit to the public will. And the power of the colorful Saturnino Cedillo, the last caudillo in Mexico, was not destroyed until the late 1930's. Miguel Alemán, who became president in 1946, was the first civilian president in the postrevolutionary era. The national army, through its ability to interfere in politics, particularly on the state level, continues to retain a significant, if at times inconspicuous, share in Mexican politics. The national administration, while undoubtedly possessing the requisite power, is often disinclined to intervene in matters affecting the individual states, and some of these federal entities often remain for considerable periods under the domination of men hardly distinguishable from the violent caudillos of the past. The state of San Luis Potosí, where in the mid-1950's the influence of the army in politics was still evident, offered a case in point.

The peasants, the workers, the military, and the middle sectors—who, in the aggregate, comprised all but a small percentage of the population—thus might reasonably expect a favorable hearing under the terms of the new charter. The Constitution had undertaken political commitments, however, which events proved were too large. Mexico had not reached the stage of economic maturity necessary to satisfy even the minimum material requirements of so large a segment of its population. From time to time first one group and then another had prior claim upon the available resources of the nation. The military held sway until the mid-1920's. The urban workers fared well for a while under Calles in the late 1920's. The rural peasants had their day under Lázaro Cárdenas, president from 1934 to 1940. The middle sectors were the last to lay claim to the nation. In the meantime they fought to protect the foundations upon which they proposed to build when they could again decisively affect policy-making on the national level.

Between 1920 and 1940 the middle sectors' influence over political life was highly indirect and negative. The revolutionary groups, translating their military and constitutional victories into political power, showed a decided preference for the leadership of persons who had distinguished themselves in the struggles of the 1910–15 period. Most of the men to whom they delegated civilian control on the national level had come originally from families that lacked social prestige, wealth, and political experience. Álvaro Obregón, president from 1920 to 1924, was a small farmer in the northwest state of Sonora before he achieved national recognition as the outstanding military figure of the Revolution. Plutarco Calles, president and president-maker from 1924 to 1934, was born into poverty in Sonora. He was a schoolteacher and bartender before joining Obregón's forces in support of Carranza. Luis Morones rose from obscurity to a position of tremendous power as head of the government-protected and -controlled Confederación Regional de Obreros Mexicanos (C.R.O.M.), Mexico's answer to the demand after 1917 that industrial labor be organized. Lázaro Cárdenas came from a family that owned a small cornfield and a horse. At the age of twelve he had become, when his father died, the chief support of his mother and seven brothers and sisters. Their early lives gave the leaders, as a group, a close acquaintance with the daily trials of the less fortunate members of society.

But these leaders, born of the armed phase of the Revolution, almost without exception had undergone notable transitions before assuming their high public offices in the peacetime civilian government. They had moved into the urban centers. They had made new contacts and had developed broader interests and understanding. They had improved their material well-being. Some, such as Calles and Morones, had become rich men. Most important, their radicalism had been tempered by the responsibilities of public office. In the heat of battle they had demanded the prompt and complete destruction of the latifundia system; they had promised once and for all to bring the Church to heel and to return Mexico to the Mexicans. As responsible officials they had to face the possibility of seriously dangerous social and economic consequences in a rapid breakup of the large landed estates. They had to consider the possible opposition of the Church, which had a strong claim upon the people and a near monopoly upon primary and secondary education. They had to recognize, too, that the government in Washington had for over a decade displayed an aggressive interest in the well-being of the American dollar in the Caribbean. Also they had to realize that Washington gave every indication of being prepared to protect the United States investor in Mexico.

In addition to the possible conflicts that might arise from land division, control of the Church, and restrictions on foreign investment, the leaders were confronted with other problems that resulted from conflicts of interest between the middle and the working groups. The social, economic, and political incompatabilities existing between the aligned peasantry and workers and the middle sectors, which had first manifested themselves in the Constitutional Convention of 1916–17, persisted. On the other hand, the leaders, who at the start of their careers had been more closely associated with the peasants and workers than with the middle sectors, had as individuals taken on many of the characteristics of the latter groups. As economic policy makers, the revolutionary leadership had come to appreciate that a successful social, economic, and political revolution would be dependent upon the utmost use of the intellectuals' academic and technological skills. But as politicians, the leaders remained beholden to the workers, who continued to look upon the intellectuals, especially the bureaucrats, as their enemies in the class struggle. The revolutionary writer, Mariano Azuela, referred to the bureaucrats as "the forces of inertia."

The revolutionary leadership also had to make arrangements with the commercial and industrial middle groups. To those struggling to stabilize their political positions any serious upsetting of the economic order would have been a catastrophe. To have attacked the urban economic middle groups or even to have ignored them might well have been serious. Thus, the leaders were continuously faced with the need of assuring the working elements, whose objectives tended to be short range and concrete, that the middle groups, whose ideological orientation was often antithetical to that of the laborer, could serve the best interests of the Revolution.

The understandings arrived at between the revolutionary leaders and the industrial elements were tenuous in the extreme. The range of agreement did not extend beyond, and could not be expected to extend beyond, the desire to see the forigner's influence reduced to a minimum and the Church kept economically and politically weak relative to the State. On the other hand, the areas in which their interests were basically antagonistic were many and often struck at the roots of the social and economic order.

The urban middle income groups were acutely concerned with the consequences inherent in precipitate land redistribution on a lavish scale. They had to be constantly on guard against the possibility that politicians would call for the implementation of the radical proposals offered as solutions to the land problem during the heat of political battles. Although agriculture was the heart and soul of Mexico's economy, the nation was in many years a net importer of foodstuffs. Any measure that would result in reduced agricultural production could upset the total economy. The wholesale redistribution of land offered such a threat. The State could dispossess the *hacendados* but it lacked the financial and technical resources to set up hundreds of thousands of penniless peasant families as independent farmers. Without financial assistance and scientific guidance those who were clamoring for land could not be expected to sustain even the low output of an antiquated agricultural system. An added handicap in maintaining production in the face of an extensive redistribution program would have been the difficulty of educating the prospective independent farmers in their economic responsibility to society as a whole. They came from a people who either had worked on large estates where the surplus was marketed by the *patrón* or who had been village farmers living in an economy based largely upon barter. Neither background had given them occasion to understand the need in a complex economic system based upon specialization for the farmer to produce not only for himself but for others performing tasks essential to his welfare.

The commercial and industrial community found at least two other reasons for opposing the rapid reallocation of land. In the early years of the Revolution such a program could not have been reconciled with Mexican nationalism, which found many of its outstanding protagonists among the middle income groups of the major cities. The widespread redistribution of land would have required the nation to funnel nearly all of its meager economic resources toward agriculture. Under the most favorable of foreseeable circumstances Mexican agriculture would not have the ability to earn foreign exchange in amounts required by industry for the purchase abroad of capital goods and certain essential raw materials. Consequently, to have devoted public revenues almost exclusively to agriculture would have condemned industry either to stagnation or to continued domination by foreign capital. Neither alternative would have been acceptable for long to the commercial and industrial components of the middle sectors.

The fact that any precipitate disintegration of the latifundia system would have left the State as the possessor of nearly all the rural land—the nation's principal source of wealth in the 1920's—was the other major concern of the middle sector leaders. They feared that should such a situation occur before a solid basis for private and locally controlled industrial enterprise was laid, the capitalist system in Mexico would be placed in serious jeopardy. And only the most radical members within the traditionally articulate groups thought seriously in terms of eliminating private ownership from all the sources of production. Of Mexico's presidents since 1917, only Cárdenas gave prolonged thought to such a possibility. The resistance to agrarian reform in the period between the promulgation of the Constitution and 1934, when Cárdenas assumed the presidency, was sufficiently great to cause his predecessors to limit official action to a minimum.

In at least one other vitally important area, the middle sectors were able to parry the thrusts of the revolutionaries' response to the demands of the peasants and the workers. In the early 1930's, the nation's leadership, under the influence of a neo-socialistic philosophy, took advantage of a surge of anti-clericalism and sponsored educational measures that seriously threatened the family as a social institution. The child was declared to belong to the community, not to the family. The child's conscience was proclaimed the property of the Revolution. Consequently it was the State's privilege to shape the child's thinking. In a further effort to weaken parental control, it was decreed that in the schools the child should be taught, in effect, that his scientific academic training and his being a product of the Revolution made him superior to his parents, whom he must, therefore, assist the State in emancipating from ignorance and superstition. The State had struck at what for generation after generation had often appeared as a primary function of the middle sector family—the privilege of educating the child. The State failed of its objective. A stalemate resulted largely because of the opposition of the middle sector women who provide the hard core of Catholic conservatism. When the issue was reopened, the ideological climate was much more favorable to the middle sectors.

The urban middle elements, meanwhile, had made rather significant gains during the decade and a half after the Revolution was legalized in 1917. Greater attention to the health and welfare of the lower sectors was accompanied by increased demands for physicians and social workers. Printing and publishing expanded as the illiteracy rate dipped slightly and the demand for textbooks rose. Privately financed national industry, behind protective tariff barriers and assisted by government encouragement, made limited advances of a nature fundamental to further expansion. Private banking and finance, although overwhelmingly in opposition to the social and economic objectives of the Revolution, were permitted to survive. At the same time, the urban laborers grew in number and came under the control of officials often named by the State. The laborers thus associated their welfare with that of the group in power, a not unimportant consideration once the middle sectors increased their political influence in the period after the outbreak of World War II.

Cárdenas was a true revolutionary. His faith in State socialism as a panacea for the ills of Mexico surpassed that of any executive before or after him in the presidency. He was dedicated to uplifting the peasants from their debased position in society. He accordingly distributed for the peasants' use, under terms laid down by the national administration, tens of millions of acres of land, seized by the State from private owners and corporations. He provided the new farm families with credit and technical assistance on a scale unprecedented in Mexico. By the end of his term of office he had broken the back of the latifundia system and had relegated the remaining vast rural estates to a precarious secondary role in the agricultural economy.

Despite Cárdenas' devotion to the peasants, his policies in the long run served the interests of the urban element no less than they did those of the farm element. In placing public education within the reach of thousands of children formerly deprived of the opportunity for academic training he also served the welfare of the middle sectors. The credit and technical facilities he created to care for the financial needs of the peasants contributed to the growth of the middle sectors by enlarging the rolls of the bureaucracies and the influence of the bureaucrats. A robust bureaucracy gave many members of the middle sectors the security (*garantías*) that had been lacking to the intellectuals since the end of the nineteenth century. The active support and protection his administration gave domestically controlled industry was urban in emphasis. The manufacturing industries made greater strides in the six years that he headed the nation than they had in the previous quarter century.

Cárdenas was an aggressive nationalist. Future historians

will probably label his decision to expropriate the large foreign-owned oil properties in March 1938 the most important act of his administration. After nearly two decades the expropriation continues to be hailed as having triggered "Mexican economic independence." As a manifestation of Mexican nationalism, the seizure was welcomed by nearly all groups. But from an economic point of view, it operated to the advantage of the urban elements far more than it did to the benefit of the peasants. This was also true of the nationalization of most of the republic's railroads in June 1937.

In breaking the latifundia system and in standing up to the foreigner, Cárdenas once and for all destroyed the myth of the residual power of the old ruling element. In so doing he served the middle sectors inestimably by giving them confidence in their ability to handle the complex problems confronting the nation.

Cárdenas was the last president of Mexico to bring to that high office ideals and convictions formulated during the militant state of the Revolution. He was a firm friend of Manuel Ávila Camacho, his successor, and actively supported him during his campaign for the presidency; but as it turned out the two men were leagues apart in their political philosophies. Cárdenas, like his predecessors in office, had not been able to achieve a reconciliation with the enemies of the Revolution. Ávila Camacho became the spokesman of a generation that was prepared to come to terms with the sons of the opponents of reform.

Ávila Camacho and those who increasingly influenced him after he attained the presidency had reached maturity after the Revolution had been accepted. They had little in common with those born of the violent period of struggle. Most of them had been reared in the cities, particularly in Mexico City. Nearly all of them had enjoyed the advantages of secondary and higher education. Many of them had profited economically from the Revolution. Some had become extremely wealthy as the 1920–40 period made "millionaires out of the Revolutionaries" on an impressive scale. The new group had viewed the agrarian revolution from its theoretical and administrative side. They did not feel the practical urgency of land reform as had those who had fought side by side with the aroused peasants. The entire experience of this rising group had made them manipulators, in contrast with the older generation of revolutionaries whose experience had taught them to rely heavily upon direct action in solving their problems. The new generation had grown up as managers in government, business, and labor. They had had an important part in the management of the convention that had given Ávila Camacho the nomination of the Partido Revolucionario Institucional (P.R.I.) in 1940. In Mexico, which since 1930 has had in effect a one-party system, nomination by the P.R.I. has been tantamount to election. Once in office and supported by this newly powerful and capitalistically minded middle sector element, Ávila Camacho gambled his political career on his ability to swing the Mexican government away from leftist agrarianism, with all that that doctrine had come to imply, and toward moderate industrialism.

During his campaign, when questioned on the Church issue, Ávila Camacho replied, *"yo soy creyente"* ("I am a believer"). In a radical departure from Mexico's foreign policy since 1910 and in the face of bitter antagonisms lingering from the expropriation of the foreign-owned petroleum holdings, Ávila Camacho made it clear that under his leadership Mexico would be on the side of the United States in the struggle against the Axis powers. When, in May 1942, he took Mexico into the war, he called for "a union of all Mexicans and love among all Mexicans." Without calling into open question the revolutionary ideal of "land for him who works it," the Ávila Camacho regime increasingly emphasized the need for agricultural productivity rather than the right of the peasant to a plot of ground. In 1945 Ávila Camacho gave assurances that the federal government would grant "all kinds" of guarantees to stimulate private initiative with a view to greater progress in industrializing the country. In rapid order the successor of Cárdenas had struck at anticlericalism, antiforeignism, the class struggle, and the revolutionary agrarian policy—all basic tenets of the Revolution. Henceforth, the official position would be that the "Indo-agrarian" phase of the Revolution had served its purpose as a necessary prelude to the capitalistic phase based upon industry, which the Revolution was entering. Little wonder that the regime's intellectual critics believed that not only had the Revolution's ascent been halted but that its ideals had been virtually reduced to mottoes on official letterheads.

By 1945, when Ávila Camacho promised "all kinds" of encouragement to industrial development, there were many indications that he and the group around him were favorably disposed to industrial expansion. Labor, in effect, had been told that domestic capital largely had replaced foreign capital in industry and that consequently the working man could not henceforth expect the same public support he had received when he had served as the "protagonist against foreign rapacity." Labor boards, on which the government held the balance of power, had increasingly sided with capital. Between 1939 and 1946 the share of national income going to wages and salaries and supplements had dropped from approximately 30 per cent to 22 per cent. Clearly, these measures were taken without any suggestion of a direct assault upon the working groups and the peasants by the middle groups. The political influence of the middle sectors in Mexico then, as now, depended upon considerable support from the urban and rural workers.

At the same time that labor was being weakened, industry was being strengthened. The total volume of industrial production rose by an annual average of 9.4 per cent from 1940 to 1945. A year after Ávila Camacho left office, the investment in industry was five times that of 1939. The tax system favored capital accumulation by the new industrial elements, while placing a heavy burden on the consumer. Most important, the State had made the sponsorship of industry a major national objective.

Ávila Camacho had given the Revolution a new direction; some said that he instituted a counterrevolution. His successor, Miguel Alemán, took the Mexicans on a wild ride down the track sketched out after 1940, and before the ride ended, the Revolution, if not discarded as many maintained, had been twisted almost beyond recognition.

The Alemán regime, continuing the policies laid down by the Ávila Camacho administration, further deemphasized the agrarian features of the Revolution. It curtailed the rate of land redistribution and modified the entire agrarian philosophy of the Revolution. The original doctrine had equated agrarian reform and social justice. The Alemán interpretation was primarily economic. It made the welfare of the rural lower income groups essentially contingent upon their ability to help the administration solve the pressing problem of feeding a rapidly growing and potentially dangerous urban population.

The urban workers fared no better than their rural counterparts under the Alemán leadership. Nearly twice as much of the income from commerce and industry continued to go for profits as went for wages, salaries, and supplements. Cost-of-living rises were permitted to outrun wages for extended periods of time. Workers' wives paraded against government-sanctioned increases in the price of basic foodstuffs. Per-capita consumption remained practically unchanged or actually declined in three of the six years that Alemán was in office. The growth of education and health and welfare services was declining greatly at a time when government investment for economic development was increasing at an accelerated pace. The lower 99 per cent of the population received only 49 per cent of the national income while the top one per cent garnered 51 per cent. Sociologist Lucio Mendieta y Núñez saw a "progressive impoverishment of the working groups." Meanwhile, labor's voice in government was markedly reduced. Ávila Camacho's critics had foreseen the end of the Revolution. Alemán's critics interpreted his administration's decisions as portending a return to nineteenth-century liberal capitalism of a neo-*científico* tinge.

Ávila Camacho publicly confessed to be a believer. Alemán and those around him chose to recognize publicly that Mexico was unalterably a Catholic country. The Revolution had not destroyed the Church's hold over the people nor was it likely to. Furthermore, the members of the Alemán clique appreciated the possible contribution a friendly Church might make toward developing their liberal capitalistic position. Also they were convinced that the State had become sufficiently powerful to defend itself against a considerably stronger Mexican Catholic Church than the one that had existed in 1947. Accordingly, they invited the Church to reassert itself. They reaffirmed the 1946 reform of Article 3, which the Ávila Camacho regime had carried out and which had opened the way for the Church to strengthen itself in the field of education. In the provincial towns religious festivals were sanctioned in defiance of the laws. Law-enforcement officers increasingly winked at the appearance of religious garb on the streets of the smaller towns, again in violation of the law. Public officials participated side by side with Church dignitaries on holidays and at the dedications of public and religious buildings.

Alemán, again pursuing a policy initiated by Ávila Camacho, worked closely with the United States. Mexican *braceros* (agricultural workers) were made available in large numbers to United States farmers hungry for field hands. United States dollars and scientists were welcomed in the fight against outbreaks of hoof-and-mouth disease, which threatened Mexico's livestock industry throughout most of the period that Alemán was in office, as it has sporadically since that time. The government resolutely resisted the efforts of the nationalists who sought to arouse the peasants by pointing to the destruction of infected animals as part of a grand plot engineered by the United States designed to keep Mexico economically subservient to the Colossus of the North. Mexico and the United States cooperated in major efforts to harness the Rio Grande River; viz., the construction of the Falcón Dam. Washington, for its part, made loans to Mexico that were vital to the rehabilitation of the republic's economic life.

The Alemán administration also courted private capital. In 1948 and 1949 United States banks made loans totaling approximately twenty million dollars, the first private United States bank loans to the Mexican government in thirty years. Foreign investors, who had been made gun-shy by the nationalistic explosions of the 1930's, began to return to Mexico, attracted in large part by the Mexican government's determination to maintain convertibility of the peso so that profits might be removed without exchange restrictions.

The direct support that industry received from the Alemán regime spoke eloquently for the new leadership's interest in that phase of the economy. Its interest stemmed from both public and private considerations. Alemán and his coterie felt strongly, and said so publicly, that Mexico had to industrialize if employment were to be provided to the nation's ever growing labor pool. (The republic's population is growing at the rate of over 3 per cent per annum.) The private consideration derived from the fact that Alemán and many of his close political associates had industrial and real estate holdings that stood to be enlarged in an expanding industrial economy. Also the more the State contributed to industrial growth the greater were the opportunities for officials in influential positions to siphon public funds into their own pockets. Under Alemán, it is widely agreed, corruption reached new heights in Mexico.

There was little that the Alemán regime was not prepared to do for industry. It poured funds into essential areas—i.e., transportation, communications, and power—in which political considerations discouraged sanctioning rates that would return sufficient profits to make them attractive to private capital. It pushed with new vigor the development of the State-controlled petroleum industry to satisfy the growing fuel demands of industry and commerce. It relied heavily on tariff walls as instruments for promoting industrial development. It employed tax exemptions for the same purpose. The tax structure continued to favor those with large incomes. In 1950 a smaller share of profits was absorbed by taxes than in 1939. The regime created the general impression that it was prepared to protect the interest of business elements in almost any foreseeable situation. The emphasis upon developing the industrial and commercial phases of the economy was reflected in the swelling stream of people who made their way from the fields to the cities in search of employment. The urban population increased from 35.1 per cent in 1940 to 42.3 per cent of the total in 1950. Most of the shift came after World War II and coincided with Alemán's presidency.

Adolfo Ruiz Cortines, who in 1952 succeeded Alemán, was the third chief executive to share the general views of the socio-economic elements that had asserted themselves politically in the 1940's. At the time of his election Ruiz Cortines was, according to Mexican custom, given a rubber-stamp Congress. The Senate was completely dominated by the P.R.I. In the Chamber of Deputies all but a handful of members owed their elections to P.R.I. backing. But Ruiz Cortines had not been selected to perpetuate Alemanism. The public's distrust of the industrial and commercial elements that Alemán had favored had reached the point where moderating influences were sought to avoid the possibilities of dangerous popular unrest. The new President invited public confidence. He came from a middle sector environment. He had served most of his adult life as a bureaucrat, in which capacity he had won a reputation for honesty and a ready willingness to place the public welfare above personal ambition.

The majority of the advisers Ruiz Cortines relied upon, the decisions that he made, and the preferences that he expressed as President strongly reflected his earlier personal experiences. From his bureaucratic training undoubtedly came his concept of the office of president as the highest managerial post in the republic. He consistently looked upon the presidency as an opportunity to serve the country, not to possess it. From his middle sector background apparently came his system of values and his dedication to such principles as private enterprise and ownership of property and to such social institutions as the family and the Church.

His desire to see the State's resources well managed led him to move cautiously in the economic field. Rather than give the industrial elements the same green light enjoyed under Alemán or launch grandiose projects, he chose to bring the economy into better balance by consolidating the gains achieved since 1940. He budgeted relatively large sums to agriculture in order not only to aid the farmer, whose position had weakened under Alemán, but to increase per capita consumption, to put breaks on the rising cost of living, and to make the farmer, over the long run, a more active bidder for manufactured goods. The renewed interest in agriculture combined with favorable climatic conditions resulted in a 30 per cent increase in agricultural production between 1953 and 1955.

In the industrial field the Ruiz Cortines administration placed major emphasis upon those areas essential to the long-range development of the economy. Accordingly, transportation, communications, and power were liberally subsidized. At the same time it made the power industry sounder economically by raising rates and guaranteeing interest on loans for developmental purposes. In 1954, 1955, and 1956 approximately 25 per cent of the national budget went to transportation and communication, the largest item in the budget. Heavy industries, notably iron and steel, received special attention from the State, but producers of nondurables and consumer goods did not suffer from neglect. The State continued to add steadily to the public funds available for assisting private investors. The currency devaluation in 1954 was advantageous to the manufacturing element in many ways, not the least being the resulting inequalities in price and wage increases. Tariffs and quantitative import restrictions were added incentives to spur industrial investment. Finally, the State maintained a climate quite favorable to the flow of foreign capital into industry.

Ruiz Cortines was far from alone in his wish to see the values and institutions associated with the "enlightened" middle sectors strengthened. By the time he came to power the current of opinion in favor of the intellectuals on the one hand and the business community on the other was running so strong that it is doubtful that Ruiz Cortines could have diverted it had he chosen to do so. The middle elements' return to favor and influence culminated in 1950 when the powerful P.R.I. officially discarded the concept of the class struggle and "democracy of the workers and agrarians" in favor of the "ideal" of the "middle classes." At the same time, the P.R.I. indicated the nation's indebtedness to the intermediate groups when it declared that the "participation of the middle classes in the history of Mexico had been constant and decidedly helpful in bringing to realization the social benefits of major magnitude."* The middle sectors had indeed come a long way since their ideological defeat in 1917.

Ruiz Cortines, backed by the P.R.I. mandate and the public confidence in his sincerity of purpose, was able to maintain an atmosphere generally favorable to a maximum of freedom of expression and assembly. He was given widespread support in his efforts to vitalize the educational program. His requests for relatively large appropriations for health and social welfare were generally applauded. The efforts to integrate the Indian into the Mexican nation went ahead without the radicalism of a Cárdenas or the demagogery of an Alemán. Ruiz Cortines built upon both of them, however. Granting the suffrage to women greatly broadened the base upon which civilian middle sector representative government in Mexico must eventually rest.

Laws governing private property in general were progressively strengthened. The courts' decisions contributed to the same end. Spokesmen for the administration repeatedly went out of their way to call attention to the conviction that State participation in the industrial sphere, far from being a cause for apprehension, would in the long run improve personal initiative by creating conditions indispensable to the growth of private enterprise. One principal source of acquiring private capital has been from dealing with the government. Cries that the Revolution had died from lack of cultivation were drowned by toasts of public officials to the well-being of the republic brought about by industrial development under the aegis of private enterprise.

The government's defense of private property was extended to the agricultural area. The regime's interpretations, for the most part, halted the tendency to reduce the size of what was held to constitute a legal privately owned agricultural holding. As a result there was ever increasing public expression of the possibility that an important property-holding rural element

* Howard Cline, *The United States and Mexico* (Cambridge, Mass., 1953), p. 326.

within the middle sectors might still evolve. This belief was strengthened in June 1957 when a Small Rural Properties Committee of the Mexican Senate reported that "Mexico's agrarian reform . . . had been a total failure," and that "chaos prevails in the countryside because of the present anarchy in . . . agrarian legislation."*

Under Ruiz Cortines' light hand, the Church built on the foundations laid down by Ávila Camacho and Alemán. The laws governing it remained essentially unaltered; their enforcement changed. The Church was ordinarily free to hold its public pageants. Religious garb was increasingly seen in provincial towns. To be a practicing Catholic was once again respectable. The State did not act vigorously in response to the insistent demands of the radical wing that the Church was violating the supreme law of the land by surreptitiously maintaining monasteries and convents.

The political role of the urban middle sectors in Mexico has increased significantly during the past decade and a half. The continued exercise of that influence is not assured. Ruiz Cortines' good faith and seemingly sincere attempt to reduce official corruption, plus his program of moderation, abated much of the resentment that built up against the middle sectors during the Alemán era. In that sense the middle sectors are being given an opportunity to consolidate the political gains won since 1940. The Ruiz Cortines administration, however, was not able to resolve the problems that gave rise to the unrest directed against the previous regime. Viewed in that context the middle sectors are still on trial. They have proclaimed that the Government, which they control, is the custodian of the Revolution. But they have not demonstrated that they could retain office in a biparty or multiparty political system. They have not established that their economic program can succeed without resort to crippling inflation. In 1955, after Ruiz Cortines had been in office approximately three years, consumption and wages continued to lag seriously behind investments and profits. Industry had not provided jobs rapidly enough to absorb all

* *New York Times*, June 25, 1957, p. 1.

those of working age. The strong demand for cheap farm labor
in the United States provided Mexico with a badly needed
safety valve. Should Mexican labor be excluded from the
United States, unemployment and underemployment would
become widespread within a short time.

The middle sector leadership has not satisfied many of
those who believe that it has lost sight of the ideals of the Revolution and has permitted commerce and industry to supersede
social justice as the major determinant of official policy. Those
who hold that the Revolution has been foresaken can be found
among both the workers and the socially and economically
radical segments of the middle sectors. Those elements have
shared power in the past. They have the ideology of the Revolution on their side. Should the economic situation deteriorate
and should the conviction prevail that social justice has been
sacrificed in the interests of technology and profit, the opposition might not find it difficult to align popular forces in the name
of the Revolution. Radical politicians might find it easy to sell
the thought that a Revolution that began with the cry for land
and liberty had ended with the creation of a plutocracy based
upon industrial capitalism—which would be tantamount to re-
viving the class struggle and reopening the wounds that have
healed during the years since 1917. The present leadership
probably could not survive such a development without adding
armed force to its present tactics in moderating social and economic differences.

8 *Brazil*

LATE BID FOR POWER

One of the striking political developments of post–World War II Latin America has been the urban middle sectors' tardy attainment of an influential position on the national level in Brazil. Equally striking is the fact that because the military has reserved the right to interfere in civilian affairs they have not been free agents. Even when the military has remained in the background, the middle sectors have not been sufficiently united to carry out programs without strong outside support. Middle sector leadership, consequently, has been forced, on the one hand, to think as the military and, on the other, to make political bargains. As a result, its conduct to date cannot be assumed to indicate the course it would pursue under more favorable political circumstances.

With the exception of having largely resolved its religious question it was apparent by 1920 that Brazil was lagging behind Argentina, Chile, Mexico, and Uruguay in those areas that were making it possible for the middle sectors to enhance their political status in Latin America. Brazil had not responded as fully as had its neighbors to the social and economic impulses of the Western world. The republic gave the impression of having grown more than it had advanced.

In Brazil, unlike in Uruguay, Argentina, and Chile, there had been no significant urbanization movements before 1920. The republic remained overwhelmingly rural, with perhaps 90 per cent of its more than twenty-seven million inhabitants living on farms or in hamlets dedicated to serving the surrounding countryside. Only Rio de Janeiro, the national capital, had become a metropolitan city of over a million population. São Paulo, Latin America's greatest industrial center today with over three million people, was just entering a rapid-growth stage and counted barely 500,000 inhabitants. The major population centers of the Brazilian "hump" were dependent almost wholly upon natural increase for any expansion, since they possessed little to attract the restless from the hinterland or the immigrant from Europe.

Modern machine industry reached Brazil about the same time as it did Mexico and Argentina. The rate of industrial growth in Brazil, however, had been somewhat slower. According to the census of 1920 the republic's machine industry was controlled by only 18,000 proprietors and afforded employment to only 6,000 administrators, 13,000 office employees, and 275,000 manual laborers.

The labor movement had not made even the limited gains it had achieved in Argentina. The workingman, distrusted and for all intents and purposes without legal status, was at the mercy of employer groups.

The Constitution of 1891 left economic and social matters largely to take care of themselves. One result of the narrow interpretation of the government's responsibilities was a small and ineffective bureaucracy. The 1920 census showed less than 140,000 individuals employed as administrators at all the levels of government.

Brazil was seriously retarded in the field of education. The aristocratic society of the empire had neglected popular education, and in 1890 not more than an estimated one in ten was literate. The nation's gains in overcoming illiteracy during the first decades of the twentieth century were not impressive. By 1920 illiteracy among persons aged fifteen and over was officially set at 64 per cent, probably an optimistic figure. The general lack of interest in education resulted in an alarmingly small teaching corps, a large part of which totally lacked professional training and possessed only a minimum academic experience. The low level of education was reflected in the immature development of the graphic arts.

In the political field, Brazil had advanced little between the fall of the empire and 1920. The Constitution of 1891, an essentially nineteenth-century liberal document, which stressed the rights of the individual and of the provincial governments as opposed to the national administration, had not undergone modification. The republic continued to be run by a narrow oligarchy. In no election prior to 1926 did the winning presidential candidate receive as many as 600,000 popular votes. As late as 1919, when the republic's population was already over 26,000,000, Epitácio da Silva Pessôa won the presidency with less than 290,000 popular votes. The oligarchy, which was dominated by the landed interests, generally exercised its power under constitutional provisions, although with frequent perversion of the electoral process. Meanwhile, the urban labor elements lacked sufficient group consciousness to be organized as a political force. In rural areas, the laborers were politically immobilized by ignorance and by paternalism.

Up to 1920 the middle sectors had not given evidence of leadership qualities. They had not displayed the will or the ability to initiate a revolution such as the middle sectors of Mexico had instituted. They had produced nothing resembling the urban-oriented and politically aggressive Radical Civic Union in Argentina, which, among other things, had served to integrate an important part of the immigrant population of the cities into the political life of the Argentine nation. Brazil's sizable immigrant population was largely ineffective politically. Neither was there a politically significant segment within the Brazilian middle groups that had begun to think in the socio-economic terms that the middle sector leadership was actually applying in Uruguay. Because of the widespread inertia that characterized the Brazilian middle elements, the narrowly circumscribed ruling elite of the republic had not felt itself under any serious compulsion to share political power with them.

During the decade of the 1920's Brazil fell still further behind Argentina, Chile, Mexico, and Uruguay in most of those spheres of growth that ease the way for the middle sectors politically. Commerce and industry suffered from the general lack of imagination displayed by the moulders of opinion and policy. Domestic capital was not discouraged from indulging its preference for exploitative agriculture, speculative investment in real estate, and those industrial ventures that promised high-unit profits and short-term gains. The tax provisions under the Constitution of 1891, whereby the income of the states came largely from export taxes while the federal income derived primarily from import taxes, served to protect the existing agricultural export economy and to hinder the rise of the manufacturing industries. The limited encouragement that manufacturing received from protective tariffs was counterbalanced by what must be termed official disregard for all forms of transportation and power development. The railroads especially suffered from official disinterest. Railroad construction was brought to a virtual standstill long before the nation had sufficient lines to satisfy its bulk-transportation needs. In fact the policy toward transportation during the 1920's resulted in a drawing upon savings.

The official disregard for industry, transportation, and power was reflected in the continued pronounced rural nature of the population. An urban movement was under way by 1930 but not on the scale of those in Argentina, Chile, and Uruguay. Brazil was still a highly rural country with an estimated 80 per cent of its population living outside the urban centers. Rio de Janeiro and São Paulo, the two principal cities, contained only 7 per cent of the total population. Nor had there been any serious attempt to incorporate the newcomers to the cities into the body politic. The lack of imagination displayed in economics and politics was manifest in the labor field where the oligarchical leadership refused to extend to the emerging working elements many of the rights and privileges those groups won during the 1920's in Uruguay, Chile, and Mexico.

The 1920's, nonetheless, become important in any political diagnosis of the middle sectors, for during that decade it became progressively apparent that educational, technological, and political retardation were symptoms rather than causes of the backward development in which the republic found itself. There were more basic considerations. The nation was suffering from the divisive forces of regionalism. No less costly was the fact that Brazil, like Argentina, was shackled economically to agricultural commodities produced in limited areas by a relatively few individuals. As in Argentina, and in contrast with Mexico and Chile, the producers of those commodities could insist upon a disproportionate share in the political life of the republic because there was no other economic element capable of challenging them. Finally, the Brazilian military, which had inherited from the empire the "moderative power" exercised by the Emperor, persistently had remained above or just below the murky political waters of the republic. Many younger officers (*tenentes*), in revolt against the established order, became the precursors of a social change favorable to the civilian middle groups.

By 1930 perceptive Brazilians were acutely aware that regionalist tendencies were rampant in their country. The problems inherent in regionalism were not new. First as a colony, then as an empire, and finally as a republic, Brazil had given the impression of seemingly infinite space fragmented into a number of distinct areas, each consciously seeking maximum self-sufficiency rather than coordinated growth through national unity.* Each region lived its particular way of life and possessed a collective mentality compounded of its peculiar geographical, economic, racial, and cultural inheritances and experiences. In certain regions, as for example the "hump," inheritances and experiences encouraged a continuation of the economic stagnation that for at least a century had plagued that area. In other sections, as for example the center-south, and more especially the state of São Paulo, a great influx of foreign capital, technicians, and trained labor into a favorable physical environment gave rise to a burst of activity which had permitted that region to surge to the forefront in major spheres of national life.

The uneven economic development of the several regions of the republic during the 1920's served to accentuate the already existing sectionalist tendencies. The center-south extended its lead in terms of material development. From the

---

* During part of the colonial period the Portuguese had spoken of their New World possession as "The Brazils."

states of that region came an overwhelming share of the national product and the federal income. In 1930 the single state of São Paulo in one way or another provided over one-third of the income of the federal government. Already the Paulistas saw their state as "a locomotive pulling twenty empty box cars." The state of Minas Gerais, the northern neighbor of São Paulo, was another large contributor to the gross national product. From the center-south came coffee, the only commodity Brazil could market abroad in sufficient quantity to earn the foreign exchange it sought.

The economic predominance of the center-south, and more especially of São Paulo and Minas Gerais, produced severe political repercussions. To guarantee themselves a political role commensurate with what they viewed as their economic importance to the nation, they had as early as World War I worked out a political arrangement that gave them a monopoly over national politics as complete as the monopoly they exercised in the economic field. The remaining states, in turn, had become increasingly resentful of the center-south and were friendly to any proposal which might thwart the São Paulo–Minas Gerais alliance. The resulting antagonism aggravated the regional animosities. The fact that industrialization and urbanization had not reached the point where they invited political alignments along urban-rural lines tended to encourage the regional approach to politics.

The political parties reflected both Brazilian provincialism and the republic's essentially rural character. The parties were at best sectional. This condition lent itself to the growth of narrowly conceived political machines in which personal ambition vied with local greed. In the less-developed states the parties were usually dominated by a few families. In those states devoted to commercial agriculture the parties were rural-oriented, but the urban financial elements were ordinarily well represented in the leadership.

The role of the urban financial elements derived from the fact that by 1930 they had gained a large share of the control of such commercially produced crops as sugar and coffee. In the late nineteenth century, following an extended period of poor management, crop failures, and competition from low-cost sugar-growing areas, the sugar producers were reduced to the point where they could not withstand the consequences of the abolition of slavery. Soon after the end of slavery in 1888, the control of the sugar-refining industry of the "hump" began to pass rapidly into the hands of the urban interests, who, before long, also began to entrench themselves as sugar-cane planters. By 1930 such an important share of the growing, refining, and marketing of sugar was controlled from the cities that protection of the industry had become as much an urban as a rural objective. This situation has persisted to the present.

Urban capitalists were also deeply involved in every stage of the coffee industry. Coffee was big business. The cost of bringing a large plantation into production and providing the apparatus for preparing the bean for market required capital ordinarily beyond the means of the individual planter. He had to be carried by city financiers. Once production was under way, the transportation, storage, and marketing of the bean were activities ordinarily carried out from the cities. In many instances urban financial interests operated coffee plantations on their own account. Politically speaking, this involvement of urban capital in coffee meant that when the coffee grower went to the government for assistance he had strong support from powerful urban financial elements.*

* We are here dealing in relative terms. The land monopolists in each of the republics in this study had depended upon urban financial assistance. In Argentina, Chile, and Uruguay, however, the dependence upon urban capital has not been as continuous as it has been in Brazil, since in the former countries periods of unusual prosperity and the rise in land values, notably in Argentina, permitted the agriculture and live-stock producers to wipe out their indebtedness from time to time. Also, in Uruguay and Argentina, meat processing and marketing were primarily in the hands of foreigners in contrast with the largely local control of processing and marketing of sugar and coffee in Brazil. As has been pointed out elsewhere, this situation had, and has, clear political implications. In Mexico, it will be recalled, a social revolution had created a condition in which the large landholders "lived outside the law" and consequently were not considered good credit risks by the urban monied interests.

In so far as the middle sectors were concerned, the share of the financial community in commercial agriculture had two major political consequences. In the first place, since the financial interests had a ready market for their surplus capital, they were not inclined to give strong support to industrialization, which might upset a foreign trade based upon the export of agricultural commodities and the import of finished goods. In the second place, the banking community was strongly inclined to align itself with the agricultural elements against any arrangement that might threaten the traditional political patterns. Thus it was that the urban middle groups in Brazil were deprived of an ally that in Uruguay and Chile, and to a somewhat lesser extent in Argentina and Mexico, was giving increasingly solid support to the nonagricultural sectors of the economy.

The most cursory review of the Brazilian political experience establishes the fact that, from the founding of the republic to 1930, the leadership of the armed forces had an overweening interest in politics. The army was instrumental in driving Pedro II into exile and in bringing the empire to an end. Two army generals ruled the new republic before a civilian was trusted to assume the presidency. No civilian chief executive prior to 1910 was sufficiently strong to disregard the whims of the military. In 1910, Hermes da Fonseca, a marshal in the Brazilian army, was elected to the presidency following a campaign generally regarded as a contest between military and civilian control. Although Hermes da Fonseca was to be the last career officer to serve as president until Eurico Gaspar Dutra was sworn into office in 1946, the armed forces did not surrender their assumed role of arbiters of the national destiny. Thus, during all of World War I and for five years thereafter, the politically powerful Military Club—which, for the most part, was under the control of ex-president Hermes da Fonseca—engaged in political intrigue to such an extent that it was unsettling to the republic first in war and then in its adjustment to peace.

The military ran its own candidate in the presidential election of 1922 only to see him swamped by Artur Bernardes, who was backed by majority elements within the monied groups of Minas Gerais, São Paulo, and Rio Grande do Sul. The military did not take its defeat gracefully. It intrigued extensively in government at the state level before disagreements in July 1924 led to a full-scale uprising of army elements assigned to the state of São Paulo. Although the revolutionaries were suppressed by forces that remained loyal to the federal government, many of the young discontents evaporated to reappear at the head of Vargas' armies in 1930.*

The senior military officers were as politically conservative as the civilian authorities. Like the civilians, the military held that the government's responsibility should largely be limited to maintaining law and order as a means of protecting private property. It followed that those who had property to protect should control the government; thus they justified the rigid suffrage requirements that remained in force. The decision-making groups within the military had not felt the full effects of nationalism as it evolved in Europe and in parts of the Western Hemisphere following World War I; consequently, they did not find it difficult to sanction the economic policies of the ruling elite. Both groups supported a coffee-oriented colonial economy as well as the maintenance of an economic climate attractive to foreign capital and European immigration.

The major contribution of the military leaders to the con-

---

* There is much that is still not in print regarding the revolt of 1924, but certain aspects have been made clearer. The revolutionaries were almost entirely army men. Few of them seemed to know what sort of changes they were seeking. Some probably wanted to protest alleged discrimination by the civilian Bernardes government. In retrospect, however, the leading figures appear to have been looking for social change, including clearing the way for greater vertical social mobility. A number of the revolutionaries of 1924 distinguished themselves during the Vargas era. Luis Carlos Prestes became the head of the Brazilian Communist Party. Eduardo Gomes, Juarez Távora, Newton Estillac Leal, Cordeiro de Farias, and João Alberto Lins de Barros emerged with Vargas in 1930 and played prominent roles in national politics during the dictatorship and after. By 1957 Estillac Leal and João Alberto Lins de Barros had died but the others were still active participants in politics; all but Prestes, who has remained the recognized leader of the Communist Party in Brazil, were associated with Center and Center-Right elements.

servative cause, however, was made through the frequent application of their assumed privilege of arbitrating political disputes between civilian elements. By preempting such an important role the officers provided a guarantee that they, rather
than the representatives of the emerging groups straining to
enter the mainstream of politics, would fill any vacuum even
temporarily created by a struggle for power between the established ruling groups.

When the Constitution of 1891 broke down under the
stresses aggravated by world-wide depression, the military, as
the moderator of civilian disputes, removed Washington Luiz
from the presidency in November 1930 and cleared the way
for Getulio Vargas' assumption of power. It thereby unin-
tentionally had a direct hand in setting the stage for Brazil's
entering a new era, during which over-all national policy
smoothed the way for the urban middle sectors' successful bid
for greater power immediately following World War II.

Vargas achieved control because in addition to his winning
over the army he was acceptable to the majority elements within nearly all the articulate civilian groups except those directly
associated with the coffee oligarchy of São Paulo. Many of
the coffee oligarchy, in fact, welcomed the Vargas rebellion
in view of Washington Luiz' refusal to extend further credit to
the sagging coffee economy. Vargas was not feared by the
regionalists, for his home state, Rio Grande do Sul, represented
the epitome of Brazilian regionalism.* His basic values did
not offer a serious threat to the status quo, and the responsible
elements, civilian and military, approved him rather than risk
a prolonged civil war that might bring new and ambitious elements into the political arena. Any major change in national
policy that Vargas might institute would almost certainly re-
dound to the advantage of the industrialists. While the Vargas
revolt was still in process the Archbishop of Pôrto Alegre re-
portedly declared publicly that the rebellion was purely po-

---

* Actually, Vargas asserted national interests at the expense of
localism and particularism. By the end of his regime the states had
been deprived of many privileges, notably in the fields of taxation, education, and public welfare.

litical in character, social and religious institutions not having suffered in the least. The conviction among interested foreigners that Vargas did not represent any radical break with the past was evidenced by the fact that Brazilian bonds on Wall Street rebounded as soon as the "rebel" victory was announced.

Vargas ruled Brazil until October 1945, much of the time under a firm dictatorship, but one largely devoid of violence. During his regime Brazil underwent a "marvelous transition." Whether the changes that transpired were for the good or otherwise is not an issue here. Nor is it necessarily relevant whether the changes should be attributed to Vargas, as he maintained they should be, or whether they were the "inevitable" result of the impact upon Brazil of developments beyond its borders. What is important is that by the time the Vargas dictatorship was forcibly terminated in 1945, Brazil had advanced so far that not even the most reactionary elements could seriously recommend turning the clock back to 1930.

Nearly all the major decisions made by Vargas directly affected the urban middle sectors, many adversely. Although Vargas successfully circumscribed the decision-making power of the military, that institution continued to be a potential threat to the smooth functioning of civil government. Furthermore, the dictator diverted large sums to the military at a time when many believed that available resources might be more profitably employed in other areas. Vargas' pledge of "political renovation," which had been taken to mean a democratization and a purification of political processes, was redeemed when he placed severe curbs on the political activities of all civilian sectors. During most of his regime the electoral process was surrendered; the political parties were abolished in 1937, not to be revived until 1945. Vargas arrogated to himself the power to determine what should be published. He nationalized a number of foreign-held railroads, but, for the most part, he neglected transportation despite the fact that a well-developed transportation system was a requisite to the sound industrial and commercial economy he claimed to foresee for the republic.

But the political advantages accruing to the middle sectors

from Vargas' programs probably outweighed the disadvantages. The dictator was an advocate of public education in the best middle sector tradition, although it often had to compete with other activities for his attention and for public funds. And considerable effort was expended on public education, although after fifteen years of Vargas' rule the average Brazilian was still an illiterate—at least 55 per cent of the population were unable to read and write. There were twice as many schools in 1945 as in 1930. Enrollment at each the primary, secondary, and superior level was up over 150 per cent. The average student was attending school longer. The teaching staff was more than doubled, and, although the public school elementary teacher in general continued to be woefully unprepared professionally and remained poorly paid, some improvement was made both in the training of personnel and in the prestige the average teacher enjoyed in the community.

Vargas' ultimate objective in promoting education was to expand industry and commerce. But the advances in education were felt in other areas as well. Not the least of the side effects were those that tended to strengthen the urban middle sectors. The greatest gains in education were made in the urban centers. The products of the schools, whether urban or rural in background, ordinarily found employment in the larger populated centers. They became the customers of merchants who often belonged to the middle groups or who were on their way to becoming middle sector. In the industrial and commercial cities—where the emerging elements first successfully challenged the elite groups—the newly educated felt most directly the political influence of the middle segments.

The prospect of being able to obtain trained personnel was only one of the inducements that Vargas held out to those who might put their capital into the essentially urban branches of the economy. A favorable climate in soft and semi-durable manufactures, created by a reduced capacity to import following the near collapse of the coffee market, was made more attractive by a series of measures designed to provide industry with federal protection and financial aid. The tariff policy of the Vargas administration sought to give added incentive to domestic industry by increasing import rates on finished products and reducing them on essential raw materials and semimanufactures unavailable in Brazil. Foreign exchange was manipulated to favor the import of capital goods, much as occurred in the other republics discussed in the earlier chapters. Numerous State-financed and -controlled institutes—i.e., coffee, cocoa, sugar, tobacco, cotton, and pine lumber—were founded to develop those industrial areas most closely associated with agriculture. The State-controlled Banco do Brasil was charged with making capital more readily available to industry. In 1937 a department of agriculture and industrial credit was added to it. Meanwhile, labor was kept under strict State regulation.

Commercial and industrial expansion was also encouraged by what the State did not do. It did not, for example, overhaul the nation's tax structure, which was seriously regressive. By keeping the burden of taxes on the low-income consumer groups, the accumulation of capital by those monied elements that might be expected to reinvest their profits in the urban sections of the economy was favored. The federal government failed to bridle speculation in urban real estate, a depressive condition as far as industry was concerned, but one that over the short range contributed importantly to the growth of the urban middle income groups. The government's neglect of transportation and power development had the effect of making funds available for manufacturing, where the demands for investment capital perpetually outran the supply.

By 1940 Vargas' efforts on behalf of commerce and manufacturing had won widespread support. Commerce and industry were, relative to agriculture, offering high-level employment to approximately three million persons in a total labor force of fourteen million engaged in nondomestic pursuits. The military, although closely allied politically with agriculture, had become more industrial minded. The federal government's "obligation" to protect domestic industry had won wide acceptance by the majority elements within the politically articulate civilian groups. Vargas had sold labor—which was becoming more politically conscious—on the advantages of cooperating with capital and on the need to sacrifice in the interest of the future welfare of society.*

Encouraged by the favorable factors mentioned above and further stimulated by a rising demand for consumer goods following the disruption of international trade that accompanied the outbreak of hostilities in Europe, Brazilian industry expanded steadily throughout the war years. By 1946 industry and commerce had arrived economically, as the value of manufacturing approached the value of agricultural and livestock production. Industry had grown to the stage where its future was assured. The owners of industry and commerce had become politically powerful in their own right. They could henceforth increasingly formulate their requirements as demands rather than as requests.

Of the governments of Latin America in the 1930's only that of Mexico promoted nationalism more assiduously than did the Vargas administration. In an effort to keep Brazilians employed, severe restrictions were placed upon immigration. The number of entries dropped from 100,000 in 1929 to less than 35,000 in 1932 and to only 23,000 in 1938. Legislation was passed which fixed the maximum per cent of foreigners that could be employed in any enterprise and the maximum share of the payroll that could go to foreigners. Many public offices which under the Constitution of 1891 were open to all citizens were by the new Constitution of 1934 reserved for native-born Brazilians. The 1934 Constitution not only prohibited foreign ownership of political and news-conveying journalistic undertakings but required that primary responsibility for, and administration of, such enterprises be exercised exclusively by Brazilians. The 1934 charter offered protection to those in the liberal professions by providing that except under specified circumstances the professions should be exercised only by native-born Brazilians and naturalized Brazilians who had rendered military service to the nation.

* The reader is reminded at this point that after his ouster in 1945 Vargas developed a new philosophy which, in essence, held that labor had been ill-treated by the employer elements and that it must assert itself.

Finally, the charter provided that the revalidation of professional diplomas issued by foreign institutions would not be permitted except to native-born Brazilians.

A wide range of nationalistically inspired measures were taken in the economic field to supplant those designed specifically to promote domestic industry. Severe restrictions were placed upon foreigners and foreign-domiciled companies in the exploitation of minerals, petroleum—including refining and distribution—and the development of water power. "Progressive nationalization" in key economic areas was written into the Constitution of 1934. Fiscal revenues were used for social welfare and public improvements rather than for resuming payments on public debts defaulted before and during the depression. Special taxes were levied on foreign companies domiciled abroad and on exchange remittances. Vargas began buying up the foreign companies that controlled the Brazilian railroads, and within a few years the bulk of the present federal railroad net was brought under the central government's control. Beginning in 1942 the dictator gave a strong impetus to domestic aviation.

The finest symbol of Brazilian economic nationalism as it developed under Vargas is the iron and steel plant at Volta Redonda. Begun during the war when plant equipment was in urgent demand, Volta Redonda was part of the United States' payment to Brazil for the use of airstrips along the "hump" and at the same time Vargas' payment to those nationalist military officers who opposed his decision to permit the use of Brazilian soil by foreign fighting forces. Volta Redonda, the largest iron and steel plant in Latin America—which in 1956 produced 740,000 metric tons of steel ingots, from which 580,000 metric tons of milled products were obtained—is to military and civilian groups alike the proof of Brazil's industrial emancipation.

Of all the decisions made by Vargas, probably none had greater political implications than his determination to bring the working groups into the political arena. The decision was not made immediately, for although Vargas created a labor ministry soon after the Revolution of 1930, and although considerable labor legislation was passed subsequently, he distrusted labor and labor distrusted him. By 1938, however, as a consequence of labor's support when he was consolidating his dictatorship under the neo-Fascist *Estado Novo* (New State), Vargas came to appreciate the political potential of the workers. He retained their approval through elaborate welfare programs and by imposing restrictions and obligations on business management. At the same time he maintained strict federal control over the labor movement as a guarantee to the business community that labor would not be permitted to get out of hand. As a consequence, an important share of the monied element continued to accept him. The dictator thus became the first person in Brazil successfully to practice on the national level "the art of getting money from the rich and support from the poor on the pretext of protecting each from the other."

By the time Vargas was driven from office the number of individuals on the electoral rolls was four times the figure for 1930; the enfranchisement of women providing a substantial portion of the enlarged electorate. The working elements had come of age and were in an improved position to influence the policies of any civilian government. Henceforth the objectives of the workingman would enter into the calculations of every successful politician.

The developments during the Vargas era were favorable on the whole to the middle sectors; their political position, however, was far from secure when the dictator was removed in 1945. Powerful forces from the past remained, and a number of them were inimical to the middle sectors. Those forces persist in varying degrees today and contribute to creating in Brazil probably the most confused political climate to be found anywhere in Latin America.

In 1945 the army still stood as the decisive factor in Brazilian politics. In the presidential election that followed on the heels of Vargas' ouster the two principal parties felt obliged to select career officers to head their tickets. Subsequently the military, particularly the army, has continued to view itself as the guarantor of the constitutional process and the defender of existing institutions. When, in its judgment, Brazilian institutions have been threatened from any source, the army has acted even against the federal government. The workers' growing influence has been of particular concern to the military and on several occasions the army has interfered with normal constitutional practices when it appeared that civilians were unprepared to resist those demands of labor that threatened the status quo.

Nationalism, which received its first sharp impulse under Vargas, has become so militant and widespread that it has ceased to be an issue and has become a fact. In recent years no major party or social group has been able to make nationalism its exclusive domain as ins and outs alike have vied in raising nationalism to an emotional political ideology that has been permitted to obscure politico-economic realities. On the other hand, those who favor a moderate approach have had difficulty in making their voices heard. A case in point is the issue of the exploitation of Brazil's petroleum resources, where an attitude of assertive nationalism probably has been decisive not only in preventing the development of a more adequate fuel supply but in effectively reducing the nation's ability to attract foreign capital in general.*

To add to the confusion created by a politically conscious military and by rampant nationalism, there has been the price to political stability extracted by a spiraling inflation, which was rooted in the Vargas era. The economic and social problems Brazil inherited from the dictator were highly complex and thus far they have defied solution. An urban population increasingly dissatisfied with its level of living and clamoring for relief from the uncertainties of urban existence placed heavy demands on leaders who in general lacked firmness. By 1950 the republic found itself confronted with runaway prices brought on in considerable part by the politicians' attempts

---

* By 1958 there were strong indications that West German and French venture capital was ready to test the economic climate of Brazil on a large scale. Significantly, the French interest in Brazil stemmed in part from its need for new investment areas concomitant to the breakup of the empire.

in some way to balance the demands of both the industrial and the working elements while they kept the producers of export commodities satisfied. From the economic disorder and inflation of the 1940's Brazil passed to near economic chaos and more inflation in the 1950's. Proceeding at a dangerous pace, inflation has in recent years colored the moves of all political forces.

Fifteen years of rule by Vargas had largely destroyed organized political parties to the political disadvantage of the middle sector leadership, which traditionally in Latin America has operated most effectively through party organizations. After the dictator's overthrow a mélange of weakly organized political parties arose, not a few of which were narrowly conceived along regional or personalist lines. The multiplicity of parties has persisted, as has the catering of many of them to localist or personalist interests. The parties, never less than ten in number since late 1945, have ranged from the Communist Party, which polled approximately 10 per cent of the vote in national elections before it was declared illegal in 1947, to such groups as the Fascist-inclined Popular Representative Party (*Partido de Representação Popular*—P.R.P.) of Plínio Salgado, who at the head of the Party's ticket in 1955 polled over 8 per cent of the votes cast for all presidential candidates. The victorious candidate in that election, Juscelino Kubitschek, polled only 34 per cent of the popular vote to defeat his nearest competitor by only 500,000 votes out of a total of approximately 8,600,000 valid ballots. The candidate who ran third received 25 per cent of the popular vote. The large number of parties, also in evidence in the composition of the national legislature, has discouraged the growth of a firm basis of support for parliamentary institutions. On the other hand, the immature party system, the continued, although lessening particularism, and the persistence of personal rivalries and ambitions have given rise to infinite and constantly shifting combinations and permutations.

The profusion of parties has contributed to political awareness, but it has not produced a clear-cut middle sector political movement. What happened was that, rather than creating a new party or new parties, the middle segments vied with the traditional ruling groups for the leadership of the existing political organizations. Members of both elements are today found in the leadership of virtually every party on the Brazilian scene. A brief examination of three of the leading parties will, it is believed, establish the contention.

The Social Democratic Party (*Partido Social Democrático* —P.S.D.), which has provided two of the three elected presidents since 1945, has relied heavily upon rural votes. Its leadership, however, has been drawn from a cross section of "privileged" urban society as well as from the landowning elite, including the coffee growers of São Paulo.

The National Democratic Union (*União Democrática Nacional*—U.D.N.), which on the basis of the 1955 elections is the second largest party and probably slightly to the right of the P.S.D. in most respects, appeals to the same socioeconomic groups as does the P.S.D. Intellectuals and professionals are probably more prominently represented in the U.D.N. leadership. This suggests the relatively conservative nature of the Brazilian middle sectors.

The Brazilian Labor Party (*Partido Trabalhista Brasileiro*—P.T.B.) offers an unusual example of the lack of class lines in politics. The party, which was the personal vehicle of Vargas after 1945, until he took his own life in August 1954, has appealed to the urban laborer. To date, however, the most prominent leaders of the party have been drawn from the traditional landowning ruling class of the southern state of Rio Grande do Sul.

Perhaps as illustrative of the confused state of Brazilian politics as the above party structure is the disregard for party lines that Vargas displayed in the election of 1950. In that year he ran successfully for the presidency on the Labor Party ticket. But he did not rely alone upon that Party. He made vote-getting deals with the local leadership of the government party (P.S.D.) in some states, and with the U.D.N in at least one state. As if this were not sufficient to emphasize the degree to which party politics in Brazil tends to be meaningless it could be pointed out that in the same election Vargas, despite his strong and at times demagogic bid for the urban labor vote, was supported by segments of both the rural and the urban wealthy elements and certain moderately conservative Catholic lay groups which considered him the only force capable of successfully coping with the Communists. Underscoring much of the political confusion that has plagued Brazil are the many instances of urban financial elements with substantial rural interests.*

The above discussion has indicated a number of circumstances influencing the political process that make it difficult to establish with any exactness the role of the Brazilian middle sectors upon decision making since 1945. They bear repeating. Because of the constant meddling of the military in civilian affairs it cannot be assumed that any given decision of an administration reflects the thinking of either its leaders or of any particular socioeconomic group. Nationalism and inflation know no class lines. The failure to develop parties dedicated to the interest of one or two socioeconomic groups and the continued reliance upon *ad hoc* arrangements in lieu of responsible party government, make it next to impossible to associate directly any given socioeconomic sector with the over-all national development since 1945. Despite these adverse characteristics of the Brazilian scene since World War II, at least one approach to determining the political influence of the middle sectors remains—that is the possibility of establishing in broad outline the extent to which certain middle group objectives and requirements have been promoted. Such an approach provides a rather impressive record of middle sector achievement.

During the months of uncertainty following Vargas' removal from office in 1945 the majority elements within the urban middle sectors joined with the landholders to form a phalanx against any radical change in the social or economic status quo. The return to representative government was given precedence over all other considérations. Plans were pushed for early elections. Although a dozen parties rushed to put up

* See pages 158–59 for a discussion of this condition as it obtained in the 1920's.

candidates, political activity soon polarized in two recently constituted parties: the P.S.D. and the U.D.N. Throwbacks to the pre-1930 era were to be found in each organization. The P.S.D., however, stood generally for what Vargas had achieved or claimed he had achieved in the social and economic fields. The U.D.N. placed its emphasis upon the return to representative, democratic government. Both parties selected a conservative military career officer to head the national ticket. The strategy offered no place for those from the middle sectors who were moving toward the Left, and in protest many of them contributed, it is believed, to the 10 per cent of the popular vote won by the Communist Party in the national election held in 1945.

The 1945 presidential race was won by unimaginative General Eurico Gaspar Dutra, who had inherited Vargas' mantle. Impelled by his own personal inclinations as well as by the temper of the times to wage a conservative campaign, Dutra had called for a prudent approach to the immediate social and economic problems confronting the "New Brazil." His principal opponent had allied himself with the old conservative coffee aristocracy and had conducted a campaign that in its emphasis upon the political and individual freedoms rather than the social and economic concerns of the popular masses was reminiscent of the 1920's and in its stress upon nationalism portended things to come.

Soon after assuming the presidency Dutra called a constituent assembly into session. By September 1946 that body had produced a new national charter. The new document evinced the continued cooperation of the Center-Right leadership that had made Dutra's election possible. It sought to return the government to the electorate by creating a system wherein power would be distributed at the various levels of government in such a way as to make impossible a dictatorship of an individual or a region. In this respect the Constitution sustained a long-established tenet of middle groups in all parts of Latin America. The imprint of the middle sector thinking was also found in the provision, later reenforced by Law No. 1164 of July 24, 1950, which sought to reduce localism in politics and to create national parties by requiring that political parties have a following in at least five electoral units (states, territories, the Federal District) or face cancellation of their charters. The liberalized suffrage requirements (literates of both sexes who had reached the age of 18 years could qualify for the vote) likewise reflected middle sector thinking.

The provision in the 1946 charter for the freedom of initiative (but only when it could be reconciled with the value of human labor) manifested the desire of the constitution-makers to legalize "the obligation of the State to the popular masses rather than to the individual." But in also providing that labor might exercise only those functions delegated to it by the public power, the members of the Assembly were expressing the generally conservative tone of both the urban middle groups and the landholding element.

The middle sectors' growing influence was particularly marked in that section of the Constitution that made the federal government ultimately responsible for developing industry and for promoting education at all levels. Middle sector influence was also apparent in the numerous provisions for the protection of nationals, natural resources, and coastwise shipping from exploitation by foreigners and companies domiciled abroad.

The decade and more since the promulgation of the Constitution has witnessed no discernible weakening of those provisions that mirrored the political philosophy of the middle sectors. Indeed, those provisions are probably currently accepted, except in detail, by all politically responsible elements of the population. Furthermore, except that power has tended to centralize in the federal authority despite constitutional restrictions, the provisions have had, for better or worse, the desired effect.

The opportunities for representative government and for national issues to supersede regional organizations and issues have been strengthened. In an environment of sustained industrialization and urban growth the political elite groups have expanded through the accretions from the industrial, commercial, professional, and bureaucratic levels. Meanwhile the political base has broadened substantially. By 1950 the number of registered voters had risen to over eleven million and five years later the figure exceeded fifteen million. More than nine million voters actually went to the polls in the presidential election held in 1955. Thus, while the Brazilian population roughly doubled in the quarter-century following 1930, the active population showed a sixfold increase and the number of eligible voters had multiplied ten times.

The apparent weakening of regional influences since 1945 is evident in the results of the 1955 presidential election. In only three of the twenty states did the winning presidential candidate poll more than 50 per cent of the vote. But he won a plurality in nine of the others, among which every major region of the republic was represented. Furthermore, he made a respectable showing in the remaining states and also in the Federal District. At the same time, the candidate who ran third —winning 25 per cent of the popular vote—polled at least 10 per cent of the vote in fourteen states and actually received a plurality in the heavily populated Federal District and in the states of Amazonas, Paraná, and São Paulo.

The 1955 election revealed at least one other political reality that would appear to portend an advantage for the middle sectors. The inhabitants of the relatively highly urbanized and literate areas where the middle sectors concentrate play a larger part in politics than their numbers warrant. This conclusion is drawn from available data on the state of São Paulo and the Federal District. The data show that those two political entities—both of which are highly urbanized and literate, relative to the remainder of the republic—although they had only about 20 per cent of the total population of the republic, actually cast approximately 30 per cent of the national vote. The same data reveal that the city of São Paulo, with approximately 5 per cent of the total population of the republic, cast about 8 per cent of the national vote.

The industrial economy has expanded at a rapid rate during the past decade. The manufacturers, their confidence shored up by the provisions of the Constitution of 1946 in support of industry, placed heavy demands upon the Dutra

regime. Among other things they extorted a fiscal policy
highly favorable to industrialization and more particularly to
manufacturing. Transportation and power, however, continued to be neglected as they had been for a generation.
Meanwhile, an easy-money policy was instituted which had
the effect of placing an important share of the cost of industrialization upon the shoulders of the urban workers. Industry's response was immediate. The index of real output
of industrial production increased from a base of 100 for
1939 to 240 in 1951. The index of manufacturing rose from a
base of 100 for 1948 to 143 by 1952 . The expansion in output
was reflected in the growth of factory employment, which rose
at an annual rate of 4.9 per cent between 1945 and 1955, one
of the highest in all of Latin America and the highest among
those republics that already had a sizable industrial economy
in 1945.

Despite the impressive industrial advance all was not well
economically. By mid-1953 a number of circumstances, including poor industrial planning, had produced a stalemate
in the industrial program and had led the republic to a point
where many feared imminent collapse. The Vargas regime
sought to meet the situation by redressing the balance between
agriculture and industry in the economy but it lacked the necessary parliamentary support. Efforts to check an accelerating
inflation failed, and Vargas' successor, Kubitschek, inherited
the problem, which by 1955 had become an impasse. The nation was confronted with the difficult and as yet insoluble task
of reconciling a rampant nationalism and the ambitious industrial elements with the republic's inability to earn foreign exchange in the amounts required to maintain the industrial
momentum to which the people had become accustomed between 1945 and 1953.

The middle sectors have benefited from increased urbanization. Industrialization and the expansion of the social and
economic responsibilities of the government which required
an enlarged public bureaucracy contributed to a significant
expansion of Brazilian cities. The urban population rose over
40 per cent between 1940 and 1950 with approximately 60

per cent of the increase resulting from internal migration. The growth of urban agglomerations has continued throughout the period since 1950. The larger cities, particularly São Paulo and Rio de Janeiro, have grown even more rapidly than the urban centers in general.

But despite the growth of its cities Brazil remains overwhelmingly a rural country. Official figures for 1950 showed the population to be over 60 per cent rural, but many scholars insist that perhaps as much as 80 per cent of the population remains strictly rural. In 1950 only one in ten or fifteen children born on farms was migrating to urban areas as compared to one in every two in the United States. The two largest cities of Brazil, São Paulo and Rio de Janeiro, combined, contained only approximately 11 per cent of the republic's total population in the mid-1950's as compared with Montevideo, which some experts estimate to contain nearly 40 per cent of the population of Uruguay; Greater Buenos Aires, with 29 or 30 per cent of the total population of Argentina; Greater Santiago, with approximately 25 per cent of the total population of Chile; and Greater Mexico City, with 15 per cent of the total population of Mexico.

Although Brazil has made considerable gains in the field of learning since 1945, it has yet much to accomplish even in terms of what its neighbors have achieved. It has built schools, enlarged the teaching staff, and vastly expanded enrollment, which by 1954 exceeded five million at all levels according to official figures. But the illiteracy rate has not been reduced significantly and the actual number of illiterates has increased. The national illiteracy rate, which in 1950 was in excess of 50 per cent for those 10 years of age and over, concealed the fact that throughout the vast northern regions the average rate was probably nearer 80 per cent. With three times the population of Argentina, Brazil was in the mid-1950's publishing about the same number of books as her southern neighbor. The republic's per capita newsprint consumption was less than a third of Uruguay's. And Brazil's daily newspaper output per 1,000 inhabitants was only one-third that of Argentina's and one-fourth that of Uruguay's.

If the above analysis is reasonably accurate there is no question but that the Brazilian urban middle sectors have been restrained by severe political handicaps. The military has served as a definite deterrent to responsible civilian government and, in those areas of development that positively affect the political role of the middle sectors, the gains have been relative. National political parties have increased in strength but party politics remains on an immature level. The republic has become more urbanized but it remains the most rural in character of the five nations. Brazil has dedicated itself to the education of its masses and the population is becoming more literate, but the fact remains that every other Brazilian is still an illiterate—not a favorable condition for the growth of representative government, which the middle sectors advocate. Industry has grown appreciably, as have commerce and the services, but the politically active urban labor force is still so small and fragmented that the formation of a middle sector–working element political amalgam—such as developed in Uruguay and Chile—has not been attractive to the middle sector leadership. In fact, it would appear that the majority within the middle sectors has tended to associate itself with those elements in the P.S.D. and U.D.N. who look askance at the political emergence of the workers. Industry contributes as much to the gross national product as agriculture and livestock production contribute, but agriculture continues to be the only branch of the economy capable of earning foreign exchange, so sought after at present. Consequently, it may be assumed that agriculturists will continue to demand a large voice in government. Nationalism has become so widespread that the middle sectors have not been able to make political capital of it.

There are forces at work in Brazil which will eventually alter the political pattern. But there appears to be only one development which might radically affect the political arrangements in the near future. The development, were it to occur, would be a successful revolt of the laborers and the salaried groups among the middle sectors. Those elements are seriously discontented. Their economic position has been eroding for several years. Their will as expressed at the polls has been countermanded by the military and the conservative leadership of the parties to which they have been forced to turn. Thus far the military, which has been basically conservative, has acted before being faced with a severe show of force. It is not known how it would react if it were faced with an explosive situation such as confronted the Argentine military in October of 1945 when Perón "returned from exile," with the support of vociferous marching mobs comprised of the working elements of society. There are some who doubt that the Brazilian military is prepared to shoot down civilians in order to keep those economic groups in power who presently control the nation.

It is the conviction of this author that in the final analysis the Brazilian military will in the foreseeable future determine the course of political events. The emergence of vigorous middle and working element amalgams—such as have appeared at different times in Argentina, Chile, Mexico and Uruguay— must await either the approval of the armed forces or the serious internal disunity within the armed forces that would prevent their united action. Until such time as one or the other development occurs, middle sector influence will be exercised primarily in conjunction with more conservative elite elements. The Brazilian government will remain unstable, and long-range projects will ordinarily be sacrificed to political opportunism.

9 Retrospect and Prospect

The middle sectors of Argentina, Brazil, Chile, Mexico, and Uruguay contributed brilliantly to the fight for freedom and to the cause of liberalism during the independence movement (1810–25). Once independence was achieved, however, they were unable to prevent the locus of power from shifting to the reactionary elements whose leaders were drawn from the elites of the land, the Church, and the military. The reactionary elements remained in unchallenged control until mid-century. To the extent that the middle sectors participated in politics and government they were limited essentially to justifying, refining, and administering the policies formulated by caudillos, whose power was based upon force and who spoke for those committed to retain the status quo.

After 1850 the middle sectors began to benefit politically from the economic transformations that were stimulated by ideas, investment capital, and technological know-how flowing from abroad and from immigrant labor. In particular, the transformations underwrote a considerable expansion of the middle sectors, primarily from among the commercial and industrial elements. The entrepreneurs, managers, technicians, and scientists associated with commerce and industry represented a new and dynamic type of wealth and influence. They were the intellectual-professional middle sectors' strong allies in the sharpening contest for power with the traditional ruling elites. But even with the additions to the commercial and industrial elements the middle groups remained numerically small, and in order successfully to challenge the elites they had to seek popular support outside their own ranks. They found it ordinarily in urban labor.* Thus were formed the political compounds that in this century have been so instrumental in breaking the monopoly of the traditional ruling elites.

The survival of amalgams composed of such disparate groups as owners of industry on the one hand and factory workers on the other was contingent upon their ability to produce results. Their social, economic, and political achievements—at least over the short range—were substantial in certain cases. The purpose of these final pages is not to summarize or conclude, but to analyze the major developments of the past several decades in terms of the middle sectors' political role in the foreseeable future. In this instance the foreseeable future is taken to mean the next decade or so.

Since the middle sector–led amalgams have asserted themselves, government by law and by the people—the nineteenth-century political trade-mark of the middle groups—has enjoyed wider acceptance than ever before in the five republics. Also, appreciable progress has been made toward institutionalizing the electoral process. The electorate has been expanded manyfold as the masses have been recalled from the political wilderness and brought inside the orbit of national affairs.† The national political parties founded upon ideological principles have made headway against the regional groupings and the personalist cliques.

On the other hand, demagoguery and the centralization of power, both of which the middle sectors have held to be antithetical to their political welfare, not only have survived but may have become more firmly entrenched. In the century following independence, demagoguery was widely employed but it was directed to a politically sophisticated element that was reasonably capable of separating fact from fancy. Furthermore, it was of such a nature as to leave the socioeconomic structure essentially unaffected. The new demagoguery in

* It will be recalled that to date the middle sector–urban labor alliance has been less pronounced in Brazil than in the other four republics.

† It is perhaps worth pointing out again that in Mexico "agrarian revolutionaries" provided the first impetus in expanding the electoral rolls and that in Argentina it was the dictator Perón who took the lead in broadening the electoral base.

which the middle sector leadership finds itself involved is directed to persons whose minds are ruled more by their immediate material needs than by reason. It emphasizes social rather than legal justice—in which the middle sectors have greatest faith. It stresses social rather than political equality —which the middle sectors traditionally have insisted is the prime requirement for social progress. It insists upon a more equitable distribution of income and, in certain extreme cases, of wealth.

Also, in order to live politically with their working sector allies the middle groups have surrendered, at least for the present and immediate future, their objective of an "equitable division" of public power and responsibility. Historically they have held that the balanced distribution of power at the various levels of government and among the three branches of government can provide the only practical guarantee against the usurpation of authority by a single individual or region. But the urgency involved in meeting the immediate minimum demands of their worker allies has resulted in the middle sector leadership's accepting the concentration of power in the central authority and in the executive branch as the most direct means of putting the meager resources of the nations to work. Under governments responsible to the amalgams, the concentration of power in the central authority and in the executive branch may have reached the point where a reversal of the trend has become little more than a remote hope. Except in Brazil, the states and towns have been deprived of nearly all financial independence. When the gains in the political area are weighted against the permanent threat to those gains both from demagogic appeals to the politically immature and economically underprivileged masses and from the concentration of power, the gains become more apparent than real.

In general, the middle sectors have been effective in popularizing public responsibility for training heads as well as for counting them. Appropriations for public education have grown. Enrollment has increased. The time spent in schools has lengthened. The percentage of illiterates has dropped, that of the functionally literate has risen. In the process the arts and attitudes of civilization to some extent have triumphed over ignorance and violence. Secondary schools and institutions of higher learning have shown a growing awareness of their responsibilities in training persons capable of contributing more fully to societies that are in the throes of a social and economic upheaval.

But the middle sectors have paid a price for the achievement in public education, and the future may well extract an even higher toll. In order to attain a share of their educational goals the middle sector leadership has sanctioned the transfer of responsibility for education from the local to the central authorities. The school curricula prepared in cosmopolitan capitals carry the threat of being woefully out of touch with the environment of the student. The opportunity for the use of the classroom for nation-wide dissemination of currently popular ideologies and the promotion of the interest of dominant political parties and groups has been enhanced. In many instances the education of the youth and at the same time the neglect of adult education have proved socially disruptive. Roles have been reversed in the home. Children have become the teachers of their parents, thereby creating some social confusion and resentments.

Despite the middle sectors' championship of public education, they have not created public elementary or secondary school systems to which they as groups by preference send their own offspring. Thus far their preference for the private training of their own children has not had significant political implications. In the not too distant future the implications may be appreciable. By keeping their children in private schools, the middle sectors are tending to perpetuate the social distinctions that, for purposes of politics, they have insisted for some time must be obliterated. Meanwhile in the public schools there is growing up a generation of citizens who are socially and economically tied to the working masses. This new generation in general is being exposed to more radical interpretations of social and economic ideologies than the offspring of the middle sectors ordinarily receive in private institutions. The "more earthy products" of the public schools who become politicians may well pose the first serious threat to middle sector control of the popular masses.

A sense of social obligation and the need to pay off political debts have combined to induce the middle sectors to support advanced labor and welfare legislation in favor of the industrial working groups. While it is true that much of the legislation still represents little more than statements of aspirations, it is also true that considerable advance has been won in terms of workers' rights and the uplifting of the dignity of the popular masses. Among the solid achievements have been the outlawing of the company store and payment in script, the recognition of the right to organize, the right to a contract, and, under specified conditions, the right to strike.

What of the middle sectors' well-being? How long can or will they continue to support the demands of the industrial workers? Originally the workers were unable to finance a labor movement and the movement as it developed in its modern form was brought into being by politicians in the control of the several governments. In turn, the State in a supervisory capacity regulated the activities of the organizations to such an extent that ordinarily the central authorities in an independent capacity determined which labor laws would be honored. The price to labor for the benevolent interest displayed by the public officials was political backing of the group in power. Labor organizations consequently were encouraged— as they still are in most instances—to place far greater emphasis upon political activities than on straight union effort as it is generally understood in the United States. But the laborers have been growing muscles and are becoming more capable of paying the costs of their trade-union movement. As their improved economic position permits them to become more concerned with wages and working conditions and less concerned with the political framework within which their economic problems are resolved, the price of their continued support may well reach the point where the dominant elements within the middle sectors will find it unbearable.

The popularizing of the suffrage in the near future may also be expected to place strains upon middle sector–labor alliances. When the middle sector leadership first turned to the workers, the factory employees were capable of exercising political influnce far out of proportion to their numbers. They were vocal. They paraded. In a society in which the practice was to restrict rigidly the number of qualified voters on the basis of literacy, a relatively large percentage of the urban workers met the legal requirements for the franchise. By the 1940's, however, the process of broadening the base of the political pyramid had reached out to make voters of many individuals before they had won for themselves a secure place within the organized industrial working movement. These additions to the electorate have reduced the relative influence of the industrial worker's vote. The expansion of the electorate to include a much larger percentage of the nonindustrial labor force has required the politicians to measure the industrial worker's share of the national income less in political terms and more in terms of his productive capacity. And the industrial worker's productive capacity, in relation to other workers, has not been increased outstandingly during the recent past.

The political relationship of the middle sectors and industrial labor is also being affected by the changes that have taken place in the ownership of industrial and commercial enterprises. When political cooperation between them began, a considerable share of machine industry was in foreign hands. Foreigners also had important holdings in commerce and particularly in transportation and foreign trade. Consequently, the foreigner and the foreign-domiciled company were made to bear directly a large portion of the original financial burdens of increased wages and other benefits that were awarded the working elements. Under such circumstances the middle sector politician could offer himself as a friend of the workers and as a watchdog against possible abuses from foreigners.

For at least two decades the trend has been for commerce and industry in the five republics to become domestically controlled. Domestic capitalists, as a result, have been called upon to carry an augmented share of the costs of wage gains and other benefits to labor. As the pressure upon them grows, they increasingly insist that the public good requires that the concern should be on expanded production rather than on equalitarian distribution. They use their legal rights and economic power to dissuade the politicians who would curry the favor of the workers by disregarding the economic realities. They have contended that it is the State's duty to alert the workingman to the fact that he cannot expect the same friendly consideration when he fights local interests as when he served as the protagonist against "foreign rapacity." The growing political influence of the industrial and commercial elements of the middle sectors has already forced the politicians to take cognizance of the argument to the current disadvantage of the laboring components.

Industrial development, which in actual practice has often meant simply the development of factory industries, has been since about 1930 the political mainspring of the middle sectors. Their leaders have ridden to giddy political heights as the champions of industrial expansion. Urban labor has given its enthusiastic support to economic emancipation. Under friendly governments the contribution of manufacturing and processing to the gross product of the republics has been expanded appreciably. Factories have been made symbols of progress.

Despite the large reservoir of favorable public opinion it enjoys, however, industry has in some cases reached the point where it has become a political bugaboo. In other cases it is rapidly approaching that point. In large part the dilemma lies in the fact that industry has not measured up to the predictions that politicians made for it.

In sponsoring industrial development, the middle sector leadership insisted that it would raise the workers' level of living. Until the late 1940's the steadily increasing output of consumer goods contributed appreciably to that end. By that time it had become apparent, however, that the expanded capacity to produce consumer goods was not built upon firm economic foundations. Rather, the increased production had resulted largely from the siphoning of available resources into the manufacturing industries to the neglect of adequate maintenance of capital investment in such vital segments of the economies as transportation and agriculture, and in Argentina, Brazil, and Uruguay agriculture has historically provided the only notable source of foreign exchange. Once the governments acknowledged that further economic progress must be predicated on heavy investment in basic industries and agriculture the rate of flow of capital into factories declined, the production of consumer goods leveled off, and the earning power of the working elements began to erode as they bid for goods in short supply. During the past half-decade the trend has been for the worker's earning power to decline.

The politicians had predicted that new industry would resolve the problem of providing employment for those entering the labor pool. In this regard industry has proved a disappointment, for although it has absorbed substantial numbers of employees, it has been the services, including the government services, and the construction industries rather than the manufacturing industries that have provided the safety valve for those entering the labor market. In the case of Mexico the demand for cheap farm labor in the United States has served a similar purpose.

The leaders also assured their electoral supporters that equalitarian distribution of income and rapid acceleration of production could be achieved simultaneously if the central government entered directly into the development of industry and the regulation of public welfare. The State has played a major role in industrial growth but it has not justified the original assumption upon which public participation in industry was predicated. Although the popular masses have undoubtedly profited from industrial development and State interference in the social field, the gap separating the rich from the poor has widened. Millionaires are being created at an ever increasing speed while millions remain economic zeros.

The politicians likewise assured the public that State participation in industry would strengthen public confidence in that segment of the economy. That assurance has been only partially fulfilled. The public has lost confidence in the utilities field as an area of private investment. The ownership of public utilities consequently has tended to pass from private to public hands. Industrial investment continues to be unattractive to the small investor who, in general, shuns the stock markets, while he displays a strong propensity for urban mortgages and speculation in real estate. Meanwhile, and to a considerable extent as a result of public intervention in the social and economic fields, the cost of government has risen faster than national income. This has served to alter the composition of the gross product. In relative terms the volume of services has increased and that of consumer and capital goods has declined. It has also led to deficit budgeting and currency depreciation.

The leaders further justified industrialization on the grounds that it would emancipate the republics from the more materially advanced countries of the world. But the fact is that industrialization, reliant as it has been to date upon equipment and raw materials from abroad, has increased their dependence on the outside. This has created complex industrial problems. The increased dependence comes at a time when the past neglect of agriculture in each of the republics except Mexico has reduced their capacity to earn foreign exchange at the rate required to maintain even a significantly reduced tempo of industrial growth. Meanwhile nationalism, which has accompanied the expansion of domestic industry, has reduced the republics' ability to attract badly needed foreign capital.

Because industrial development has in fact failed to satisfy either of the two groups most directly concerned, the republics during the foreseeable future may be expected to live under the dual threat of: (1) labor erupting against the immediate price it must pay for greater industrialization and (2) owners of industry seeking more forceful solutions to their foreign-exchange problems. The resort to direct action by either labor or capital could destroy the political amalgams that since World War I have played such an important part in the social and economic reorientation of the five republics.

Modern-integrated nationalism represents the collective demand of frustrated people for direct action by the State. In each of the five republics the middle sectors have played a leading role in lifting nationalism in its modern form to the level of a major political ideology. The nationalism of the new leadership has been of an essentially economic nature—the nationalism of people impatient for more rapid material progress. This type of nationalism gave the new leadership, in its bid for office, the opportunity to associate the old ruling elite with foreign exploitation and raw-material economies while they presented themselves as the promoters of indigenous values and modern-diversified economies. As policy-makers the new leaders placed themselves in the forefront of those who demanded legislation that would protect the national workers, capitalists, and resources from foreign exploitation during the transitional periods that would lead to the republics' emancipation from foreign domination. The leaders asked that during the transitions the workers, in return for the material and political sacrifices nationalism entailed, accept the spiritual and emotional rewards the ideology offered. But the question arises: Has nationalism reached the point where the presently dominant middle sector elements can no longer benefit from it to the extent that they could when the ideology was going through its formative stages? There are reasons to believe that such may be the case.

The middle sectors have done such an excellent job of selling nationalism that they can no longer claim an option on it. The ideology is today embraced by all the articulate elements, some of whom hold to it more ardently than do the dominant element within the middle sectors. In fact it may be that the middle sectors in certain instances have assumed—and in other instances in the near future will assume—a moderator's role on the nationalist issue. Already in Chile the Communists have seized the nationalist label and are running with it. Meanwhile, the Chilean middle sector leadership has urged moderation and has cleared the way for greater foreign private participation in economic development. In Brazil, João Goulart, the Vice-President of the republic and head of the Labor Party (P.T.B.), at a convention of the Party in late 1957 declared that "we [the workers] have *de facto* authority and the legitimate right to exercise the function of the vanguard in the nationalistic struggle in which the Brazilian people are involved."* What Goulart was saying was that labor must assume the responsibility for seeing that the middle sector leadership does not weaken on nationalistic issues. In Mexico the xenophobic nationalism of the agrarian radicals under Lázaro Cárdenas has been modified under the middle sector leadership of the past decade to the point where Mexico is currently hailed as one of the more favorable areas for foreign capital investment and foreign business. In Argentina an exaggerated nationalism has left very little room for rational thinking. That small space, however, appears to be occupied almost exclusively by middle sector components.

Both internal and external developments seem to favor the middle sectors' holding for the most part to a moderately nationalistic position in the foreseeable future. The record repeatedly reveals that they are less radical in office than in seeking office. Many within the increasingly influential commercial and industrial components have come to appreciate that nationalism, when carried to extremes, can be economically disruptive. The leadership in general has recognized that assertive nationalism is often incompatible with the desire for international prestige and the expectation of assistance from major powers of the West.

Several developments and changes in attitudes abroad may encourage the middle sectors' pursuit of moderate nationalistic courses. In international relations narrowly defined, the growing interdependence of the nations of the Western world has made the less-developed nations feel that their cooperation is urgently desired. From that point they have argued with considerable success that cooperation is possible only among equals. Having attained equality, at least theoretically, they have been able to contend that their backwardness is not exclusively their own problem but also a problem of those with whom they cooperate. The acceptance, especially by the United States, of the republics as equals and the recognition that under-

* *Correio da Manhã*, October 4, 1957, and *Estado de São Paulo*, October 4, 1957.

development is an international problem may serve to make easier the justification of international cooperation.

Developments in economic relations also favor the lessening of the antipathies and tensions that first bred nationalism and then were nurtured by it. Governmental and particularly international lending agencies are replacing private foreign lenders in many areas of economic activity. These new agencies attach fewer safeguards in their financial transactions than do private investors and, especially in the case of the UN agencies, are scarcely susceptible to the charge of imperialism. To the extent that public agencies replace the private lender, one of the favorite whipping boys of the Latin American nationalists will be removed from the scene. Directly related to this consideration is the evident decline of foreign private-capital investment in public utilities. In terms of the lessening of tensions this change may be particularly significant. Nearly every citizen living in urban areas must make use of utilities that, because of their public nature, are subject to regulation by the politicians. The charges and countercharges resulting from regulation of the utilities have served as a constant irritant. The sooner that all Argentines, Chileans, and Mexicans can pay an electric-light bill without believing or being reminded that they are paying "a hidden foreign tax" the sooner the nationalist politicians will have to discard one of their popular weapons. Finally, the fact that science and technology have reached a point where the borrowing of an idea is often more important than the borrowing of personnel or capital holds promise of healing some of the national wounds caused by what often in the past have been considered abrasive economic practices.

Meanwhile, as the ties that have bound the middle sectors and the workers together politically are being tested, changes have taken place which seem to insure the middle sectors a continuing prominent role with or without the support of the industrial laboring elements. The steady extension of the political base would appear to promise the middle sectors an increasing maneuverability in any situation dominated by civilian groups. Most significantly an enlarged electorate offers the middle sectors the possibility of finding popular support among voters whose price, at least in the beginning, would be lower than that of the industrial laboring elements, whose members are often looked upon and resented as the "aristocrats of labor" by other workers.

On the other hand, as public responsibility moderates the middle sectors' views, the middle groups have become more acceptable to the old elites. The middle sectors in general have systematically protected domestic property and have reserved an important segment of commerce and industry for individual initiative. This fact has tended to obscure their social and economic radicalism in the eyes of the conservative monied elements. The amelioration of the clerical issue since 1930 has reduced tensions to the point where the enlightened representatives of the Catholic Church can successfully cooperate with the progressive middle sector leadership. Such cooperation is currently effective in Chile and appears to be gaining strength in Argentina and Mexico. The Church and Catholic lay organizations in league with the middle sector political leadership might inject into politics a moral force for the most part lacking at present. They also might be highly effective in discouraging workers from deserting to the extreme Left Wing organizations, especially to the Communists, for many workers have a deep and abiding loyalty to the Roman Catholic Church.

The middle sectors may in the foreseeable future expect to exercise considerable influence in policy-making during those "unfortunate interludes" when the republics suffer from the incubus of military domination. The officer corps of the armed forces come almost entirely from middle sector homes. The military in each of the republics appears to be as committed to industrial progress as is the middle sector leadership. In the past the military associated itself with the old elite elements because of their influence and prestige. The armed forces may be expected to remain associated with the middle sectors as those groups continue to gain in prestige and influence vis-à-vis the old elites. Furthermore, the day has passed when the military in any one of the five republics can usurp power and rule in disregard of civilian wishes. Military rulers will have civilian advisers who have their fingers on the public pulse. At the moment individuals from the middle sectors would seem most often to satisfy this requirement.

The middle sectors' political position is also strengthened by the fact that interested foreign powers, in general, have come to accept them as providing the most responsible leadership that can be expected from the republics at this time. The direct and indirect support offered the Western bloc in the UN by the middle sector leadership of the five republics has been basically, if not uniformly, satisfactory. On all major issues the republics have voted with the Western bloc or have abstained. Perhaps more important, the remaining fifteen Latin American republics have shown a strong tendency to follow the leadership of the five republics, especially that of Mexico and Brazil.

Past and present developments directly affecting the middle sectors themselves offer abundant evidence that the future holds considerable political promise for them. They are in their present state the legitimate product of an evolutionary process which they played a major role in initiating and subsequently in guiding. They are experiencing rapid numerical growth in each of the republics. It is almost literally true that each new set of statistics makes them a larger segment of the total population. Publications of international agencies commonly fix the middle sectors in Argentina and Uruguay as constituting approximately 50 per cent of the total population of those republics, and in Chile 40 per cent. More important than any statistical designation is the recognition that they are finally receiving from the experts.

Their economic significance also promises them an important political role in the future. The age of the farmer is giving way to the age of the merchant and manufacturer. As the shift of wealth toward the urban economies develops the voice of the commercial and industrial elements in decision-making will become firmer. To their voice will be added that of high-level bureaucrats who direct the towering structure of government-controlled institutes charged with the protection and promotion of industry. Government participation in the economic field has given thousands upon thousands of bureaucrats the prestige of being associated with the planning and management of industrial and commercial undertakings—a prestige that their own financial resources deny them. They have become, consequently, firm converts to progress through technological advance. Their underlings look to governments for security in their jobs.

The solid body of political experience the middle sectors have acquired in this century also strongly suggests that their political influence will grow rather than decline in the next decade. In a society where economic concerns have become the primary political concern the middle sectors have had an opportunity to learn practical lessons in political economy. Their experience has taught them that it is easy to stimulate demands but that it is difficult to satisfy them. They have also learned some of the problems involved in attempting to telescope the economic process. These lessons will neither prevent them from making honest mistakes in the future nor prevent them from exploiting economic misfortunes for political ends. Undoubtedly they will often be guilty of placing their collective head in the lion's mouth in order to operate on a sore tooth. Progress does not move in a straight line but deviously, and the middle sectors will from time to time probably compete with both the Left and the Right in exploiting the nadirs. But more than any other groups, they possess the equipment for dealing with realities; consequently, they may not be confused by the economic fictions they formulate for political purposes.

Included in the body of political experience the middle sectors have accumulated in this century are valuable lessons in the art of compromise. In an area where, prior to the middle group's appearance in a major role, political compromise was unknown or distasteful, the middle sectors have elevated to a new level the art of achieving some equilibrium by balancing a mass of political antagonisms. They have consequently become stabilizers and harmonizers and in the process have learned the dangers of dealing in absolute postulates. Their political experience has also given them a positive psychology as opposed to the negative one so often held by opposition groups.

The middle sectors' cultural experience may be their greatest political asset. It gives them access to the great avenues leading to the past. But it also gives them, more than any other group, faith that the golden age lies not behind but ahead. Their faith in the future may keep them from becoming the slaves of antecedent circumstances. If it does, they may in the years ahead be up to the herculean task of providing the type of leadership requisite to advance before the fires they themselves lighted overtake them.

Bibliography

This Bibliography is divided to correspond with the chapters of the volume. Official publications are ordinarily not annotated; those by individuals and private agencies in general are, unless the titles appear to be self-explanatory.

CHAPTER 1

This section includes works which are primarily concerned with the entire Latin American area in the twentieth century.

Acosta, Cecilio. "Causas generales de las revoluciónes en América Española," *Boletín de la Academia Nacional de la historia* (Caracas), XX, No. 78 (April-June, 1937), 276–82.—An enumeration of factors contributing to political instability.

Aguirre, Manuel Agustín. "¿Revolución burguesa o revolución proletaria para la América Latina?" *Universidad* (Oruro, Bolivia), I, No. 1 (1952), 201–10.—Has a definitely Marxist slant.

Aguirre Cerda, Pedro. *El problema industrial.* Santiago, 1933.—The author was president of Chile from 1938–41. In this volume he contended that he and his contemporaries were living in an industrial world and that small countries would have to industralize or collapse. Education must be directed to increasing industrial production.

Aikman, Duncan. *The All-American Front.* New York, 1940.—Complex problems presented in quite readable style and with limited distortion.

Alba, Víctor. *Historia del comunismo en América Latina.* Mexico, 1954. The surest defense against Communism is the lifting of the level of living of the working groups.

———. "Mitología del movimiento obrero: el nacionalismo proletario," *Cuadernos Americanos,* XIII, No. 5 (Sept.-Oct., 1954), 43–57.

———. *Le mouvement ouvrier en Amérique Latine.* Paris, 1953.—The author is concerned that the greed of the "aristocrats" of labor will destroy the labor movement.

———. "El movimiento obrero en la América Latina—presente y futuro," *Cuadernos Americanos,* XII, No. 3 (May-June, 1953), 33–51.

Alberto Rangel, Domingo. "Una interpretación de las dictaduras latinoamericanos," *Cuadernos Americanos,* XIII, No. 5 (Sept.-Oct., 1954), 33–42.—Education and the foreigner are the primary problems that the Latin American must recognize. Latin America is undergoing change and riches are becoming increasingly important as a social determinant.

Alexander, Robert J. *Communism in Latin America.* New Brunswick, N.J., 1957.—A descriptive history of communism in each of the republics. The best source available to the general public.

———. *Labour Movements in Latin America.* London, 1947.—Emphasis is upon socialism in the Latin American labor movement.

———. "The Latin American Aprista Parties," *Political Quarterly,* XX, No. 3 (July-Sept., 1949), 236-47.—Sympathetic. Although "indigenous" parties have grown up separately they have developed in a parallel way.

Álvarez, T. E. "El drama de la América Latina," *Cuadernos Americanos,* XII, No. 4 (July-Aug., 1953), 7-63.—Highly emotional. The author places the blame for Latin America's misfortunes on the foreigners and the oligarchs.

Anuario estadístico interamericano. Raúl C. Migone, ed.—The work appeared in 1940 and 1942. It represents one of the first serious efforts to compile statistics on a hemispheric scale.

Arciniegas, Germán. *The State of Latin America.* Translated from the Spanish by Harriet de Onís. New York, 1952.—An excellent expression of a liberal's concern and indignation over the state of democracy in Latin America following World War II.

———. "Revolutions," *Américas,* I, No. 1 (March 1949), 22-24 ff.

Ayala, Francisco. "Los intelectuales en la crisis social presente," *El trimestre económico,* VII, No. 1 (April-June, 1940), 75-95.—The author believes that the intellectuals have failed to meet the challenge of the new socioeconomic environment, explains why.

———. "El nacionalismo sano y el otro," *Sur.* No. 242 (Sept.-Oct., 1956), 5-10.—Middle groups are largely to blame for keeping nationalism alive.

———. "Notas sobre la cultura nacional," *Cuadernos Americanos,* XIV, No. 3 (May-June, 1955), 85-97.—The great danger to national culture is not internationalism but the State that tends to determine cultural development.

———. "Unity and Variety in Hispanic America," *The Michigan Alumnus Quarterly Review,* LXII, No. 18 (May 1956), 185-92.—The people of Latin America, because they are members of Western civilization but untouched by the ravages of its later development, can act as mediators between Western civilization and the other great cultures.

Bain, Harry F., and Thomas T. Read. *Ores and Industry in South America.* New York, 1934.—Each republic and major foreign possession receives attention. There are concluding chapters on financing of mining and the industry's future.

Bara, Walter. "The Publishing Renaissance in Latin America," *Publisher's Weekly,* CLX, No. 2 (July 14, 1951), 102-5.

Barcos, Julio R. "Our Professors of Idealism in America." *Inter-America,* English III, No. 2 (December 1919), 84-102; No. 3 (February 1920), 173-75.—Friendly to the realism he believes he perceives in the United States, the author points out what he considers to be the unrealistic features of the teachings of several Latin Americans who won wide recognition before World War I.

Barón Castro, Rodolfo. *Españolismo y antiespañolismo en la América hispana.* Madrid, 1945.—Seeks to explain the attitudes of Latin Americans toward Spain and the Spanish people from the early colonial period to the present.

Basadre, Jorge. "Why Nationalism?" *Américas,* I, No. 7 (September 1949), 12–14 ff.—A thoughtful statement of the contribution that nationalism may make toward overcoming "provincialism" and "cosmopolitanism" in Latin America.

Bastide, Roger. "The Negro in Latin America," *International Social Science Bulletin,* IV, No. 3 (1952), 435–42.—The thinking of an outstanding authority on the Negro in America.

Beals, Carleton. "Aprismo; the Rise of Haya de la Torre," *Foreign Affairs,* XIII, No. 2 (January 1935), 236–46.—Friendly.

Beals, Ralph. "Social Stratification in Latin America," *American Journal of Sociology,* LVIII (1952–53), 327–39.—Authoritative insights on a major problem.

Belaunde, Víctor Andrés. "The Frontier in Hispanic America," *The Rice Institute Pamphlets,* X, No. 4 (October 1923), 202–13.—Holds that the absence of a frontier has caused "the rigidity of our structure and our lack of youth and vitality."

———. "Hispanic America: Its Culture and Its Ideals." *The Rice Institute Pamphlets,* X, No. 4 (October 1923), 165–83.—Quite representative of intellectual thinking in the early 1920's.

Bemis, Samuel Flagg. *The Latin American Policy of the United States, An Historical Interpretation.* New York, 1943.—A strong defense of the Latin American policy of the United States by a highly able scholar.

Blanco-Fombona, Rufino. "Historia del ogro yanqui y de la caperucita isleña," *Nosotros,* XXXVII, No. 141 (February 1921), 137–43.— Bitterly anti–United States.

Blanksten, George I. "Technical Assistance and the Political Instability of Latin America," *Economic Development and Cultural Change,* II, No. 5 (June 1954), 350–56.—Divides revolutions into three types: "real," "antiforeign," and "typical."

Bolton, Herbert E. "Some Cultural Assets of Latin America," *The Hispanic American Historical Review,* XX, No. 1 (February 1940), 3–11.—There is much to be learned from the old cultural traditions of Latin America.

Burden, William A. M. *The Struggle for Airways in Latin America.* New York, 1943.—History of the development and status of air transport in Latin America in the early 1940's.

Burr, Robert N. and Roland D. Hussey. *Documents on Inter-American Cooperation.* 2 vols. Philadelphia, 1955.—Sixty-eight documents on the rise and decline of Inter-American cooperation, 1810–1948. A useful reference.

Caldwell, Robert G. "Exile as an Institution," *Political Science Quarterley,* LVIII, No. 2 (June 1943), 239–62.—Provides interesting insight on the thinking of the political elite.

Campbell, John C. "Political Extremes in South America," *Foreign*

Affairs, XX, No. 3 (April 1942), 517–34.—Valuable as a document of the times.

Carillo Flores, Antonio. "El nacionalismo de los países latinoamericanos en la postguerra," in *Jornadas,* (Mexico City, Colegio de México, Centros de Estudios Sociales), No. 28 (1945).

Carneiro Leão, A. "Regionalismo e internacionalismo en la educación," *Revista mexicana de sociología,* X, No. 1 (January-April, 1949), 7–20.—One of Brazil's leading educators warns that schools must not become so preoccupied with national problems as to neglect internationalism.

Centro de estudios de derecho internacional público. *La nacionalidad en las repúblicas americanas.* Buenos Aires, 1936.—Contains requirements for citizenship in several of the republics.

"Changes in Employment Structure in Latin America, 1945–55," *Economic Bulletin for Latin America,* II, No. 1 (February 1957), 15–42. —Divided into two major parts: the first deals with alterations in employment structure during the decade 1945–55; the second seeks to analyze changes in the employment structure in relation to agriculture, mining, industry, and services, and, finally, to consider the characteristics of Latin American urban employment.

Christensen, Asher N. *The Evolution of Latin American Government.* New York, 1951.—For the most part reprints of articles from scholarly journals. A useful compilation.

The Christian Science Monitor, 1920–57. Boston.—The day-to-day coverage of the *Monitor* cannot be favorably compared with that of the *New York Times,* but the special reports are often unusually good.

Ciencias Sociales (1950—).—Published by the Pan-American Union, the journal contains articles of considerable merit but is perhaps more important as a bibliographical aid. The reader interested in either the Caribbean area or those republics with large Indian components will find the publication especially useful.

Clagett, Helen L. *The Administration of Justice in Latin America.* New York, 1952.—A "subject-matter" approach to the administration of justice in the several republics.

Colmo, Alfredo. *La revolución en la América Latina.* 2d ed. Buenos Aires, 1933.—A penetrating examination of the revolutions that swept over Latin America in 1930. Approximately half the volume is devoted to the events immediately preceding and following the overthrow of Irigoyen in Argentina.

Comas, Juan. "El mestizaje y su importancia social," *Acta Americana,* II, Nos. 1 & 2 (Jan.-June, 1944), 13–24.—The mestizo has abilities equal to others. If he has not been successful it has been because he was born into an inferior social and economic class.

"El concepto latinoamericano de la buena vida," *Revista de América,* XIII, No. 38 (February 1948), 145–53.—Views expressed at a round-table discussion held in Mexico City with Robert Redfield, Alfonso Reyes, and Daniel Cosío Villegas as participants.

Cosío Villegas, Daniel. "España contra América en la industria editorial." *Sur* (Buenos Aires), XVII (April 1949), 74–88.—The author warns Latin America of the danger to its culture if it does not develop its own graphic arts.

————. *Extremos de América*. Mexico, 1949.—Essays of exceedingly high quality previously published in leading journals.

————. "Los problemas de América," *Cuadernos Americanos*, VIII, No. 2 (March-April, 1949), 7–23.—The problems are how to develop the art of living together and how to benefit from the common experiences of the Western world in order to hasten the forward march.

————. "Las relaciones de Estados Unidos e Iberoamérica," in *Jornadas* (Mexico City, Colegio de México, Centros de Estudios Sociales), No. 10 (1944).—Concerned with the meaning to Latin America of the United States in the role of world leader.

Crawford, William Rex. *A Century of Latin-American Thought*. Cambridge, Mass., 1944.—The author quotes heavily from the writings of thirty-eight Latin American experts in an effort to depict the main lines of thinking in the area during the nineteenth and twentieth centuries.

Cuadernos Americanos. Mexico, 1942—.—Covers the entire range of the humanities and the social sciences with highly stimulating and often polemical articles. A treasury of ideas and interpretations on current problems.

Dávila, Carlos G. *El imperialismo Norte Americano*. New York, 1930.— A warm defense of the United States by an influential Chilean politician.

Davis, Harold Eugene, ed. *Government and Politics in Latin America*. New York, 1958.—Written as a college text for courses in Latin American government and politics, this volume contains a number of quite stimulating chapters by recognized experts in the field.

Davis, Kingsley. "Future Migration into Latin America," *The Milbank Memorial Fund Quarterly*, XXV, No. 1 (January 1947), 44–62.— Contended correctly that Latin America would not absorb large numbers of immigrants. Observes that the fundamental problem of Latin America is not a lack of people but the lack of skills and capital.

————. "Latin America's Multiplying Peoples," *Foreign Affairs*, XXV, No. 4 (July 1947), 643–54.—Demographic growth with some attention to the political significance thereof.

————. "Political Ambivalence in Latin America," *Journal of Legal and Political Sociology*, I (October 1942), 127–50.—Political forms a result of the total institutional structure.

Davis, Kingsley and Ana Casis. "Urbanization in Latin America," *The Milbank Memorial Fund Quarterly*. XXIV, No. 1 (January 1946), 186–207.—Leaves little doubt as to the propensity of the Latin American for city living.

Dinámica social, Buenos Aires, 1950—. Published by the Centro de Estudios Económicos Sociales.—Worthwhile provided it is kept in mind that it began publication under the Perón tyranny.

Dozer, Donald M. "Roots of Revolution in Latin America," *Foreign Affairs*, XXVII, No. 2 (January 1949), 274–88.—The author finds his answer in traditional institutions.

Duggan, Laurence. *The Americas: The Search for Hemisphere Se-*

curity. New York, 1949.—Historical and social background of Hemisphere unity and its present and future prospects.

Dunn, W. E. "The Post-War Attitude of Hispanic America Towards the United States," *The Hispanic American Historical Review*, III, No. 2 (May 1920), 177–83. Interesting for comparative purposes.

Economic Bulletin for Latin America (1956—). Published twice yearly by the Economic Commission for Latin America of the United Nations, this journal is "designed to supplement and bring up to date" the information published in the annual *Economic Survey of Latin America.* Apart from the summary, special articles on subjects related to the economy of Latin America are also included.

"Economic Diplomacy with Latin America: A Symposium Presented at the Annual Convention of the Mississippi Valley Historical Association, Cincinnati, April 19–21, 1951," *Inter-American Economic Affairs,* IV, No. 4 (Spring, 1951), 3–47.—Contains articles by Harris G. Warren, Arthur P. Whitaker, Wendell C. Gordon, J. Fred Rippy, and Simon G. Hanson.

Economist Intelligence Unit, London. Publishes a series of economic reviews containing information about economic developments in all Latin American republics. The major republics are reviewed on a yearly basis.

Edwards Bello, Joaquín. *Nacionalismo continental.* Santiago, 1935.— Strongly antiforeign, the author is critical of the lack of concern over foreign dominance shown by his contemporaries.

"Energy Consumption in Latin America," *Economic Bulletin for Latin America,* I, No. 2 (September 1956), 36–51.—Statistical evidence of Latin America's energy deficiencies.

Fitzgibbon, Russell H. "Constitutional Development in Latin America: A Synthesis," *The American Political Science Review*, XXXIX, No. 3 (June 1945), 511–22. A careful introduction to the subject.

——, ed. *The Constitutions of the Americas, as of January 1, 1948.* Chicago, 1948.—Translations of the texts of constitutions in force in each of the republics.

——. "Measurement of Latin American Political Phenomena: A Statistical Experiment," *American Political Science Review,* XLV (June 1951), 517–23. Also see his follow-up under the title "How Democratic Is Latin America?" *Inter-American Economic Affairs,* IX, No. 4 (Spring, 1956), 65–77.

——. "How Democratic Is Latin America?" *Inter-American Economic Affairs,* IX, No. 4 (Spring, 1956), 65–77.—A statistical approach to the problem.

——. "The Pathology of Democracy in Latin America: A Political Scientist's Point of View," *The American Political Science Review,* XLIV, No. 1 (March 1950), 118–29.

——. "Revolution: Western Hemisphere," *South Atlantic Quarterly,* LV, No. 3 (July 1956), 263–79.—The fact that the Latin American countries are no longer colonies but continue in large measure to behave as colonies goes far to explain realities in the area.

Flournoy, Richard W. and Manley O. Hudson. *A Collection of Nationality Laws of Various Countries as Contained in Constitutions,*

Statutes, and Treaties. New York, 1929.—The road to naturalization was, at the time, a relatively easy one.

Franklin, John Hope. *From Slavery to Freedom: A History of American Negroes.* New York, 1947.—Contains a good chapter on the Negro in Latin America.

Frondizi, Arturo. *La lucha antiimperialista; etapa fundamental del proceso democrático en América Latina.* Buenos Aires, 1955.—Written as part of his successful campaign for the presidency of Argentina, the author insists that the republics must form their own international policies.

Frondizi, Risieri. "Tendencies in Contemporary Latin-American Philosophy," *Inter-American Intellectual Interchange* (University of Texas, Institute of Latin American Studies, Austin, 1943), pp. 35–48. —What is usually called Latin American philosophy is a restatement of European philosophical problems. Contemporary Latin American philosophy has grown out of the struggle against positivism and of the search for an autonomous philosophy which should be dependent on neither theology nor science.

———. "Is There an Ibero-American Philosophy?" *Philosophy and Phenomenological Research,* IX, No. 3 (March 1949), 345–55.—The answer is No. The deliberate wish to have a philosophy of "our own" has been the greatest impediment to the rise of such a philosophy.

Galíndez Suárez, Jesús. *La era de Trujillo; un estudio casuístico de dictadura Hispanoamericana.* 4th ed. Santiago, 1956.—A bitter attack upon dictatorship in general and more particularly that of Trujillo in the Dominican Republic. It is believed by many that the author was murdered by henchmen of Trujillo.

———. "Revolución socio-económica en iberoamérica," *Cuadernos Americanos,* XIII, No. 2 (March-April, 1954), 7–18.

García, Antonio. "Hacia una teoría de los países atrasados," *Cuadernos Americanos,* XIV, No. 2 (March-April, 1955), 24–36.—Stresses need for regional unity. Bitterly anti–United States.

García Calderón, Francisco. "Dictatorship and Democracy in Latin America," *Foreign Affairs,* III, No. 3 (April 1925), 459–77.—Shows unusual insight considering the date that it was written.

Gil, Federico G. "Responsible Parties in Latin America," *Journal of Politics,* XV, No. 3 (August 1953), 333–48.—Stresses "indigenous" aspects of political parties in Latin America.

Gillin, John. "Mestizo America," in *Most of the World,* Ralph Linton, ed. New York, 1949. Pp. 156–211.—An excellent review of Indo-America.

———. "Modern Latin American Culture," *Social Forces,* XXV, No. 3 (March 1947), 243–48.—Necessarily highly generalized.

Gordon, Wendell C. *The Economy of Latin America.* New York, 1950. —A survey which sacrifices depth for breadth.

Griffin, Charles C., ed. *Concerning Latin American Culture.* New York, 1940.—A collection of high-quality papers dealing with cultural relations, social change, music, art, and literature.

Hanson, Simon G. *Economic Development in Latin America.* Washington, D.C., 1951.—The author takes the Latin Americans to task for their lack of economic planning and their willingness to see private enterprise supplanted by State controlled agencies.

Haring, Clarence H. "Federalism in Latin America," in *The Constitution Reconsidered,* Conyers Read, ed. New York, 1938. Pp. 341–47. —Historical.

Haya de la Torre, Víctor Raúl. *¿A dónde va Indoamérica?* 2d ed. Santiago, 1935.—Views of the leader of the Aprista Party.

———. *El antiimperialismo y el APRA.* 2d ed. Santiago, Chile, 1936.— The author has moderated his views on imperialism considerably since writing this volume.

———. *Por la emancipación de América Latina.* Buenos Aires, 1927.

———. "Sobre la 'historia del comunismo en América' y una rectificación," *Cuadernos Americanos,* XIV, No. 4 (July-Aug., 1955), 14–26. —Takes the occasion of commenting on Víctor Alba's views to point out that unlike the Communists who hold imperialism to be the last stage of capitalism, the Apristas hold imperialism to be the first stage in capitalism.

Henríquez-Ureña, Pedro. *Literary Currents in Hispanic America.* Cambridge, Mass., 1945.—More than a literary survey, the volume is a stimulating synthesis of Latin American culture from the discovery to the 1920's.

Holmes, Olive. "Army Challenge in Latin America," *Foreign Policy Reports,* XXV, No. 14 (December 1, 1949), 166–75.—Early recognition of the changing character of the military following World War II.

Hoselitz, Bert F. "Non-Economic Barriers to Economic Development," *Economic Development and Cultural Change,* I, No. 1 (March 1952), 8–21.—Although Hoselitz in this article is not primarily concerned with Latin America, his observations and interpretations regarding underdeveloped areas are so astute that his article becomes required reading for those interested in social and economic change in the area.

Ingenieros, José. *Por la unión latino americana.* Buenos Aires, 1922.— Probably one of the outstanding thinkers and scientists ever produced in Latin America, Ingenieros in this work comes out strongly for union against the economic and cultural invasion of the "Northern Colossus."

Inman, Samuel G. "Which Way Latin America?" *World Affairs,* n.s. IV, No. 1 (January 1950), 83–98.—Survey of political, social, and economic conditions and objectives in a period of rapidly rising populations.

Inter-American Affairs; An Annual Survey . . . 1941—. Arthur P. Whitaker, ed. New York, 1942–46. Five volumes appeared covering the war years.—The articles, written by highly qualified experts, make this a major source for the years of conflict.

Inter-American Economic Affairs. Washington, D.C., 1947—.—The quality of the articles varies widely, but there are a sufficient number of good ones to make the journal a valuable source of material.

Inter-American Labor Bulletin. Washington, D.C., 1951—. Official organ of the pro-democratic Inter-American Regional Organization (O.R.I.T.) of the International Confederation of Free Trade Unions (I.C.F.T.U.).

Inter-American Municipal Review. 1950—. Published in English and Spanish by the Pan American Commission of Intermunicipal Cooperation, Havana, Cuba.—The *Review* serves as a sounding board for those concerned with municipal development. A most worthwhile source.

International Labour Review (Geneva, 1921—). The official publication of the International Labour Office contains numerous articles on and notices of labor legislation, and social and economic policy.

Ireland, Gordon. *Boundaries, Possessions and Conflicts in Central and North America and the Caribbean.* Cambridge, Mass., 1941.—Historical background of all major territorial disputes in the area since independence.

———. *Boundaries, Possessions and Conflicts in South America.* Cambridge, Mass., 1938.—Historical background of all major territorial disputes in the area since independence.

Iturriaga, José E. "El tirano en la América Latina," in *Jornadas* (Mexico City, Colegio de México, Centros de Estudios Sociales), No. 15 (1945).—Despotism in Latin America fed by imperialists, was headed in the direction of fascism.

Izquierdo Araya, Guillermo. "La clase media en la América del Sur," *Dinámica social,* II, No. 17 (January 1952), 21–22.—The political future of the middle sectors lies more in unions than in political parties.

———. "Las clases medias en la configuración social latino-americana," *Dinámica social,* I, No. 10 (June 1951), 9–10.

———. "Las clases medias en la sociedad contemporánea," *Dinámica social,* I, No. 9 (May 1951), 9–10.

———. "Visión de la clase media en Latinoamérica," *Dinámica social,* I, No. 12 (August 1951), 9–10.

James, Preston E. *Latin America.* New York, 1942.—A comprehensive treatise on the geography and economic resources of Latin America. Probably the best one-volume geography of Latin America to appear to date.

Jiménez, Rafael Bernal. "A Sociological Appraisal of Cultural, Political and Economic Problems in Latin America," *International Social Sciences Bulletin,* IV, No. 3 (1952), 461–70.—Concerned with the need of interpreting political and economic developments in sociological terms.

Johnson, John J. "The Latin American Municipality Deteriorates," *Inter-American Economic Affairs,* V, No. 1 (Summer, 1951), 24–35.—The loss of local autonomy to the central government.

———. "The New Latin America and the United States," *The Pacific Spectator,* IX, No. 3 (Summer, 1955), 244–55.

Jornadas. Mexico, 1943—. Published by the Colegio de México, Centros de Estudios Sociales. Fifty-seven numbers appeared between 1943 and 1947. Publication apparently ceased with number 57.—Written by experts in the social sciences and humanities from several of the

Western Hemisphere republics, including the United States, the articles in *Jornadas* constitute a major collection of thoughts on the internal and external problems of Latin America during and immediately after World War II.

Kandel, Isaac L., ed. *Educational Yearbook of the International Institute of Teachers College, Columbia University.* New York, 1925–44.—Over half of the yearbooks contain articles on the republics of Latin America and the volume for 1942 is entirely devoted to the Latin American area. The articles are of varying quality but are on the whole useful surveys.

Kandel, Isaac L. "Education in Latin America," in *Some Educational and Anthropological Aspects of Latin America* (University of Texas, Institute of Latin American Studies, Austin, 1948), pp. 17–26.

Kantor, Harry. *The Ideology and Program of the Peruvian Aprista Movement.* Berkeley, 1953.—Historical study of the most successful indigenous movement in Latin America to date.

Kelchner, Warren H. *Latin American Relations with the League of Nations.* Boston, 1929.—A country-by-country analysis which deals with entrance into the League, and participation in that international body, with a chapter on relations with the International Labor Organization.

"Latin America: Area of Population Explosion," *Population Bulletin,* IX, No. 6 (October 1953), 65–75.—Rapid population growth cannot fail to create serious problems.

Leonard, Olen E. and Charles P. Loomis. *Readings in Latin American Social Organization & Institutions.* Lansing, Mich., 1953.—A good selection of articles from United States journals.

Lessing, Juan A. *La nacionalidad, sus diversos sistemas en los 21 países americanos.* Buenos Aires, 1941.—Good summaries of requirements for citizenship.

Lewis, Cleona. *America's Stake in International Investments.* Washington, D.C., 1938.—An invaluable source book for the period prior to the mid-1930's.

Lippmann, Walter. "Vested Rights and Nationalism in Latin America," *Foreign Affairs,* V, No. 3 (April 1927), 353–63.—Early recognition of the rise of nationalism to the level of a political ideology.

Lloréns, Noel. "América irredenta," *Cuadernos Americanos,* XIII, No. 5 (Sept.-Oct., 1954), 26–32. — Strongly anti-United States. Puerto Rico must be free. The problem of Puerto Rico is the problem of America.

Lôbo, Hélio. *O pan-americanismo e o Brasil.* São Paulo, 1939.—A strong defense of international unity as a means of reducing the excesses of authoritarianism.

Mariátegui, José Carlos. *Siete ensayos de interpretación de la realidad peruana.* Lima, 1928.—Considered by some to be Latin America's first Marxist, Mariátegui in his "seven Essays" was concerned with "all" hemispheric problems as he saw them.

Martin, Percy A. *Latin America and the War.* Baltimore, 1925.—The best single source on the subject.

Mecham, J. Lloyd. *Church and State in Latin America.* Chapel Hill, N.C., 1934.—Still the best single volume on the subject.

Mejía Nieto, Arturo. *El perfil americano (ensayo de interpretación de la realidad americana).* Buenos Aires, 1933.—Assumes that the North American and Latin American cultures are different and then proceeds to indicate what he considers to be the strengths and weaknesses of each culture.

Mendieta y Núñez, Lucio. *Las clases sociales.* Mexico, 1947.—Lucio Mendieta y Núñez may well be Latin America's outstanding sociologist. This study as well as those immediately following and still others included in the bibliography on Mexico show a fine combination of indignation, sensitiveness, scientific investigation, and precise presentation.

——. *Urbanismo y sociología.* Mexico, 1952.

——. "Racial and Cultural Tensions in Latin America," *International Social Science Bulletin,* IV, No. 3 (1952), 442–51.

——. "The Social Classes," *American Sociological Review,* XI, No. 2 (April 1946), 166–76.

Miller, Edward G., Jr. "Economic Aspects of Inter-American Relations," *Department of State Bulletin,* XXIII, No. 599 (December 25, 1950), 1011–16.

——. "A Fresh Look at the Inter-American Community," *Foreign Affairs,* XXXIII, No. 4 (July 1955), 634–47.—At the time the article was published, Miller was Under Secretary of State for Latin America.

——. "Inter-American Relations in Perspective," *Department of State Bulletin,* XXII, No. 561 (April 3, 1950), 521–23.

Mosk, Sanford A. "Latin America and the World Economy, 1850–1914," *Inter-American Economic Affairs,* II, No. 3 (Winter, 1948), 53–82.—A plea for historians to interest themselves in the last one hundred years of economic development in the Latin American area and an analysis of the major impulses for economic change prior to World War I.

——. "Latin American Economics: The Field and Its Problems," *Inter-American Economic Affairs.* III, No. 2 (Autumn, 1949), 55–64.—Views of a highly qualified authority.

——. "El nacionalismo económico en la América Latina," *Revista de economía continental* I, No. 4 (November 1946), 401–11.—Scholarly analysis of factors contributing to the growth of economic nationalism.

——. "The Pathology of Democracy in Latin America: An Economist's Point of View," *The American Political Science Review,* XLIV, No. 1 (March 1950), 129–42.—A reasoned point of view concisely presented.

Munro, Dana G. "Economic Nationalism in Latin America," *Latin America in World Affairs, 1914–1940.* Philadelphia, 1941.—Written when the Hemisphere was preparing for war.

Murkland, Harry B. "Appeal to Masses New Trend in Latin America," *Foreign Policy Bulletin,* XXX, No. 38 (July 20, 1951), 3–4.—The *peronista* revolution, based on a direct appeal to the *descamisados,* is a rejection of the traditional Latin American political pattern of wooing the economic "oligarchy" and the army.

―――. "Argentine Political Pattern Affects Latin America," *Foreign Policy Bulletin,* XXX, No. 39 (August 3, 1951), 3–4.—Concerned with the spread of Perón's methods to Bolivia, Colombia, and Guatemala.

National Planning Association. *Technical Cooperation in Latin America: Recommendations for the Future.* Washington, D.C., 1956.

The New York Times, 1920–1957. New York.—Absolutely indispensable.

Oliveira Lima, Manoel de. "New Constitutional Tendencies in Hispanic America," *Hispanic American Historical Review,* V, No. 1 (February 1922), 24–29.—Early recognition of "state socialism" in Latin America.

―――. "Pan-Americanism and the League of Nations," *Hispanic American Historical Review,* IV, No. 2 (May 1921), 239–47.—The "Pan-American League" emerged on top when a firm friend of the United States compared it with the League of Nations.

Oropesa, Juan. "Imparidad del destino Americano," *Revista nacional de cultura* (Caracas), VII, No. 51 (July-Aug., 1945), 18–37.—Finds that United States education teaches conformity and that Latin American education teaches differentiation.

Otero, Gustavo Adolfo. *Sociología del nacionalismo en Hispano-América.* Quito, 1947.—A significant contribution. The treatment of contemporary nationalism is weak. The sociological background of nationalism, however, is good.

Padilla, Ezequiel. *Free Men of America.* Chicago, 1943.—A strong plea, by a leading Mexican public official, for hemispheric unity in the face of the Fascist threat. The volume contains considerable evidence of the friendlier attitude of Mexico toward the United States after President Camacho assumed control.

Page, Charles A. "Labor's Political Role in Latin America," *Virginia Quarterly Review,* XXVIII, No. 4 (Autumn, 1952), 481–99.—Interesting ideas, well presented.

Palacios, Alfredo L. *Nuestra América y el imperialismo yanqui.* Madrid, 1930. Views of the "Grand Old Man" of Argentine socialism.

Pan American Union. Congress and Conference Series No. 60. *Final Act of the American Committee on Dependent Territories; Signed at Habana on July 21, 1949.* Washington, D.C., 1949.—The future status of dependent territories of the Western Hemisphere has been a favorite theme of the nationalists of Latin America. This represents an effort to formalize the position of those most directly concerned at the time.

―――. *Economic Survey of Inter-American Agriculture.* 2 vols. Washington, D.C., 1949.

―――. Consejo Interamericano Económico y Social. *La administración pública en la América Latina.* Washington, D.C., 1955.—A good survey.

―――. Oficina de Ciencias Sociales. *Materiales para el estudio de la clase media en la América Latina*. Theo R. Crevenna, ed. 6 vols. Washington, D.C., 1950–51. Processed.—A pioneer effort to present the middle sectors to the reading public and to encourage further research. Most articles on the various republics are by nationals.

Pendle, George. "Perón and Vargas," *Fortnightly Review*, CLXXVI, n.s. 170 (November 1951), 723–28.—The rise, personalities, and problems of the two leaders.

Perkins, Dexter. *A History of the Monroe Doctrine*. Boston, 1955.— This is the widely known and read *Hands Off; A History of the Monroe Doctrine* brought up to date. Indispensable.

Perry, Edward. "Anti-American Propaganda in Hispanic America," *The Hispanic American Historical Review*, III, No. 1 (February 1920), 17–40.—Actions of the United States in its relations with Latin America contributed significantly to ill-feeling during and immediately following World War I.

Plaza Lasso, Galo. *Problems of Democracy in Latin America*. Chapel Hill, N.C., 1955.—A highly optimistic report on post-World War II Latin America by a former president of Ecuador.

Poblete Troncoso, Moisés. *La economía agraria de América Latina y el trabajador campesino*. Santiago, 1953.—A useful survey of the conditions under which the farm worker lives and of legislation on his behalf.

———. *El movimiento obrero latinoamericano*. Mexico, 1946.—The first serious attempt to present a picture of the labor movement in all the republics. Still has value.

———. *Standard de vida y desarrollo económico-social*. Santiago, 1956. —The author's primary concern is Chile, but the volume contains important insights on Latin America in general.

Prebisch, Raúl. "El desarrollo económico de la América Latina y algunos de sus principales problemas," *El trimestre económico*, XVI, No. 3 (July-Sept., 1949), 347–431.—Written to stimulate interest in economic investigation in Latin America, the article surveys in clear and concise form the gains and gaps in internal economic development as well as international considerations affecting continued growth.

———. "O desenvolvimento econômico da América Latina e seus principais problemas," *Revista brasileira de economia*, III, No. 3 (September 1949), 47–111.—Prebisch, generally considered to be one of Latin America's outstanding economists of the post-World War II era, is here concerned with terms of trade and scarcity of dollars.

"Problems and Progress in Latin America," *Journal of International Affairs*, IX, No. 1 (1955).—This special issue contains articles by José Figueres, Jesús de Galíndez, Germán Arciniegas, Frank Tannenbaum, Robert Alexander, Serge Fliegers, Donald Grant, Julio Vielman, Norman Bailey, Alexander Marchant, and Charles G. Fenwick.

Quintanilla, Luis. *A Latin American Speaks*. New York, 1943.—A Mexican official, deeply attached to the United States, indicates his likes and dislikes.

Radvanyi, Laszlo. "Planning the Industrialization of Latin America,"

The Social Sciences in Mexico and South and Central America, I, No. 4 (1948), 25–34.—Too often problems involved in successful industrial planning are not fully considered.

"Recent Trends in United States Imports of Latin American Products," *Economic Bulletin for Latin America,* I, No. 2 (September 1956), 52–58.

Revista brasileira de economia. Rio de Janeiro, 1947—.—The Vargas Institute which publishes this journal is producing perhaps the best economic studies currently coming out of Latin America.

Revista mexicana de sociología. Mexico, 1939—.—This journal under the guidance of Lucio Mendieta y Núñez is unexcelled in its field in Latin America.

Reyes Heroles, Jesús. "El papel del estado en el desarrollo económico," *Cuadernos Americanos,* XII, No. 3 (May-June, 1952), 83–98.—Industrial growth in underdeveloped areas is dependent upon State support.

Rippy, J. Fred. "British Investments in Latin America at Their Peak," *Hispanic American Historical Review,* XXXIV, No. 1 (February 1954), 94–102.—Primarily on the year 1928 after which British investments began to decline.

Rivas, Rafael Paniagua. "Interpretación de las luchas políticas de Hispano-América," *Revista de estudios políticos,* XIV, Nos. 25–26 (1946), 209–23.—The observations of a Hispanophile Nicaraguan.

Robles, Gonzalo. "Obstáculos a la industrialización de los países latinoamericanos," in *Jornadas* (Mexico City, Colegio de México, Centros de Estudios Sociales), X (1944).—A survey of the difficulties to be overcome, by an individual strongly committed to industrialization.

Rodó, José Enrique. *Ariel.* 2d ed. Montevideo, 1900.—Addressed to the youth of Latin America. The author answers in the negative the question he poses; "does that society [the United States] realize, or at least tend to realize the ideals of such rational conduct as satisfies to the heart's desire the intellectual and moral dignity of our civilization?" There are several English translations.

Rogge, Benjamin A. "The Role of Government in Latin American Economic Development," *Inter-American Economic Affairs,* IX, No. 3 (Winter, 1955), 45–66.—A serious contribution on a subject which is demanding much greater scholarly attention.

Romualdi, Serafino. "Labor and Democracy in Latin America," *Foreign Affairs,* XXV, No. 3 (April 1947), 476–89.—A good report on political parties and the role of labor at the end of World War II.

Roura Parella, Juan. "Formación de la consciencia nacional," *Revista mexicana de sociología,* XVI. No. 1 (Jan.-April, 1954), 39–60.—Discusses the basis of nationalism and ends with a reasoned plea for an appreciation of internationalism.

Sáenz, Vincente. *Latin America Against the Colonial System.* Mexico, 1949.—One of the more abusive of the Yankeephobes directs his attack at the British for holding peoples of the Western Hemisphere in subjugation and for depriving independent republics of their territorial patrimony.

Sánchez, Luis Alberto. "Dos mundos, dos generaciones," *Cuadernos*

Americanos, XII, No. 3 (May-June, 1953), 24–32.—A strong defender of the Latin American way of life warns his generation that the youth of Latin America must be more broadly trained.

———. "A New Interpretation of the History of America," *Hispanic American Historical Review,* XXIII, No. 3 (August 1943), 441–56.—Primarily a discussion of the Aprista movement.

Scorza, Manuel. "Una doctrina americana," *Cuadernos Americanos,* XI, No. 1 (Jan.-Feb., 1952), 20–35.—Discusses *aprismo* as an indigenous doctrine.

Séché, Alphonse "¿Existen las clases sociales?" *Dinámica social,* II, No. 16 (December 1951), 7–8.—Social groups are artificial creations of politicians.

Seoane, Manuel A. *Nuestra América y la guerra.* Santiago, 1940.— Latin American, Pan American, and world unity in that order.

Siegfried, André. *Impressions of South America.* Translated by H. H. Hemming and Doris Hemming. New York, 1933.—This world-renowned French scholar visited Latin America at a time when the republics were in turmoil following the collapse of international trade in 1930. His highly astute social and economic interpretations of the political instability he noted everywhere, place him in the ranks of the keenest observers of the Latin American scene in the early 1930's.

Sierra, Manuel J. "Unidad interamericana," *Cuadernos Americanos,* XII, No. 1 (Jan.-Feb., 1953), 64–70.—Sierra warns that in the UN cannot be permitted to weaken the unity of Latin America or Latin American–United States cooperation.

Singer, H. W. "Obstacles to Economic Development," *Social Research: An International Quarterly of Political and Social Science,* XX, No. 1 (Spring, 1953), 19–31.—A quite thoughtful article containing findings that are highly applicable to the Latin American scene.

Smith, Henry L., and Harold Littell. *Education in Latin America.* New York, 1934.—A survey.

Stanford, G. Alonso. "Cultura latino-americana y los Estados Unidos," *Atenea,* XXI, No. 232 (October 1944), 34–43.—A favorable presentation of the intellectual interest of the United States in Latin America.

Stimson, Henry L. *American Policy in Nicaragua.* New York, 1927.— A defense of United States policy in the Caribbean at a time when that policy was under bitter attack.

Stokes, William S. "Parliamentary Government in Latin America," *American Political Science Review,* XXXIX, No. 3 (June 1945), 522–36.—The parliamentary system has never worked successfully in the area.

———. "Violence as a Power Factor in Latin-American Politics," *Western Political Quarterly,* V (September 1952), 445–68.—Discusses the various forms that violence takes in the political area.

Suslow, Leo A. "Democracy in Latin America—U.S. Plan," *Social Science,* XXVI (1951), 5–14.—Contains interesting views of the role of labor in Latin America.

Tannenbaum, Frank. "Agrarismo, Indianismo, y Nacionalismo," *His-*

panic American Historical Review, XXIII, No. 3 (August 1943), 394–423.—You may not agree with Tannenbaum but there is no doubt of the points he wishes to make. A forceful article.

———. "A Note on Latin American Politics," *Political Science Quarterly*, LVIII, No. 3 (September 1943), 415–21.—In Latin American politics a!l that really counts is personalities.

Ugarte, Manuel. *The Destiny of a Continent.* New York, 1925.—Highly critical of the United States and more particularly of the conduct of the United States in Central America and the Caribbean.

United Nations. Bureau of Social Affairs, Population Branch. *The Population of South America, 1950–1980.* (ST/SOA/Series A/21), New York, 1955.

———. Bureau of Social Affairs. "Urbanization in Latin America," in *Report on the World Social Situation Including Studies of Urbanization in Underdeveloped Areas.* (E/CN.5/324/Rev. 1), New York, 1957, pp. 170–92.

———. Department of Economic Affairs, Economic Commission for Latin America. *Economic Survey of Latin America, 1948—.* (E/Cn.12/82) Lake Success, New York, 1949—.—An annual concerned with trends in the area as a whole and in selected countries. It fills, in part, what was a few years ago a great void in the economic literature of Latin America.

———. Department of Social Affairs, Population Division. *The Population of Central America (Including Mexico), 1950–1980.* (ST/SOA/Series A/16). New York, 1954.—Statistical.

United States. Department of Commerce, Bureau of Foreign Commerce, Office of International Trade. *Factors Limiting U.S. Investment Abroad:* Part I, Survey of Factors in Foreign Countries. Washington, D.C., 1953.

———. Office of Business Economics. *U.S. Investment in the Latin American Economy.* Washington, D.C., 1957.—Highly useful up-to-date statistical information.

———. Department of State, Division of Publications, Office of Public Affairs. *Ninth International Conference of American States: Bogotá, Colombia, March 3–May 2, 1948.* International Organization and Conference Series II, American Republics, 3. Washington, D.C., 1948.—Contains excellent material on Latin American attitudes on "colonies" and "submerged lands."

University of California, Los Angeles. Committee on Latin American Studies. *Statistical Abstract of Latin America* (Processed). Los Angeles? 1956—.—This annual brings together in clear and concise form available data on the area. The *Abstract* is rapidly establishing itself as an invaluable research tool.

Urquidi, Víctor L. "La participación del estado y de la iniciativa privada," in *Jornadas* (Mexico City, Colegio de México, Centros de Estudios Sociales), X (1944).

Vasconcelos, José. *La cultura en Hispanoamérica.* La Plata, 1934.— At the time that the author composed this work his friendship for the United States was somewhat less apparent than it became following World War II.

————. *Hispanoamérica frente a los nacionalismos agresivos de Europa y Norteamérica.* Buenos Aires, 1934.

Violich, Francis. *Cities of Latin America.* New York, 1944.—A noteable breakthrough in a still largely unexplored field.

————. "Urban Problems and the University in Latin America," Processed, Berkeley, 1957.—Distributed by the author. Discusses the challenge that city planning offers in Latin America.

Vivas, Eliseo. "The Spanish Heritage" [in Latin America], *American Sociological Review*, X, No. 2 (April 1945), 184–91.—In the traits of character displayed by the conquerors can be seen "clearly" the sources of many of the traits displayed by the dominant classes of Spanish today.

Wagley, Charles. "An Introduction to Latin American Culture," Mimeographed by the Foreign Service Institute, Department of State, Washington, D.C., 1953.—A quite useful survey.

Watnick, Morris. "The Appeal of Communism to the Peoples of Underdeveloped Areas," *Economic Development and Cultural Change*, I, No. 1 (March 1952), 22–36.—Although not concerned primarily with Latin America, this article is an indispensable source to those interested in Communist tactics in underdeveloped areas.

Waiss, Oscar. *Nacionalismo y socialismo en América Latina*, Santiago, 1954.—Capitalism has failed.

Whitaker, Arthur P., ed. *Inter-American Affairs: An Annual Survey.* 5 vols. New York, 1942–46.—Brings together the observations of many of the outstanding experts in the field during a period of crisis.

Whitaker, Arthur P. "The Pathology of Democracy in Latin America: A Historian's Point of View," *The American Political Science Review*, XLIV, No. 1 (March 1950), 101–18.

————. *The Western Hemisphere Idea: Its Rise and Decline.* Ithaca, 1954. The impact of the emergence of the United States as world leader upon the "Western Hemisphere Idea" which had its roots in the eighteenth century and which was nourished to maturity in the twentieth.

World Federation for Mental Health. *Cultural Patterns and Technical Change.* Margaret Mead, ed. Paris, 1953.—Latin America is dealt with only incidentally in this United Nations, Education, Scientific and Cultural Organization, Tensions and Technological Series publication, but the basic problems raised by technological change appear to be quite similar in many underdeveloped areas.

Wythe, George. *Industry in Latin America.* 2d ed. New York, 1949.—The standard work on the history of industrial development in Latin America.

Y. "On a Certain Impatience with Latin America," *Foreign Affairs*, XXVIII, No. 4 (July 1950), 565–79.—Perhaps the most widely discussed article to appear in the United States on Latin America during the last ten years. The author concluded that although the trend in Latin America was toward democracy the area had only reached the stage of political maturity that "we" had in 1776.

Ycaza Tigerino, Julio. "Elementos de la anarquía hispanoamericana,"

Revista de estudios políticos, Año 7, Vol. XVII, Nos. 31-32 (1947), 273-306.—Holds the Indian and Negro primarily accountable for the anarchy that Latin America has experienced but recognises that the lack of racial homogeneity is also a factor.

Zamora, Juan Clemente. "New Tendencies in Latin American Constitutions," *Journal of Politics,* III, No. 3 (August 1941), 276-96.— New views on the concept of property, freedom of contracts, social security, economic nationalism, and the necessity of a technical bureaucracy are considered.

Zea, Leopoldo. *América como conciencia.* Mexico, 1953.—Interesting interpretations by one of Latin America's more practical philosophers.

———. "¿Bondad norteamericana e ingratitud mundial?" *Cuadernos Americanos,* XIV, No. 1 (Jan.-Feb., 1955), 99-119.—A friendly view of the United States.

Zum Felde, Alberto. "Generalidades sobre el inmediato porvenir de la democracia en la América Latina," *Universidad Nacional de Colombia: Revista trimestral de cultura moderna,* No. 7 (July-Sept., 1946), 295-304.—Those who proclaim democracy most loudly must be watched.

———. *El problema de la cultura americana.* Buenos Aires, 1943.— Spanish America traditionally has depended upon Europe, especially Spain and France, but is capable of creating a distinctive culture of its own. Nationalism and Hispanidad are the major obstacles.

CHAPTER 2

The entries below deal chiefly with the period 1810–50.

Literally hundreds of foreigners visited and then wrote on Latin America during the years between 1800 and 1870. Although liberally consulted, only a few such items are included in this Bibliography. For a quite good sampling of the thinking of the others see Tom B. Jones, *South America Rediscovered,* Minneapolis, 1949. See also Tom B. Jones, Elizabeth A. Warburton, and Anne Kingsley, *A Bibliography on South American Economic Affairs: Articles in Nineteenth-Century Periodicals,* Minneapolis, 1955.

Alberdi, Juan Bautista. *Las bases.* Buenos Aires, 1915.—First published in 1852 the ideas set forth formed the basis for the Argentine Constitution of 1853.

Amunátegui y Solar, Domingo. *Formación de la nacionalidad chilena.* Santiago, 1943.—Forces that shaped Chilean development during the colonial period and the independence era.

———. *Nacimiento de la República de Chile (1808–1833).* Santiago, 1930.—A careful analysis by an expert in the period.

Barreda, Gabino. *Estudios.* Mexico, 1941.—Selections from the writings of the man generally credited with introducing positivism into Mexico during the 1860's.

Belaúnde, Víctor Andrés. *Bolívar and the Political Thought of the Spanish American Revolution.* Baltimore, 1938.—Highly useful for an understanding of the change in ideological emphasis that took place during the long struggle for independence.

Blanco Acevedo, Pablo. *El federalismo de Artigas y la independencia nacional.* Montevideo, 1939.—By insisting upon independence for Uruguay, Artigas became the father of Uruguayan nationalism.

Blanco-Fombona, Rufino. *La evolución política y social de Hispano-América.* Madrid, 1911.—Deals primarily with the period prior to 1830 but the author could not resist launching an attack upon interference of the U.S. in Latin America.

——. *El pensamiento vivo de Bolívar.* Buenos Aires, 1942.—The biases of an author who still commands considerable respect in Latin America.

Bolívar, Simón. *Selected Writings of Bolívar.* Compiled by Vicente Lecuna, edited by Harold A. Bierck, Jr., translated by Lewis Bertrand. 2 vols. New York, 1951.—Essential primary material.

Burgin, Miron. *Economic Aspects of Argentine Federalism, 1820–1852.* Cambridge, Mass., 1946.—The best work on the subject in any language.

Cady, John F. *Foreign Intervention in the Rio de la Plata, 1835–1850.* Philadelphia, 1929.—Still one of the best sources for the period it covers.

Chapman, Charles E. "The Age of the Caudillos: A Chapter in Hispanic American History," *Hispanic American Historical Review,* XII, No. 3 (August 1932), 281–300.—A pronounced impatience with both the caudillos and the societies in which they flourished.

Chávez Orozco, Luis. *Historia de México (1808–1836).* Mexico, 1947.—Seeks to explain the many facets affecting the course of development in Mexico during a critical period in the nation's history. Scholarly.

Eyzaguirre, Jaime. *O'Higgins.* Santiago, 1946.—Sympathetic.

Freyre, Gilberto. *The Masters and the Slaves.* Translated by Samuel Putnam. 2d ed. New York, 1956.—A classic. Brazil's historical development has been determined by its peculiar economic system and the attitude of the Portuguese toward race.

——. "Social Life in Brazil in the Middle of the Nineteenth Century," *Hispanic American Historical Review,* V, No. 4 (November 1922), 597–630.—Stresses the backwardness of Brazil in the period under discussion.

Galdames, Luis. *La evolución constitucional de Chile.* Santiago, 1925.—Excellent treatment of constitutional development to 1833.

García Samudio, Nicolás. *La independencia de Hispanoamérica.* Mexico, 1945.—The foreign influences upon the Latin American independence movements are stressed.

Gondra, Luis R. *Historia económica de la República Argentina.* Buenos Aires, 1943.—Three-fourths of the volume are devoted to the period prior to 1850.

——. *Las ideas económicas de Manuel Belgrano.* Buenos Aires, 1923.

—Contains a number of Belgrano's communications relating to economic matters.

González, Joaquín V. *La tradición nacional.* 2 vols. Buenos Aires, 1912.—A distinctly nationalistic approach to Argentine history to approximately 1830.

Great Britain, Foreign Office. *British and Foreign State Papers.* London, 1841—.—Uniquely important. Contains numerous key political and social documents dating from the period of independence. Translations are often crude.

Griffin, Charles C. "Economic and Social Aspects of the Era of Spanish-American Independence," *Hispanic American Historical Review,* XXIX, No. 2 (May 1949), 170–87. Calls for more research on the period and suggests profitable avenues of approach.

Humboldt, Alexander von. *Personal Narrative of Travels to the Equinoctial Regions of America During the Years 1799–1804.* 3 vols. London, 1907–8.—A classic on conditions at the end of the colonial period.

Humphreys, Robert A., ed. *British Consular Reports on the Trade and Politics of Latin America, 1824–1826.* London, 1940.—A highly useful source.

Ingenieros, José. *La evolución de las ideas argentinas.* Buenos Aires, 1937.—A bitter denunciation of the mentality that dominated Argentine thought during the colonial period and the early nineteenth century.

Isabelle, Arsène. *Emigração e colonização, na província brasileira do Rio Grande do Sul, na República Oriental do Uruguai e em toda a bacia do Prata.* Tradução de Belfort de Oliveira. Rio de Janeiro, 1950.—First published in 1830 as a guide for prospective immigrants from Europe.

Jane, Cecil. *Liberty and Despotism in Spanish America.* Oxford, 1929.— Particularly useful for the independence period. Stresses the extremism of the Latin American people on the one hand and their search for perfection on the other hand.

Johnson, John J. "Foreign Factors in Dictatorship in Latin America," *The Pacific Historical Review,* XX, No. 2 (May 1951), 127–41.

Kaufmann, William W. *British Policy and the Independence of Latin America, 1804–1828.* New Haven, 1951.—Scholarly synthesis which in certain particulars supplements C. K. Webster's unusually perceptive introduction to his *Britain and the Independence . . . q.v.*

Kroeber, Clifton B. *The Growth of the Shipping Industry in the Rio de la Plata Region 1794–1860.* Madison, Wis., 1957.—Scholarly study based upon a vast amount of original materials.

Lastarria, José V. *La América.* 2 vols. Madrid, 1917.—On the one hand Lastarria stoutly defends Latin American society from "unjust" attacks by Europeans and North Americans, and on the other he is highly critical of what he observes around him.

Lecuna, Vicente, ed. *Cartas del libertador.* 10 vols. Caracas, 1929–30.— A major source for the history of the Independence era and the years immediately thereafter when the new republics sought vainly for the formula which would give them stability without tyranny.

Levene, Ricardo. "Contribución al estudio de las clases sociales en la Argentina durante el período hispánico," *Revista mexicana de sociología*, XI, No. 2 (May-August, 1949), 197–205.—A restatement of the position that the author has held for years, to wit : "miscegenation began immediately. The mixing of blood made for social democracy."

Manchester, Alan K. *British Preëminence in Brazil: Its Rise and Decline.* Chapel Hill, N.C., 1933.—Serves as a dependable statement of political development during the first half of the nineteenth century.

Manning, William Ray. *Diplomatic Correspondence of the United States Concerning the Independence of the Latin American Nations.* 3 vols. New York, 1925.—These three volumes and the twelve cited immediately below are indispensable for the periods they cover.

———. *Diplomatic Correspondence of the United States: Inter-American Affairs, 1831–1860.* 12 vols. Washington, D.C., 1932–39.

Martin, Percy Alvin. "Artigas, the Founder of Uruguayan Nationality," *Hispanic American Historical Review,* XIX, No. 1 (February 1939), 2–15.—By opposing both Argentine and Portuguese domination Artigas sowed the seeds of nationality in the Banda Oriental.

Masur, Gerhard. *Simón Bolívar.* Albuquerque, N.M., 1948.—The best single volume on Bolívar.

Martineau, Harriet. *A History of the Thirty Years' Peace, 1816–1846.* 4 vols. London, 1877–78.—Volume two contains a good account of Great Britain's financial adventures in Latin America during the 1820's.

Mecham, J. Lloyd. "The *Jefe Político* in Mexico," *The Southwestern Social Science Quarterly,* XIII, No. 4 (March 1933), 333–52.—The historical background of the *Jefe Político* to 1914 with emphasis on the independence period.

———. "The Origins of Federalism in Mexico," in *The Constitution Reconsidered,* Conyers Read, ed. New York, 1938, pp. 349–65.

Melo Franco, Afonso Arinos de. *Desenvolvimento da civilização material no Brasil.* Rio de Janeiro, 1944.—The last chapter deals with the early nineteenth century. Statistics are employed freely.

Oddone, Jacinto. *El factor económico en nuestras luchas civiles.* Buenos Aires, 1937.—Oddone writes as a spokesman for the Socialist Party of Argentina. The volume covers the period to approximately 1860.

O'Leary, Daniel F. *Bolívar y la emancipación de Sur-América; memorias del General O'Leary.* Translated by Simon B. O'Leary. 2 vols. Madrid, 1915.—O'Leary was closely associated with and highly regarded by Bolívar. This segment of the author's thirty-two volume work was edited by his son and published in Caracas between 1879 and 1888.

Oliveira Lima, Manoel de. *The Evolution of Brazil Compared with that of Spanish and Anglo-Saxon America.* Stanford, 1914.—Except for the final chapter examples are drawn almost entirely from the colonial period and the independence era.

Palmer, Thomas W. "A Momentous Decade in Brazilian Administrative History, 1831–1840," *Hispanic American Historical Review,*

XXX, No. 2 (May 1950), 209–17.—Regionalism on the rampage.
Pan American Union. Departamento de Asuntos Culturales, División de Filosofía, Letras y Ciencias. Sección de Bibliografía. *Las actas de independencia de América.* Edited and preliminary notes by Javier Malagón. Preface by Charles C. Griffin. Washington, D.C., 1955.— Handy compilation.
Pereda Valdes, Ildefonso. "Negroes in Uruguay." *Phylon,* IV, No. 3 (1943), 213–21.—Estimates that at the end of the colonial period the population of Montevideo was a third African or mulatto.
Piccirilli, Ricardo. *Rivadavia y su tiempo.* 2 vols. Buenos Aires, 1943. A scholarly examination of the contributions of one of the outstanding thinkers of the independence era.
Ramos Mejía, Francisco. *El federalismo argentino.* Buenos Aires, 1915. —Separatism, which was rooted in the colonial period, was nourished by differences arising from the struggle for independence.
Rippy, J. Fred. "Bolívar as Viewed by Contemporary Diplomats of the United States." *Hispanic American Historical Review,* XV, No. 3 (August 1935), 287–97.—Praised as a revolutionary, Bolívar was generally condemned by U.S. diplomats for his political beliefs.
Robertson, William Spence. "Foreign Estimates of the Argentine Dictator, Juan Manuel de Rosas," *Hispanic American Historical Review,* X, No. 2 (May 1930), 125–37.—Primarily a French view of a "consummate poseur."
Robertson, William S. *France and Latin-American Independence.* Baltimore, 1939.—Provides valuable insights on the Latin American mentality of the independence period.
———. *Iturbide of Mexico.* Durham, N.C., 1952.—Scholarly.
———. *The Life of Miranda.* 2 vols. Chapel Hill, N.C., 1929.—Sound research and scrupulous objectivity.
———. *Rise of the Spanish-American Republics as Told in the Lives of Their Liberators.* New York, 1918.—Brief, scholarly essays on Miranda, Hidalgo, Iturbide, Moreno, San Martín, Bolívar, and Sucre, as well as observations on some of the lesser figures.
Rojas, Ricardo. *La argentinidad, ensayo histórico sobre nuestra conciencia nacional en la gesta de la emancipación, 1810–1816,* Vol. 3 of *Obras de Ricardo Rojas,* 2d edition, 4 vols., Buenos Aires, 1922.— Written from a strongly nationalistic point of view.
Sánchez Viamonte, Carlos. *Historia institucional de Argentina.* Mexico, 1948.—Essentially a political history with the stress on the period prior to 1830.
Shaw, Paul Vanorden. "José Bonifacio and Brazilian History." *Hispanic American Historical Review,* VIII, No. 4 (November 1928), 527–50.—A satisfactory brief account of Brazil's outstanding champion of independence from Portugal.
Sierra, Justo. *Evolución política del pueblo mexicano.* Mexico, 1950.— First published nearly a half-century earlier, this volume by one of Mexico's *pensadores* interprets the major trends in the republic's development to 1867.
Sprague, William Forrest. *Vincente Guerrero, Mexican Liberator.* Chicago, 1939.—Sympathetic treatment of a Mexican revolutionary.

Sousa, Octavio Tarquínio de. *José Bonifacio: emancipador del Brasil.*
Mexico, 1945.—The turbulent decade of the 1820's interpreted by an
outstanding authority on the period.
Stevenson, William B. *On the Disturbances in South America.* London,
1830.—At this early date the author, who had resided in South
America, was concerned over the tendency of Englishmen and
Europeans to look upon Latin America as a single entity, politically,
economically, and socially.
————. *On the Recognition of Chile and Peru,* n.p., 1830.
Vanderburgh, John Bolan. "The Government of Bernardo O'Higgins."
Unpublished doctoral dissertation, Stanford University, 1954.—Par-
ticularly good on the economic sphere.
Vasconcelos, José. *Apuntes para la historia de México; desde la conquista hasta la revolución de 1910.* Mexico, 1943.—The colonial
period looked better to the author than it had two decades earlier.
Villoro, Luis. *La revolución de independencia: ensayo de interpretación
histórico.* Mexico, 1953.—A philosopher's interpretation of the conflicts of interest during and immediately following the independence
movement in Mexico.
Webster, Charles K., ed. *Britain and the Independence of Latin America,
1812–1830; Select Documents from the Foreign Office Archives.*
2 vols. London, 1938.—The British followed the independence movement quite closely. The observations of British officials are consequently a major source of information for the early period.
————. *Britain and the Independence of Latin America, 1812–1830.* London, 1944.—This is a reprint of Webster's excellent introduction to
his two volumes of documents on the subject of Latin American independence. See above.
Whitaker, Arthur P., ed. *Latin America and the Enlightenment.* New
York, 1942.—Six essays by recognized authorities.
Zimmerman, A. F. "Spain and Its Colonies, 1808–1820," *Hispanic
American Historical Review,* XI, No. 4 (November 1931), 439–63.—
Discontent of the creoles over their failure to secure equal rights
is emphasized.

CHAPTER 3

*The materials contained in this section generally stress develop-
ments in the five republics emphasized in this volume during the period
1850 to 1915.*

Abasolo Navarrete, Jenaro. *La personalidad política y la América del
porvenir.* Santiago, 1907.—Men of learning must play a greater role
in government.
Alberdi, Juan Bautista. *Estudios económicos; interpretación económica
de la historia política argentina y sud-americana; con un estudio
sobre las doctrinas sociológicas de Alberdi, por José Ingenieros.*
Buenos Aires, 1916.
————. *Del gobierno en Sud-América,* Vol. XIII of *Obras selectas,*

new ed., Buenos Aires, 1920.—Alberdi wrote this particular study late in life. He had lost much of his faith in the ability of the Latin American people to create viable governments under the federalist system.

Alberini, Coriolano. "La enseñanza de la historia en las universidades alemanas." *Nosotros,* VI, No. 36 (January 1912), 56–64.—Uses the German universities in order to point up the dangers of teaching nationalism.

Altamira y Crevea, Rafael. *La huella de España en América.* Madrid, 1924.—The central theme is the need of strengthening the ties between Spain and its former colonies.

American Academy of Political and Social Science. *Political and Social Progress in Latin America.* "The Annals," XXXVII, No. 3 (May 1911). Philadelphia, 1911.—Interesting as an early effort to define the basis for closer United States–Latin American relations. The entire issue is devoted to the problem and nine experts, several of them Latin Americans, express views.

Argentine Republic, Comisión del Censo Agropecuario. *Agricultural and Pastoral Census of the Nation . . . 1908.* Buenos Aires, 1909.

Argüedas, Alcides. *Pueblo enfermo.* 2d ed. Barcelona, 1910.—This is such good social history that it is included despite the fact that it deals primarily with Bolivia.

Ayarragaray, Lucas. *La anarquia argentina y el caudillismo.* 2d ed. Buenos Aires, 1925.—The mestizo is the anarchistic element in Latin American society.

———. "La mestización de las razas en América y sus consecuencias degenerativas," *Revista de filosofía, cultural, ciencias, educación.* II (1916), 21–41.—The mixing of races is degenerative.

Bastos, Humberto. *O pensamento industrial no Brasil.* São Paulo, 1952. —Historical development of industrial capitalism with the stress on the nineteenth century.

Blakeslee, George H., ed. *Latin America.* New York, 1914.—Views of United States and Latin American "experts" on the future of Latin America and United States–Latin American relations. Highly valuable as a serious look at Latin America at a time when United States interest in the area was sharpening.

Boehrer, George C. *Da monarquia à república; história do Partido Republicano do Brasil (1870–1889).* Rio de Janeiro, 1954.—This quality study is available in English on microcards as an unpublished doctoral dissertation, Catholic University of America, 1951.

Bryce, James. *South America: Observations and Impressions.* New York, 1912.—Views of probably the keenest observer to visit Latin America during the century after independence was won.

Bunge, Carlos O. *Nuestra América.* Barcelona, 1903.—A racist. Latin America is so unruly that it cannot be governed by moderation. Contains interesting sketches on Rosas, García Moreno, and Díaz.

Bunkley, Allison Williams. *The Life of Sarmiento.* Princeton, 1952.— A readable, objective treatment of one of Latin America's great thinkers and statesmen. Strongest on the period prior to the time that Sarmiento assumed the presidency of the republic.

——. "Sarmiento and Urquiza," *Hispanic American Historical Review*, XXX, No. 2 (May 1950), 176–94.—Similar aims and conflicting methods of two strong-willed men.

Burr, Robert N. "The Balance of Power in Nineteenth Century South America: An Exploratory Essay," *Hispanic American Historical Review*, XXXV, No. 1 (February 1955), 37–60.—A challenging thesis.

Calderón, Francisco R. *La vida económica en la República restaurada, 1867–1876*. Mexico, 1955.—A searching account of the Mexican economy for the period covered.

Cárcano, Miguel Angel. *Evolución histórica del régimen de la tierra pública, 1810–1916*. 2d ed., rev. Buenos Aires, 1925.

Cárcano, Ramón J. *Historia de los medios de comunicación y transporte en la República Argentina*, 2 vols. Buenos Aires, 1893.—Scholarly.

Carrancá y Trujillo, Raúl. *La evolución política de Ibero-América*. Madrid, 1925.—Racism, nationalism, and Hispanism presented in exaggerated form.

Chapman, Mary Patricia. "Yankeephobia: an Analysis of the Anti-United States Bias of Certain Spanish South American Intellectuals (1898–1928)." Unpublished doctoral dissertation, Stanford University, 1950.

Cochut, André. "Le Chili en 1859," *Revue des deux mondes*, XXIV (Nov.-Dec., 1859), 822–61.—A generally favorable review of political, economic, and educational developments.

Cosío Villegas, Daniel. *Historia moderna de México*. Mexico, 1955.—This is the first volume of a multi-volume work. A scholarly interpretation of the turbulent 1867–1876 period. Juárez fares well in general.

Cruz Costa, João. *Contribuição à história das idéias no Brasil (O desenvolvimento da filosofia no Brasil e a evolução histórica nacional)*. Rio de Janeiro, 1956.—Conflicting interests which explain the evolution of ideas in Brazil. Strongest on the nineteenth century.

Delmez, Albert J. "The Positivist Philosophy in Mexican Education, 1867–1873," *The Americas*, VI, No. 1 (July 1949), 32–44.—Synthesis.

De Onís, José. *The United States as Seen by Spanish American Writers, 1776–1890*. New York, 1952.—Views of Latin American writers during a period when the United States was to them the example *par excellence* of revolutionary accomplishment as distinguished from the following period when to the Latin Americans the United States represented conservatism.

Englekirk, John E. "El hispanoamericanismo y la generación de 98," *Revista iberoamericana*, II, No. 4 (November 1940), 321–51.—The attitudes of Spanish intellectuals toward Spanish America early in this century.

Foerster, Robert F. *The Italian Emigration of Our Times*. Cambridge, Mass., 1919.—Four chapters are devoted to Argentina and Brazil; they constitute some of the most lucid writing on immigration yet to appear on Latin America.

García Calderón, Francisco. *Latin America; Its Rise and Progress*.

London, 1913.—Highly recommended as an example of "intellectual confusion" at the time when large segments of Latin America were breaking with the Hispanic tradition.

Giusti, Roberto F. "La restauración nacionalista," *Nosotros,* IV, No. 26 (February 1910), 139–54.—This is an extended review of the book by Ricardo Rojas. The reviewer takes Rojas to task for his exaggerated nationalism.

González-Blanco, Andrés. *Escritores representativos de América.* Madrid, 1917.—Observations on Rodó, Blanco Fombona, and Bunge are particularly pertinent.

Great Britain, Foreign Office. *Diplomatic and Consular Reports.* London, 1886–19—.—An excellent source for technological and industrial development prior to 1920 when Great Britain exercised great influence in the area.

Groussac, Paul. *El viage intelectual.* 2 vols. Madrid, 1904.—Much of this is the rantings of a leading Yankeephobe.

Hanson, Simon G. "The Farquhar Syndicate in South America," *Hispanic American Historical Review,* XVII, No. 3 (August 1937), 314–26.—The rise and collapse early in this century of a great industrial empire which centered in Brazil.

Hudson, William H. *Far Away and Long Ago.* New York, 1918.—A vivid description of rural Argentina in the late nineteenth century.

International Labour Office. *Emigration and Immigration: Legislation and Treaties.* Geneva, 1922.—A catalog.

Jefferson, Mark S. W. *Peopling the Argentine Pampa.* New York, 1926.—Thorough examination of immigration and the impact of the immigrant upon Argentina's developmental pattern.

Jeffrey, William H. *Mitre and Urquiza; a Chapter in the Unification of the Argentine Republic.* Madison, Wis., 1952.—Mitre comes out on top when compared with a number of his contemporaries.

Knapp, Frank A. *The Life of Sebastián Lerdo de Tejada, 1823–1889.* Austin, Tex., 1951.—Scholarly treatment of a leading Mexican "Liberal."

Levene, Ricardo. *Historia de las ideas sociales argentinas.* Buenos Aires, 1947.—The contribution of a number of outstanding Argentines to the development of social thought. The emphasis is decidedly on the nineteenth century.

Marchant, Anyda. "A New Portrait of Mauá, the Banker: A Man of Business in Nineteenth-Century Brazil," *Hispanic American Historical Review,* XXX, No. 4 (November 1950), 411–31.—Objective study of one of Latin America's first farsighted businessmen.

Martin, Percy Alvin. "Causes of the Collapse of the Brazilian Empire," *Hispanic American Historical Review,* IV, No. 1 (February 1921), 4–48.—Thoughtful and concise.

———. "Federalism in Brazil," in *The Constitution Reconsidered,* Conyers Read, ed. New York, 1938, pp. 367–84.—Primarily concerned with the period prior to 1890.

Mazade, Ch. de. "Les révolutions et les dictatures de l'Amérique du Sud en 1859," *Revue des deux mondes,* XXVII (May-June, 1860), 435–79.—A general survey of political instability in Latin America during the late 1850's.

Melfi, Domingo. "El héroe de la clase media en la novela chilena," *Atenea,* Año VII, Tomo XIII, No. 61 (March 1930), 65–69.—Deals largely with the nineteenth century.

Morse, Richard M. "São Paulo in the Nineteenth Century: Economic Roots of the Metropolis," *Inter-American Economic Affairs,* V, No. 3 (Winter, 1951), 3–39.—Thorough.

Mulhall, Michael G. *Handbook of the River Plate, Comprising the Argentine Republic, Uruguay, and Paraguay,* 6th ed. Buenos Aires, 1892.—Probably the best known "guide" of the nineteenth century for the area involved.

Muñoz Tebar, Jesús. *El personalismo i el legalismo.* New York, 1890.— Holds the press in large part responsible for the turmoil in Latin America.

Nichols, Madaline W. *The Gaucho.* Durham, N.C., 1942.—Highly condensed. Skillfully drawn portraiture of the Argentine cowboy.

Oddone, Jacinto. *La burgesía terrateniente argentina,* 2d ed. Buenos Aires, 1936.—The loss of the public domain, the creation of the landed estates, and the origins of the great fortunes in Argentina prior to 1890.

Pletcher, David M. "The Building of the Mexican Railway," *Hispanic American Historical Review,* XXX, No. 1 (February 1950), 26–62. —Scholarly account of efforts on the part of Mexico to establish railroads prior to the opening, in 1873, of its first line.

———. "The Development of Railroads in Sonora." *Inter-American Economic Affairs,* I, No. 4 (March 1948), 3–45.

Prado, Eduardo. *Fastos da dictadura militar no Brasil.* 4th ed. (Oporto, 1890).—Violent attack upon those responsible for the overthrow of Pedro II.

Quesada, Ernesto. *Alocución patriótica.* Buenos Aires, 1895.—Nationalistic.

Read, John Lloyd. *The Mexican Historical Novel, 1826–1910.* New York, 1939.—History was interpreted by novelists in terms of the ideals of the nineteenth century when Mexico was attempting to constitute itself a new nation.

Reclus, Élisée. "Les républiques de l'Amérique du Sud, leurs guerres et leur projet de fédération." *Revue des deux mondes,* LXV (Sept.-Oct., 1866), 953–80.—The project of federation referred to was the proposal which followed the Spanish attack upon Peru and Chile in the early 1860's. The value of the article lies in its survey of political dynamics during a decade of serious unrest.

Rippy, J. Fred. "The British Investment 'Boom' of the 1880's in Latin America," *Hispanic American Historical Review,* XXIX, No. 2 (May 1949), 281–86.—Statistical.

———. "British Investments in Latin America, End of 1913," *Inter-American Economic Affairs,* V, No. 2 (Autumn, 1951), 90–100.

———. *Latin America and the Industrial Age.* New York, 1944.— Largely concerned with the introduction of various technological developments.

———. "The Peak of British Investment in Latin-American Mines," *Inter-American Economic Affairs,* II, No. 1 (Summer, 1948), 41–48.

Rojas, Ricardo. *El profeta de La Pampa.* Buenos Aires, 1945.—A friendly account of Sarmiento's contribution to the formation of the Argentine nationality by one of that nation's outstanding literary figures.

Sánchez, Luis Alberto. *Nueva historia de la literatura americana.* Asunción, 1950.—A detailed study by an established authority.

Sarmiento, Domingo Faustino. *Facundo; ó civilización i barbarie en Las Pampas Arjentinas,* 4th ed. New York, 1868.—A classic on the problem of caudillism.

Scholes, Walter V. *Mexican Politics During the Juárez Regime, 1855–1872.* The University of Missouri Studies, Vol. 30. Columbia, Mo., 1957.—The leaders of the Reform were successful in initiating certain aspects of democratic capitalism, yet many of the fundamental theses of the Reform never developed to any degree. Particularly did personalism in politics persist.

———. "A Revolution Falters: Mexico, 1856–1857," *Hispanic American Historical Review.* XXXII, No. 1 (February 1952), 1–21.— Straightforward discussion of the liberal-conservative conflicts that led to a decade of strife.

United States. Bureau of Foreign Commerce. *Consular Reports,* Washington, D.C., 1880–1903.—The numbers contain valuable information on economic development in the several republics.

———. Department of State. *Foreign Relations of the United States: Diplomatic Papers,* Washington, D.C., 1861—.—Invaluable for the period prior to 1920.

Vargas Vila, José M. *Ante los bárbaros.* Barcelona, 1917.—A real "Yankeebaiter."

Walford, A. J. "Economic Aspects of the Argentine War of Secession (1852–1861)," *Inter-American Economic Affairs,* I, No. 2 (September 1947), 70–96.—Scholarly coverage of a confused era.

George Washington University, Washington, D.C., Seminar Conference on Hispanic American Affairs. *South American Dictators during the First Century of Independence,* Vol. 5 of *Studies in Hispanic American Affairs,* edited by A. Curtis Wilgus. Washington, D.C., 1937.—A standard reference work.

Williams, Mary Wilhelmine. *Dom Pedro the Magnanimous, Second Emperor of Brazil.* Chapel Hill, N.C., 1937.—Thorough and friendly study of one of Latin America's most charming personalities.

Zea, Leopoldo. *Dos etapas del pensamiento en Hispanoamérica: del romanticismo al positivismo.* Mexico, 1949.—The best survey of the field.

CHAPTER 4

The works included below are chiefly concerned with Uruguay in the twentieth century.

Acevedo, Eduardo. *Anales históricos del Uruguay.* 6 vols. Montevideo, 1933–36.—A reference work for the history of Uruguay from pre-Colombian times to 1930. Little in way of interpretation.

Araujo, Orestes. *Historia compendiada de la civilización uruguaya.* 2 vols. Montevideo, 1907.—Worthwhile chapters on education, immigration, population, and the growth of Montevideo are to be found in volume 1.

Ardao, Arturo. *La filosofía en el Uruguay en el siglo XX.* Mexico, 1956.—Examines the writings of more than a dozen Uruguayan thinkers beginning with Rodó.

Arena, Domingo. *Batlle y los problemas sociales en el Uruguay.* Montevideo, 1939.—Makes no serious pretense of being objective. However, the volume contains important material on Batlle's views on a number of major issues.

Blanco Acevedo, Pablo. *Estudios constitucionales.* Montevideo, 1939.—Scholarly essays on the constitutions of 1830, 1917, and 1934.

Charlone, César. "The Economic and Social Situation of Uruguay," *International Labour Review,* XXXIII, No. 5 (May 1936), 607–18.—An essentially legal approach by a high official in the Uruguayan government.

Chiarino, Juan Vicente, and Miguel Saralegui. *Detrás de la ciudad, ensayo de síntesis de los olvidados problemas campesinos.* Montevideo, 1944.—The authors were closely associated with projects designed to correct existing evils in the rural areas.

Collado, E. G., and Simon G. Hanson. "Old-Age Pensions in Uruguay," *Hispanic American Historical Review,* XVI, No. 2 (May 1936), 173–89.—The authors use the experiences of the old-age pension plans as a basis for generalizations upon the nature of Uruguayan attitudes on economic and social problems.

Demicheli, Alberto. *Los entes autónomos; régimen jurídico de los servicios públicos descentralizados.* Montevideo, 1924.— Seeks greater autonomy for state industrial entities.

Espalter, José. *El problema nacional.* Montevideo, 1905.—Brief. The national problem was the anachronistic political parties which were incompatible with the regular functioning of democratic institutions.

Fitzgibbon, Russell H. "Adoption of Collegiate Executive in Uruguay," *Journal of Politics,* XIV, No. 4 (November 1952), 616–42.

———. "Argentina and Uruguay: A Tale of Two Attitudes," *Pacific Spectator,* VIII, No. 1 (Winter, 1954), pp. 6–20.

———. *Uruguay: Portrait of a Democracy.* New Brunswick, N.J., 1954.—Quite friendly account with emphasis on the period since World War I. Heavily relied upon by the present author.

Giudici, Roberto B. *Batlle y el batllismo.* Montevideo, 1928.—Laudatory.

Great Britain. Board of Trade. *Uruguay; Economic and Commercial Conditions* in . . . "Overseas Economic Surveys." London, 1954.

Grompone, Antonio Miguel. "Las clases medias en el Uruguay," *Materiales para el estudio de la clase media en la América Latina.* I, 76–91. Unión Panamericana, La oficina de ciencias sociales, Departamento de asuntos culturales, Washington, D.C., 1950.—A good statement given the limited materials available to the author.

Hall, John O. *La administración pública en el Uruguay.* Montevideo, 1954.—A concise statement.

Hanson, Simon G. *Utopia in Uruguay.* New York, 1938.—Still the best published account in English of Batlle's reform program and its affect upon foreign investment.

International Bank for Reconstruction and Development. "Studies in Economic Development . . . No. 2: Uruguay," n.p., 1951.—This study was processed for limited distribution. The copy used by this author was held by the Documents Division of the University of California, Berkeley. Contains valuable statistical information and highly pertinent observations on the economic condition of Uruguay during the late 1940's.

Kitchen, James D. "National Personnel Administration in Uruguay," *Inter-American Economic Affairs,* IV, No. 1 (Summer, 1950), 45–58.—Finds the quality and *esprit de corps* in the Uruguayan bureaucracy to be good.

Lôbo, Hélio. *A democracia uruguaya.* Rio de Janeiro, 1928.—Sympathetic account by a Brazilian whose interest was primarily in Uruguayan-Brazilian relations.

Martin, Percy A. "The Career of José Batlle y Ordóñez," *Hispanic American Historical Review,* X, No. 4 (November 1930), 413–28.—Scholarly, sympathetic.

Martínez Lamas, Julio. *Economía uruguaya.* Montevideo, 1943.—A satisfactory survey.

——. *Riqueza y pobreza del Uruguay; estudio de las causas que retardan el progreso nacional.* 2d ed. Montevideo, 1946.—A serious examination of the urban-rural imbalance.

Pan American Union. Department of International Law. *A Statement of the Laws of Uruguay in Matters Affecting Business.* 3d ed. Washington, D.C., 1957.

Pendle, George. *Uruguay, South America's First Welfare State.* London, 1952.—A useful compendium of current developments.

Pintos, Francisco R. *Historia del Uruguay, 1851–1938.* Montevideo, 1946.—A materialistic interpretation of Uruguayan development. Stresses the need for united public support of agrarian reform and industrial development.

Pivel Devoto, Juan E. *Historia de la República Oriental del Uruguay (1830–1930).* Montevideo, 1945.—Somewhat critical of Batlle and the State intervention which he espoused.

Rodríquez Fabregat, Enrique. *Batlle y Ordóñez; el reformador.* Buenos Aires, 1942.—A careful and friendly study of Uruguay's foremost statesman.

Sanguinetti Freire, Alberto. "Social Legislation in Uruguay," *International Labour Review,* LIX, No. 3 (March 1949), 271–96.—Review by a high official of Uruguay's National Labor Institute.

Solari, Aldo E. *Sociología rural nacional.* Montevideo, 1953.—A serious attempt to fit life in the rural areas into the national scene.

Taylor, Philip Bates. "The Executive Power in Uruguay." Unpublished doctoral dissertation, University of California, 1950.—Essentially a constitutional study.

——. "The Uruguayan Coup d'État of 1933," *Hispanic American Historical Review,* XXXII, No. 3 (August 1952), 301–20.—A clear statement of the background and aftermath of one of Uruguay's few undemocratic aberrations since 1905.

Uruguay. Dirección General de Estadística. *Anuario 1884* . . . Montevideo, 1885—.—An invaluable source for the period prior to 1920.

———. Dirección General de Instrucción Primaria. *La instrucción pública primaria en la República Oriental del Uruguay.* Montevideo, 1911.

———. Dirección General de Instrucción Pública. *Memoria.* Montevideo, 1903—.—Particularly useful for the early years of the twentieth century. Quality and usefulness decline during the second decade of the century.

———. Ministerio de Industrias. *Memoria* . . . *1907–17.* Montevideo, 1908–1918.—Primarily valuable for the statistics it contains.

———. Ministerio del Interior. *Memoria* . . . *1907*—Montevideo, 1908—. —A good statistical source.

Vanger, Milton. "Uruguay Introduces Government by Committee," *American Political Science Review* XLVIII, No. 2 (June 1954), 500–513.—A thoughtful examination of developments leading up to the institution of the plural executive in 1952.

Vidart, Daniel D. *La vida rural uruguaya.* Montevideo, 1955.—Views contemporary problems in light of the historical development of the republic. Urges sweeping reforms.

Zayas, Edison V. "Las instituciones financieras del Uruguay y la movilización de los ahorros," *El trimestre económico,* XX, No. 2 (April-June, 1953), 242–91.—Particularly valuable is the author's discussion of the role of the State and of autonomous public institutions in the promotion of economic development.

Zum Felde, Alberto. *Evolución histórica del Uruguay.* 3d ed., Montevideo, 1945.—A sociological interpretation of Republic's development.

———. *Proceso histórico del Uruguay.* Montevideo, 1919.—Social and political evolution of the republic by one of its outstanding historians.

CHAPTER 5

This portion of the Bibliography contains works primarily concerned with Chile in the twentieth century.

Abbott, Roger S. "The Role of Contemporary Political Parties in Chile," *American Political Science Review,* XLV, No. 2 (June 1951), 450–63.—Considerable cooperation between the executive and legislative branches; parties support the principle of relative cabinet stability and believe in government support of the economy.

Alarcón Pino, Raúl. *La clase media en Chile; orígenes, características e influencias.* Santiago, 1947.—Superficial in many respects but one of the few studies on class structure to be done in Chile.

Alessandri, Arturo. *Recuerdos de gobierno.* Santiago, 1952.—Primarily concerned with the author's first term as president of the republic.

Alvarado Maldonado, Germán. *Organización de los servicios públicos y su influencia en la economía nacional.* Santiago, 1945.—The State can participate in economic development without threatening the democratic process.

Alvarez Andrews, Oscar. "Las clases sociales en Chile," *Revista mexicana de sociología,* XIII, No. 2 (May-Aug. 1951), 201-20.—Particular attention is paid to the middle sectors. The author identifies the middle sectors by occupation and seeks to fix their numbers, and discusses the role of the membership in modern society.

———. *Historia del desarrollo industrial de Chile.* Santiago, 1936.— Substantive rather than interpretative.

Azócar Gauthier, Octavio. *La enseñanza industrial en relación con la economía nacional.* Santiago, 1951.—Develops the interdependence of industry and education.

Bermúdez Miral, Oscar. *El drama político de Chile.* Santiago, 1947.— An objective examination of parties and party programs.

Blasier, S. Cole. "Chile: a Communist Battleground," *Political Science Quarterly,* LXV, No. 3 (September 1950), 353-75.—Stresses the role of Communists in Chilean politics between 1936 and 1939.

Butland, Gilbert J. *Chile: An Outline of Its Geography, Economics and Politics.* London, 1951.—Useful primarily for the statistical data it contains.

Cabero, Alberto. *Chile y los chilenos.* Santiago, 1926.—A thoughtful, panoramic view of Chile that has retained much of its original popularity.

Campos Harriet, Fernando. *Manual de historia constitucional de Chile.* Santiago, 1951. — Constitutional development during the various presidential regimes.

Carmona de la Fuente, Augusto. *Examen crítico y comparativo de la nacionalidad, la ciudadanía y los conflictos derivados.* Santiago, 1925. —A legal treatise.

Chile. Dirección General de Estadística. *Anuario . . . 1909 . . .* Santiago, 1910—.—From 1909 to 1927 when broken down into several components this was the best single published statistical source on developments in Chile.

———. *XII censo general de población y 1. de vivienda; levantado el 24 de abril del año 1952.* Santiago, 1953.—A summary of findings.

———. *Estadística chilena.* Santiago, 1928.—Official monthly statistical compilation. Invaluable.

———. *Industrias . . . 1947—.* Santiago, 1950—.—Contains occasional brief statements on economic policy.

Chile, Dirección del Registro Electoral. *Elección ordinaria del Congreso Nacional en 6 de marzo de 1949.* Santiago, 1949.—Distribution of votes by electoral districts.

———. *Elección ordinaria del senadores y diputados al Congreso Nacional (período constitucional 1953-57).* Santiago, n.d. — Handy guide to the distribution of the vote geographically and by party.

Chile, Inspección Jeneral de Ferrocarriles. *Ferrocarriles del estado.* Santiago, 1910.—A brief history of railroad development on the occasion of the centenary of Chilean independence.

Chile, Oficina Central de Estadística. *X censo de la población efectuado en 27 de noviembre de 1930.* 3 vols. Santiago, 1931–35.—Compares findings with those obtained at earlier dates.

———. *Veinte años de legislación social.* Santiago, 1945.

Chile, Presidente. *Mensaje . . . 1828—.* Santiago, 1829?—.—Consulted only occasionally for this study, but a highly useful source.

Chile, Universidad. *Anales . . . 1843—.* Santiago, 1843?—.—A major depository for an important part of the thinking to come out of Latin America in the nineteenth century.

———. *Desarrollo de Chile en la primera mitad del siglo XX.* 2 vols. Santiago, 1953.—Essays of varying worth by a number of social scientists and humanists. The ones which proved most valuable are entered separately in this Bibliography.

———. Instituto de Economía. *Desarrollo económico de Chile; 1940–1956.* Santiago, 1956.—An inventory of economic development in Chile in light of a desire on the part of the Ibáñez administration "to diminish State interventionism" in the economy. Five chapters treat of the general aspects of the economy and six chapters examine in some detail major sectors of the economy.

Cornejo Bravo, Octavio. *Tendencias modernas del movimiento de asociación professional.* Santiago, 1948.—Deals with professional labor organizations since 1920.

Cruz-Coke Madrid, Ricardo. *Geografía electoral de Chile.* Santiago, 1952.—Highly useful. Discusses the parties and their success in each of the major geographical regions in recent elections.

Donoso, Ricardo. *Alessandri, agitador y demoledor: cincuenta años de historia política de Chile.* 2 vols. Mexico, 1952–54.—Alessandri is flailed unmercifully but in the process fifty years of Chilean political development is closely scrutinized by a thorough scholar.

———. *Desarrollo político y social de Chile desde la constitución de 1833.* Santiago, 1933.—Scholarly and reasonable in most respects, the section dealing with Alessandri is polemical.

———. *Las ideas políticas en Chile.* Mexico, 1946.—A thoughtful discussion of liberal reform in Chile during the nineteenth century.

Echaiz, René León. *Evolución histórica de los partidos políticos chilenos.* Santiago, 1939.—Harking back to the nineteenth century, the author discovers that some parties have preferred liberty even in anarchy to order in despotism.

Edwards, Alberto. *La fronda aristocrática en Chile.* Santiago, 1928.—Reflective. The aristocracy is defended against the emerging urban elements.

———. *La organización política de Chile.* Santiago, 1943.—Scholarly.

Edwards, Alberto and Eduardo Frei Montalva. *Historia de los partidos chilenos.* Santiago, 1949.—The parties to 1891 were done by Edwards, from that date to 1938 by Frei Montalva.

Ellsworth, Paul T. *Chile, an Economy in Transition.* New York, 1945.—The first serious examination in English of Chile's shift toward a State-controlled economy.

Encina, Francisco A. *Historia de Chile.* 20 vols. Santiago, 1940–52.—The author knew no idols. He challenged numerous traditional interpretations while raising nationalism to new heights in serious historical writing in Chile.

———. *Resumen de la historia de Chile.* Edited, with illustrations and appendixes, by Leopoldo Castedo. 3 vols. Santiago, 1954–55.—A condensation of Encina's twenty-volume history of Chile, *q.v.*

Frei Montalva, Eduardo. *La verdad tiene su hora.* Santiago, 1955.— The author, a Christian Democrat, had his eye on the presidency of the republic when he wrote this volume.

Fuenzalida Villegas, Humberto, *et al. Chile; geografía, educación, literatura, legislación, economía, minería.* Buenos Aires, 1946.—Six lectures given in Argentina by a group of Chilean scholars. The tone is generally pessimistic.

Galdames, Luis. *A History of Chile.* Translated and edited by Isaac Joslin Cox. Chapel Hill, N.C., 1941.—The standard text in English.

———. *Educación económica e intelectual.* Santiago, 1912.—Calls for a reexamination of public education in view of Chile's changing economy.

———. *Jeografía económica de Chile.* Santiago, 1911.—An early effort to arouse interest in the economic geography of Chile.

Guerra, José G. *La constitución de 1925.* Santiago, 1929.—A comprehensive legal treatise.

Haring, Clarence H. "Chilean Politics, 1920–1928," *Hispanic American Historical Review,* XI, No. 1 (February 1931), 1–26.—A clear account of a decade of political instability, social unrest, and economic change.

———. "The Chilean Revolution of 1931," *Hispanic American Historical Review,* XIII, No. 2 (May 1933), 197–203.—The overthrow of Ibáñez was brought about by the professional classes, students, and labor.

Heise González, Julio. *La constitución de 1925 y las nuevas tendencias político-sociales.* Santiago, 1951.—Extremely good analysis of developments leading to the change that came in 1925.

Horst H., Heriberto. "El comercio en los últimos 50 años," in Chile, Universidad, *Desarrollo . . . ,* I, 249–61.—The *ambiente* in which the commercial sector has developed in this century.

Huneeus y Gana, Jorge. *Cuadro histórico de la producción intelectual de Chile.* Santiago, 1910?—Largely devoted to the nineteenth century, the volume ranges widely and often superficially over various intellectual pursuits. Few names are missed in the process.

International Bank for Reconstruction and Development. "The Agricultural Economy of Chile." Santiago, 1952 (Processed).—Urges determined action in order to overcome backwardness in the agricultural area of the economy.

Jefferson, Mark S. W. *Recent Colonization in Chile.* New York, 1921.— Good statistics but lacks interpretation.

Jobet, Julio César. "Movimiento social obrero," in Chile, Universidad, *Desarrollo . . . ,* I, 51–106.—A good statement of the Chilean Socialist position.

———. *Ensayo crítico del desarrollo económico-social de Chile.* Santiago, 1955.—Gives a strongly economic interpretation to Chilean history.

Keller R., Carlos. *La Eterna crisis chilena.* Santiago, 1931.—Written at a time of widespread instability. Assesses the tools with which Chile must face the future.

Labarca Hubertson, Amanda. "Apuntes para estudiar la clase media en Chile," *Materiales para el estudio de la clase media en la América Latina,* VI, 68–89. Unión Panamericana, La oficina de ciencias sociales, Departamento de asuntos culturales. Washington, D.C., 1950.—Based upon knowledge derived from a long and successful career in education and public welfare, there is no evidence of field work.

———. "Evolución femenina," in Chile, Universidad, *Desarrollo . . . ,* I, 107–29.—Worthwhile information on a sadly neglected subject in Latin America.

———. *Historia de la enseñanza en Chile.* Santiago, 1939.—The best single volume on education in Chile.

Lagos Valenzuela, Tulio. *Bosquejo histórico del movimiento obrero en Chile.* Santiago, 1941.—Mining and manufacturing made possible an aggressive labor movement. A short section is devoted to labor and politics.

Latcham, Ricardo A. "El ensayo en Chile en el siglo XX," in Chile, Universidad, *Desarrollo . . . ,* II, 343–84.—Useful for its observations on those essayists who concerned themselves with nationalism and social problems.

McBride, George M. *Chile; Land and Society.* New York, 1936.—A scholarly examination of the landholding system and use of land in Chile.

Marín Vicuña, Santiago. *Los ferrocarriles de Chile.* 4th ed. Santiago, 1916.—A full account.

Marshall, Enrique L. "Finanzas y sistema monetario," in Chile, Universidad, *Desarrollo . . . ,* I, 263–89.—The historical development of monetary institutions, credit, and public finance.

Martner, Daniel. *Estudio de política comercial chilena e historia económica nacional.* 2 vols. Santiago, 1923.—Good economic history through World War I.

Montenegro, Ernesto. "La novela chilena en medio siglo," in Chile, Universidad, *Desarrollo . . . ,* II, 321–42.—Actually better on the nineteenth century than on the twentieth.

Müller Hess, Walter. "La industria chilena en la primera mitad del siglo XX," in Chile, Universidad, *Desarrollo . . . ,* I, 189–213.—Economic growth and its effect upon living standards.

Pan American Union, Department of International Law. *A Statement of the Laws of Chile in Matters Affecting Business.* 2d ed. Washington, D.C., 1956.

Pfeiffer, Jack B. "Notes on the Heavy Equipment Industry in Chile, 1800–1910," *Hispanic American Historical Review,* XXXII, No. 1 (February 1952), 139–44.—Suggestive of development after 1880 rather than 1800 as indicated by the title.

Pinochet Ugarte, Augusto. *Síntesis de geografía de Chile.* Santiago, 1955.—Geography as reflected in politics and economics.

Pinto Santa Cruz, Aníbal. *Hacia nuestra independencia económica.* Santiago, 1953.—Thoughtful discussion of the problems of economic planning in a free economy.

Pinto Santa Cruz, Aníbal, *et al. La inflación: naturaleza y problemas.* Santiago, 1951.—Seven essays by as many authors. Deals with monetary expansion, fiscal action as it affects inflation and deflation, prices in inflationary periods, appraisal of inflation upon income, and international trade as it is influenced by inflation.

Ruiz Bourgeois, Julio. "Desarrollo de la minería chilena en la primera mitad del siglo XX," in Chile, Universidad, *Desarrollo . . . ,* I, 215–47.—Particularly interesting for the degree of objectivity the author displays in discussing the role of foreign capital in the mining sector.

"Some Aspects of the Acceleration of the Inflationary Process in Chile," *Economic Bulletin for Latin America,* I, No. 1 (January 1956), 45–53.—Considerable information on government spending and its effects.

Stevenson, John Reese. *The Chilean Popular Front.* Philadelphia, 1942. —The economic impact upon politics is stressed.

Subercaseaux, Guillermo. *Historia de las doctrinas económicas en América y en especial en Chile.* Santiago, 1924.—A survey for college students, contains worthwhile chapters on protectionism and Pan-Americanism.

Thomson, Charles Alexander. "Chile Struggles for National Recovery," *Foreign Policy Reports,* IX, No. 25 (February 14, 1934), 282–92.

Topaze. Santiago, 1933—.—A weekly. Political satire and cartoons at their very best in Latin America.

United States. Department of Labor. Bureau of Labor Statistics. "Labor in Chile," *Foreign Labor Information* [bulletin], No. 3 (July 1956). Processed.—A concise statement. Concerned more with labor statistics than policy.

————. Tariff Commission. *Mining and Manufacturing Industries in Chile.* Washington, D.C., 1949.

Vega, Julio. "La clase media en Chile," *Materiales para el estudio de la clase media en la América Latina,* III, 60–92. Unión Panamericana, La oficina de ciencias sociales, Departamento de asuntos culturales. Washington, D.C., 1950.

————. *La racionalización de nuestra enseñanza.* Santiago, 1954.—The entire education system in need of a complete revamping.

Vial, Carlos. *Cuaderno de la realidad nacional.* Santiago, 1952.—The role of the worker in Chilean society is examined, and means of improving living standards within the framework of democratic government are recommended.

Walker Linares, Francisco. "Evolución social," in Chile, Universidad, *Desarrollo . . . ,* I, 35–49.—Sees 1920 as the dividing line in social growth. Attempts to fix the number belonging to each of the major social groups.

Washington, Samuel Walter. "A Study of the Causes of Hostility

Toward the United States in Latin America; Chile." Washington, D.C., 1956. (Processed.) An External Research Paper, Department of State.

Zañartu Prieto, Enrique. *Hambre, miseria e ignorancia.* Santiago, 1938.
—Nationalism as expressed by a man long in public life.

CHAPTER 6

The entries contained in this section are chiefly concerned with Argentina since 1900.

Alexander, Robert J. *The Perón Era.* New York, 1951.—The primary value of the volume lies in its attention to labor in politics under Perón.

Amadeo, Octavio R. *Vidas argentinas.* 2d ed. Buenos Aires, 1934.—Brief sketches of seventeen Argentine personalities most of whom were at one time or another actively engaged in politics.

Argentina. Dirección General de Estadística. *Resúmenes estadísticos retrospectivos.* Buenos Aires, 1914.

Argentine Republic. *Anuario oficial de la República Argentina.* Buenos Aires, 1912—.—A mine of statistical information.

——. Congreso. *Debates parlamentarios sobre instrucción pública.* Buenos Aires, 1904.

——. Constitution. *Constitución de la nación argentina . . . 1949.* Buenos Aires, 1949.

——. Dirección de Comercio e Industria. *Censo industrial y comercial de la República, 1908–1914.* Buenos Aires, 1915.—Detailed.

——. Dirección de Inmigración. *Memoria.*—Began publication in the 1860's. Probably the best single source on immigration in Latin America.

——. Dirección General de Estadística. *Censo de los empleados administrativos, funcionarios judiciales y personal docente de la República Argentina correspondiente al 31 de diciembre de 1892.* Buenos Aires, 1893.

——. Dirección General de Estadística. *Estadística industrial . . . 1934/35—.* Buenos Aires, 1938—.

——. Dirección General del Servicio Estadístico Nacional. *Resultados generales del censo de población, 1947.* Buenos Aires, 1951.—Includes data on employment.

——. Dirección Nacional de Estadística y Censos. *Informe demográfico, 1944–1954.* Buenos Aires, 1956.—Contains valuable data from earlier censuses, information on immigration, and a chapter on population growth as compared with other Latin American republics.

——. Dirección Nacional del Servicio Estadístico Nacional. *Anuario estadístico de la República Argentina.* Buenos Aires, 1948—.

——. Dirección Nacional del Servicio Estadístico Nacional. *IV censo general de la nación; censo industrial de 1946.* 2 vols. Buenos Aires, 1952—.

———. Ministerio de Justicia e Instrucción Pública. *Antecedentes sobre enseñanza secundaria y normal.* Buenos Aires, 1903.

———. Ministerio de Relaciones Exteriores y Culto. *La República Argentina ante el "Libro Azul."* Buenos Aires, 1946.—Argentina's answer to the "Blue Book," published by the United States Department of State in February 1945, which sought to bring about Perón's defeat in the presidential elections by associating him and his group with European totalitarianism.

———. Servicio Estadístico Nacional. *IV censo general de la nación, 1945; comparación de los resultados del censo de población.* Buenos Aires, 1951.—Provides comparative data from censuses of 1869, 1895, 1914, and 1946.

———. Servicio Estadístico Nacional. *La actividad industrial, Argentina en 1951.* Buenos Aires, 1952.—Statistics for 1946-1950 compared with those for 1951.

Bagú, Sergio. "La clase media en la Argentina," *Materiales para el estudio de la clase media en la América Latina,* I, 34-65. Unión Panamericana, La oficina de ciencias sociales, Departamento de asuntos culturales. Washington, D.C., 1950.—Thoughtful.

———. "Diagrama político de la Argentina de hoy," *Cuadernos Americanos,* XV, No. 6 (Nov.-Dec., 1956), 38-57.—Workers will henceforth play an important political role. No reason why the middle sectors cannot cooperate with workers.

Bank of London & South America Limited. *The Prebisch Plan.* London, 1955.—An outstanding economist recommends the path to recovery for Argentina following the overthrow of Perón.

Berraz Montyn, Carlos. "Indole de la tercera posición," *Hechos e ideas,* XIII, No. 105 (December 1952), 323-52.—May be considered an official version of Perón's "third position" between capitalism and communism.

Berrutti, José J. *Escuela y democracia.* Buenos Aires, 1932.—"National" education at great sacrifice if necessary.

Bertotto, José G. "La educación en el Plan Perón," *Hechos e ideas,* XII, No. 90 (September 1951), 39-50.—A defense of Perón's educational objectives.

Beveraggi Allende, Walter. *El dilema económico de la revolución.* Buenos Aires, 1956.—Critical of the recommendations for economic recovery made by Raúl Prebisch, *q.v.* under Bank of London . . .

Bidabehere, Fernando A. *Acción de la economía dirigida en la República Argentina.* Buenos Aires, 1937.—Examines measures taken by the State to control the depression. Doubts that such measures can be warranted except in cases of extreme emergency and then more adaptable to industry than agriculture.

Blanksten, George I. *Perón's Argentina.* Chicago, 1953.—Valuable for day-to-day developments during a crucial period of Argentine and world history.

Bosch, Mariano Gregorio Gerardo. *Historia del Partido Radical, la U.C.R., 1891-1930.* Buenos Aires, 1931.—Vehemently anti-U.C.R.

Buenos Aires, Universidad Nacional. *La Universidad Nacional de Buenos Aires: 1821-1910.* Buenos Aires, 1910.—Concerned more with growth of the institution than with University policy.

————. Instituto de Política Económica. *Entidades de economía dirigida en la República Argentina.* Buenos Aires, 1938. — An excellent study. Traces development of several of the State economic enterprises. Calls for closer control of such activities.

Bunge, Alejandro E. *Una nueva Argentina.* Buenos Aires, 1940.—An early warning that population was outrunning economic development, a fact only too apparent by 1958.

Bunge, Augusto. *La inferioridad económica de los argentinos nativos.* Buenos Aires, 1919.—Because the immigrants as a group possessed superior training they surpassed the "native" in the industrial and commercial areas. The answer to the problem was more "positive" and "utilitarian" general education.

[Ceppi, José.] *Los factores del progreso de la República Argentina: por Aníbal Latino.* 2d ed. Buenos Aires, 1910.—The various immigrant groups, according to the author, were factors of progress.

Chambers, Edward J. "Some Factors in the Deterioration of Argentina's External Position, 1946–1951," *Inter-American Economic Affairs,* VIII, No. 3 (Winter 1954), 27–62.—Emphasis is upon balance of payments, industrial development through inflation and foreign economic policy.

Dickmann, Enrique. *Recuerdos de un militante socialista.* Buenos Aires, 1949.—These memoirs of a leading Argentine Socialist constitute an interpretation of a half-century of social and political development based upon the author's firsthand acquaintance with his subject.

Doherty, George. "The Cross and the Sword," *Harper's Magazine,* CXC, No. 1136 (January 1945), 106–15.—A Catholic attacks the nationalism of Argentina as pagan and anti-Catholic.

Dorfman, Adolfo. *Evolución industrial argentina.* Buenos Aires, 1942. —One of the early serious examinations of the industrial scene.

Egoroff, Pavel Petroff. *Argentina's Agricultural Exports During World War II.* Stanford, 1945.—Scholarly.

Etkin, Alberto M. *Bosquejo de una historia y doctrina de la Unión Cívica Radical.* Buenos Aires, 1928.—Defends U.C.R. against its detractors.

Frondizi, Arturo. *Petróleo y política: contribución al estudio de la historia económica argentina y de las relaciones entre el imperialismo y la vida política nacional.* Buenos Aires, 1954.—Highly nationalistic. A good example of extremist thinking in Argentina following the overthrow of Perón, by a "responsible" politician who became president of Argentina in May 1958.

Frondizi, Silvio. *La realidad argentina.* Buenos Aires, 1955.—Published approximately a month after the overthrow of Perón, this study seeks to explain Argentina's problems in terms of the capitalistic system.

Gandía, Enrique de. *Historia de la República Argentina en el siglo XIX.* 2d ed. Buenos Aires, 1948.—An unusually good synthesis.

Germani, Gino. "La clase media en la Argentina con especial referencia a sus sectores urbanos," *Materiales para el estudio de la clase media en la América Latina,* I, 1–33. Unión Panamericana, La oficina de ciencias sociales, Departamento de asuntos culturales. Washington, D.C., 1950.—The author is outstanding in his field in Argentina.

———. "La clase media en la ciudad de Buenos Aires," *Boletín del Instituto de Sociología,* No. 1 (1942), 105–26.—A useful statistical study of the social groups of Buenos Aires in the late 1930's based primarily upon industrial and demographic censuses of the city.

———. *Estructura social de la Argentina.* Buenos Aires, 1955.—Largely a statistical study, but a section is devoted to the political attitudes of the various groups.

Gómez, Rosendo A. "Intervention in Argentina 1860–1930," *Inter-American Economic Affairs,* I, No. 3 (December 1947), 55–73.—Intervention of the central government in the states.

González, Joaquín V. *The National University of La Plata: Report Relative to Its Foundation.* Translated by George Wilson-Rae. Buenos Aires, 1906.

Gori, Gastón. *La Pampa sin gaucho.* Buenos Aires, 1952.—Brief but discerning examination of the influence of the immigrant upon the culture of the Pampa.

Great Britain, Department of Overseas Trade. *Economic Conditions in the Argentine Republic,* in "Overseas Economic Surveys." London, 1920.

———. *Report on Economic and Commercial Conditions in the Argentine Republic,* in "Overseas Economic Surveys." London, 1937.

Hanson, Simon G. *Argentine Meat and the British Market.* Stanford, 1938.—History of the Argentine meat industry and its impact on the growth of the republic to approximately 1920, although a brief concluding chapter carries the story forward to the early 1930's.

Haring, Clarence H. *Argentina and the United States.* Boston, 1941.—Written with clarity and understanding, this "condensed comment" provides a sound beginning for a basis of understanding Argentina at a time when the world was being drawn into war.

Hasbrouck, Alfred. "The Argentine Revolution of 1930," *The Hispanic American Historical Review,* XVIII, No. 3 (August 1938), 285–321.—Largely descriptive.

Hoffmann, Fritz L. "Perón and After; A Review Article," *Hispanic American Historical Review,* XXXVI, No. 4 (November 1956), 510–28.—An excellent digest of serious literature on Perón.

Holmes, Olive. "Perón's 'Greater Argentina' and the United States," *Foreign Policy Reports,* XXIV, No. 14 (December 1, 1948), 158–71.—A keen understanding of the problems that an Argentina bent on rapid industrialization would have to face in a world recovering from war.

Ingenieros, José. *Sociología argentina.* Buenos Aires, 1946.—First published in 1918 this is a highly critical examination of Argentine society by an outstanding social scientist.

Iñigo Carrera, Hector. *El engaño de las nacionalizaciones totalitarias: una estafa al descubierto.* Buenos Aires, 1955.—Discusses in a scholarly manner some of the problems raised by the State's interference in the economy during the Perón regime.

Justo, Juan Bautista. *Discursos y escritos políticos.* Buenos Aires, 1933.—A collection of essays and addresses on a wide variety of subjects. The author was a leader of the Socialist Party and his views may in general be considered those of the Party.

Korn, Alejandro. *Influencias filosóficas en la evolución nacional.* Buenos Aires, 1936.—Scholasticism, *la filosofía moderna,* romanticism, and positivism.

La Prensa. *Defense of Freedom.* New York, 1952.—Published by the "editors" of *La Prensa,* the volume constitutes a statement of the position of the enterprise in the face of Perón's appropriation of the plant.

Levene, Ricardo. "La misión de la escuela," *Nosotros,* VIII, No. 63 (July 1914), 106–10.—The school must teach idealism and social responsiiblity.

Llamazares, Juan. *La Argentina en el comercio ibero-americano.* Buenos Aires, 1941.—Statistics on trade in general and with the individual republics.

Macdonald, Austin F. *Government of the Argentine Republic.* New York, 1942.—Considerable stress is placed upon similarities between the Argentine Constitution of 1853 and the United States Constitution.

Maciel, Carlos Néstor. *La italianización de la Argentina.* Buenos Aires, 1924.—Italians pose a threat to Argentine national culture.

Magnet, Alejandro. *Nuestros vecinos justicialistas.* 10th ed. Santiago, 1955.—By a Chilean, this widely read work—ten editions in 25 months—is generally considered to be one of the best studies of the Perón era written while the dictator was still in power.

Mazo, Gabriel del. *El radicalismo: notas sobre su historia y doctrina, 1922–1952.* Buenos Aires, 1955.—Sympathetic. Perón was still in office when the volume was published; the *Concordancia* of the 1930's, consequently, becomes the bête noire and receives the brunt of the author's attack.

Miguez, Francisco. *La patria y el patriotismo.* Quilmes, 1942.—Looks to leaders such as San Martín, Sarmiento, Alberdi, and Monteagudo for values.

Montemayor, Mariano. "Los corrientos políticos en Hispanoamérica," *Dinámica social,* II, No. 13–14 (Sept.-Oct., 1951), 18–19.—Anti-United States. Sees Pan-Americanism, Marxism, and nationalism as the "political currents" most significantly affecting the Hemisphere.

Moyano Llerena, Carlos, *et al. Argentina social y económica.* Buenos Aires, 1950.—Comprehensive.

Munger, William L. "Academic Freedom Under Perón," *The Antioch Review,* VII, No. 2 (June 1947), 275–90.—Perón sought to integrate the educational system into his "despotic state." Considerable attention is paid to Peron's use of the Catholic Church.

Nudelman, Santiago I. *Proceso contra la dictadura.* 2 vols. Buenos Aires, 1953–55.—Largely drawn from congressional debates, the materials are supposed to establish the author's defense of the U.C.R. position on a number of issues against the *peronista* majority.

———. *El radicalismo al servicio de la libertad.* Buenos Aires, 1947.— A justification of the Radical Party position in the upheavals of 1930 and 1943 by a prominent member of the U.C.R.

Oddone, Jacinto. *Gremialismo proletario argentino.* Buenos Aires, 1949.—The Argentine labor movement from about 1910 to 1944 with emphasis upon the role of the Socialist Party, by a trade unionist and scholar.

———. *Historia del socialismo argentino.* 2 vols. Buenos Aires, 1934.— Probably the best study of the Socialist Party for the period of its rise and greatest influence.

Orfila Reynal, Arnaldo. "Breve historia y examen del peronismo," *Cuadernos Americanos,* XIV, No. 6 (Nov.-Dec., 1955), 7–37.— Violently anti-Perón and almost as violently anti-U.S. Department of State for supporting his regime.

Palacios, Alfredo L. *La defensa de valor humano; legislación social argentina.* Buenos Aires (1939).

———. *Soberanía y socialización; industrias, monopolios, latifundios, y privilegios del capital extranjero.* Buenos Aires, 1946.—The "Grand Old Man" of Argentine socialism presents his views on a number of matters vital to Argentina.

Pan American Union, Department of International Law. *A Statement of the Laws of Argentina in Matters Affecting Business.* Washington, D.C., 1951. Supplements appeared in 1955 and 1957.

Pendle, George. *Argentina.* London, 1955.—Highly compressed social science.

Perón, Eva (Duarte). *La razón de mi vida.* Buenos Aires, 1951.—May be considered an official version of the Perón social ideology.

———. *The Writings of Eva Perón.* Buenos Aires, 1950.—Collection of articles and speeches in translation.

Perón, Juan Domingo. "Bases para la organización del Partido Peronista," *Hechos e ideas,* XIV, No. 52 (July 1948), 21–42.—Perón's views on how a political party should be organized.

———. *Perón Expounds His Doctrine,* Translated by the Argentine Association of English Culture. Buenos Aires, 1948.

———. *Doctrina peronista, filosofía política, social.* Buenos Aires, 1947. —The development of Perón's political philosophy.

———. *Doctrinary Principles of the Social Policy of General Juan Perón.* Buenos Aires, 1947.—An address before the General Confederation of Labor in February, 1947.

———. *The Theory and Complete Doctrine of General Perón.* [Buenos Aires], 1946.—Propaganda, but important propaganda.

———. *The Voice of Perón.* Buenos Aires, 1950.

Phelps, Vernon L. *The International Economic Position of Argentina.* Philadelphia, 1938.—A descriptive analysis of international economic relations with particular reference to Argentine–United States relations.

Poviña, Alfredo. "Concepto de la clase media y su proyección argentina," *Materiales para el estudio de la clase media en la América Latina,* I, 66–75. Unión Panamericana, La oficina de ciencias sociales, Departamento de asuntos culturales. Washington, D.C., 1950. —A thoughtful statement.

Prebisch Plan. See Bank of London . . .

Quesada, Ernesto. *La universidad y la patria.* Buenos Aires, 1921.— More nationalism.

Rabinovitz, Bernardo. *Sucedió en la Argentina, 1943–1956; lo que no se dijo.* Buenos Aires, 1956.—Short, penetrating account of the Perón dictatorship.

Reissig, Luis. "El fin de un ciclo histórico en Argentina," *Cuadernos Americanos,* XV, No. 4 (July-Aug., 1956), 7–34.—In 1955 Argentina was at a crossroads. More than anything else the republic needed a prolonged period of social, economic, and political stability, the prospects for which were not entirely favorable.

Rennie, Robert A. "Argentine Fiscal Policy," *Inter-American Economic Affairs,* I, No. 1 (June 1947), 51–76.—The scope and significance of changes in fiscal policy following the coup of June 4, 1943.

Rennie, Ysabel. *The Argentine Republic.* New York, 1945.—Scholarly, well-written, synthetic history of Argentina with interesting interpretations of the developments leading up to the military coup of 1943.

Repetto, Nicolás. *Política internacional.* Buenos Aires, 1943.—Generally critical addresses on the state of the Argentine nation by a leader of the Socialist Party.

Rojas, Ricardo. *Blasón de Plata.* 4th ed. Buenos Aires, 1940.—Nationalism stimulated by preparations to observe the centenary of independence in 1910.

———. *Eurindia.* Buenos Aires, 1924.—The title is supposed to suggest the merging of European and indigenous cultures to form a new way of life in America.

———. *La guerra de las naciones.* Buenos Aires, 1924.—Argentina should have entered the war as it would have provided an opportunity to further nationalistic aspirations.

Romero, José Luis. *Argentina: imágenes y perspectivas.* Buenos Aires, 1956.—A collection of essays by one of Argentine's outstanding historians.

———. *Las ideas políticas en Argentina.* Mexico, 1946.—Authoritarianism, liberalism, democracy to 1930 with the stress on the era to 1910. Sees revolution of 1890 as a struggle between the landed oligarchy and the urban middle sectors.

Saavedra Lamas, Carlos. *Luis María Drago; su obra, proyecciones y trascendencia.* Buenos Aires, 1943.—The contributions of a distinguished Argentine statesman and authority on international law by a fellow countryman who, as a statesman, won the Nobel Peace Prize.

Sammartino, Ernesto E. *La verdad sobre la situación argentina.* Montevideo, 1950.—One of the more reasoned but nonetheless strong attacks upon the Perón government.

Sánchez Zinny, Eduardo F. *La revolución inconclusa.* Buenos Aires, 1943.—The revolution of 1943 opened a new and better era in Argentine history during which the objectives of 1810 would finally be realized.

Santos Gollán, José. "Argentine Interregnum," *Foreign Affairs,* XXXV, No. 1 (October 1956), 84–94.—Divergent forces joined to overthrow Perón. With the removal of the common enemy traditional rivalries reappeared.

Silva, Carlos A. *La política internacional de la nación Argentina.* Buenos Aires, 1946.—A chronology of Argentine foreign policy. Laudatory.

Síntesis estadística mensual de la República Argentina, I. Buenos Aires, 1947—.—Demographic and economic data in quantity, issued by the Dirección General de Estadística.

"The Situation in Argentina and the New Economic Policy," *Economic Bulletin for Latin America,* I, No. 1 (January 1956), 26–45.—Contains highly pertinent economic data.

Sommi, Luis V. *Los capitales alemanes en la Argentina, historia de su expansión.* Buenos Aires, [1945].—Factual.

———. *La revolución del 90.* Buenos Aires, 1948.—Political-social explanation of the overthrow of Celmán.

Taylor, Carl C. *Rural Life in Argentina.* Baton Rouge, La., 1948.—A careful study of the rural contribution to national life. Particularly significant observations on the role of the "newcomer" to Argentina.

Tinker, Edward Larocque. "The Cult of the Gaucho and the Creation of a Literature," *American Antiquarian Society, Proceedings,* LVII, Pt. 2 (1947), 308–48.—The legend of the gaucho has become a national symbol around which various elements, including the recent arrivals in Argentina, rally.

United States, Tariff Commission. *Mining and Manufacturing Industries in Argentina.* Washington, D.C., 1949.

Urruela, Rafael J. *Argentine Journey.* New Orleans, 1948.—Highly eulogistic of Perón by the founder and first director of the Office of International Relations of the City of New Orleans.

Vedia y Mitre, Mariano de. *La revolución del 90.* Buenos Aires, 1929.—Causes and consequences of the revolution of 1890 and the origins of the U.C.R.

Villafañe, Benjamin. *Irigoyen el último dictador.* 6th ed. Buenos Aires, 1922.—A vitriolic attack which associates Irigoyen with Quiroga and Rosas.

Whitaker, Arthur P. *Argentine Upheaval.* New York, 1956.—A "wrap-up" of the Perón dictatorship and a look into the future.

———. *The United States and Argentina.* Cambridge, Mass., 1954. Broader than the title suggests, this study presents a sound basis for an understanding of the collapse of democratic government and the rise of dictatorship after 1943.

Z. "Argentina in The Tunnel," *Foreign Affairs,* XXX, No. 3 (April 1952), 391–401.—Perón's system was his own but he borrowed from the teachings of Hitler, Stalin, and Mussolini.

Zorraquín Becú, Ricardo. *El federalismo argentino.* Buenos Aires, 1939.—Conservative, protectionist interior versus liberal, free-trade and "immigrant" Buenos Aires. The capital has triumphed and federalism does not exist in fact.

CHAPTER 7

Mexico in the twentieth century is stressed in the studies included in this section.

Alemán, Miguel. *Program of Government.* San Antonio, 1946.—A pamphlet in support of Alemán's candidacy for the presidency.

Alzati, Servando A. *Historia de la mexicanización de los ferrocarriles nacionales de México.* Mexico, 1946.—Concerned primarily with the replacement of foreign operatives by Mexicans and the formation of the Union of Mexican Railroad Employees to 1913. A concluding chapter brings the story to 1933.

American Academy of Political and Social Science. *Mexico Today,* in "The Annals," CCVIII, No. 208 (March 1940). Philadelphia, 1940.—The entire issue is devoted to Mexico and contains articles by seventeen Mexicans and North Americans, each an expert in the field in which he writes.

―――. *The Purposes and Ideals of the Mexican Revolution,* in "The Annals," LXIX, No. 158 (January 1917), Supplement. Philadelphia, 1917.—Four of the five contributors were high officials in the Mexican Government.

Armour Research Foundation. *Technological Audit of Selected Mexican Industries with Industrial Research Recommendations.* Chicago, 1946.—Results of a survey conducted at the request of the Banco de México, S.A. Calls attention to certain developments in the Mexican economy which tended to dim an otherwise relatively bright picture.

Aubrey, Henry G. "Structure and Balance in Rapid Economic Growth: The Example of Mexico." *Political Science Quarterly,* LXIX, No. 4 (December 1954), 517–40.—Excellent.

Ávila Camacho, Manuel. *México coopera con las naciones aliadas.* Mexico, 1944.—An appeal by the president of the republic for unity in the face of the Fascist threat.

Azuela, Mariano. *Two Novels of Mexico: The Flies. The Bosses.* Translated by Lesley Byrd Simpson. Berkeley, 1956.—Bitter attacks upon the conduct of the middle sectors during the Revolution.

Bal y Gay, Jesús. "El nacionalismo y la música mexicana de hoy," *Nuestra música,* IV (April 1949), 107–13.—A reasoned statement.

Beals, Carleton. *Porfirio Díaz; Dictator of Mexico.* Philadelphia, 1932.—Written from a liberal point of view, the author finds little in Díaz's favor after he came to power.

Beteta, Ramón. *The Mexican Revolution: a Defense.* Mexico, 1937.—Lectures delivered in the United States from 1930 to 1935.

―――. *Pensamiento y dinámica de la revolución mexicana.* Mexico, 1950.—A sympathetic statement of the economic and social philosophy of the Alemán administration, but criticizes certain shortcomings of the regime.

Booth, George C. *Mexico's School-Made Society.* Stanford, 1941.—Education as a reflection of political philosophy in the 1930's.

Bosch García, Pedro. *Antecedentes para el control de las empresas del estado en México.* Mexico, 1947.—Suggests ways that the government-controlled enterprises might more efficiently fulfill their functions.

Bulnes, Francisco. *Los grandes problemas de México.* Mexico, 1927.—Brief essays on personages and problems by a conservative.

―――. *El verdadero Díaz y la revolución.* Mexico, 1920.—A vicious attack upon the system that obtained under Díaz.

[Cabrera, Luis.] *La revolución de entonces (y la de ahora).* Mexico,

1937.—Compares objectives of the 1910–17 period with those at the time he wrote. The author, one of the original revolutionaries, felt that the liberties provided for in the Constitution of 1917 were being abrogated and that Mexico was heading toward a dictatorship

Callcott, Wilfrid H. *Liberalism in Mexico, 1857–1929.* Stanford, 1931.— Scholarly and impartial.

Carreño, Alberto María. "Las clases sociales de México," *Revista mexicana de sociología,* XII, No. 3 (Sept.-Dec., 1950), 333–50.—Primarily concerned with the middle sectors after World War II. Their grave economic conditions demanded serious public attention.

———. *La evolución económica de México en los últimos cincuenta años.* Mexico, 1937.—Corruption and neglect of the industrial investor were among the serious problems confronting the Mexican industrial sector at the time of writing.

Caso, Antonio. *Discursos a la nación mexicana.* Mexico, 1922.—Essays on Mexican culture and philosophy by one of the nation's most respected intellectuals.

———. *México.* Mexico, 1943.—A brief but thoughtful examination of Mexican civilization and intellectual life.

Castillo, José R. del. *Historia de la revolución social de México: la caída de General Díaz.* Mexico, 1915.—A primary source for the early months of the Revolution.

Chico Goerne, Luis. *Hacia una filosofía social en el siglo XX.* Mexico, 1943.—The Revolution, a nationalist movement with strong Indianist manifestations, made its greatest strides under President Cárdenas.

Clark, Marjorie Ruth. *Organized Labor in Mexico.* Chapel Hill, N.C., 1934.—Scholarly account of the labor movement to 1929.

Cline, Howard F. *The United States and Mexico.* Cambridge, Mass., 1953.—Much more inclusive than the title suggests, this is one of the clearest presentations and in the opinion of this author the most plausible interpretation thus far written of the Mexican Revolution of 1910 and its aftermath.

Combined Mexican Working Party. *The Economic Development of Mexico, Report.* Baltimore, 1953.—An examination of the Mexican economy between 1939 and 1950. The *Report* finds the policies of the national government largely responsible for the imbalance in the economy. Contains highly useful statistical data.

Cumberland, Charles Curtis. *Mexican Revolution: Genesis Under Madero.* Austin, 1952.—The political and military background to a major social revolution.

———. "Precursors of the Mexican Revolution of 1910." *Hispanic American Historical Review,* XXII, No. 2 (May 1942), 344–56.— Attention is focused on Ricardo Flores Magón.

Durán Ochoa, Julio. "El crecimiento de la población mexicana," *El trimestre económico,* XXII, No. 3 (July-Sept., 1955), 331–49.— Emphasis is on population growth in Mexico since 1920. Contains some data on urban expansion.

———. *Población,* Mexico, 1955.—A good demographic survey and examination of the problems presented by Mexico's rapidly growing population.

Ebenstein, William. "Public Administration in Mexico," *Public Administration Review,* V, No. 2 (Spring, 1945), 102–12.—Contains significant observations on the Mexican civil service.

Echánove Trujillo, Carlos A. *Sociología mexicana.* Mexico, 1948.— Among other things, the author finds that racial prejudices exist in Mexico.

Flower, Elizabeth. "The Mexican Revolt Against Positivism," *Journal of the History of Ideas,* X, No. 1 (January 1949), 115–29.—Why positivism was introduced into Mexico, the form it took, and Antonio Caso's opposition to it.

Fuentes Mares, José. *México en la hispanidad.* Madrid, 1949.—Mexican culture, an adaptation of Hispanic culture, will retain its identity.

Galarza, Ernesto. *La industria eléctrica en México,* Mexico, 1941.— Carefully done.

Gamio, Manuel. *Algunas consideraciones sobre la salubridad y la demografía en México.* Mexico, 1939.—Sees considerable advantage to be derived from further mixing of the European and Indian strains in Mexico.

———. "Cultural Patterns in Modern Mexico," *The Quarterly Journal of Inter-American Relations,* I, No. 2 (April 1939), 49–61.—The adaptation of the Indian and the European to the Mexican environment goes far to explain the republic's cultural pattern.

———. *Forjando patria (pro nacionalismo).* Mexico, 1916.—Argues for unity of the Mexican people through racial and cultural fusion and greater economic equality.

Germán Parra, Manuel. *La industrialización de México,* Mexico, 1954. —In answer to the thesis set forth by Tannenbaum in his volume *Mexico, the Struggle for Peace and Bread, q.v.,* the author insists that the industrial process in Mexico is not the product of economic policy but on the contrary economic policy is a reflection of the industrial revolution that Mexico has been undergoing.

González Peña, Carlos. *History of Mexican Literature.* Rev. ed. Translated by G. B. Nance and F. J. Dunstan. Dallas, 1943.—The author is generally considered to be one of the outstanding critics of Mexican literature.

González Ramírez, Manuel. "La política internacional de la revolución mexicana," *Cuadernos Americanos,* XIV, No. 4 (July-Aug., 1955), 27–48.—Finds that Mexico's international policies have been fitted into a framework of regionalism and nationalism.

Goodspeed, Stephen S. "The Role of the Chief Executive in Mexico: Policies, Powers, and Administration," Unpublished doctoral dissertation, University of California (Berkeley), 1947.—The president is all powerful since the Constitution gives him many prerogatives and he controls the only political party.

Gordon, Wendell C. *The Expropriation of Foreign-Owned Property in Mexico.* Washington, D.C., 1941.—Written before the dispute was settled the conclusion was that the interested nations should accept the situation and reach an amiable agreement.

Great Britain, Board of Trade. *Mexico: Economic and Commercial Conditions in Mexico . . . 1949,* in "Overseas Economic Surveys," London, 1949.

Great Britain, Department of Overseas Trade. *Report on Economic and Financial Conditions in Mexico, 1920–1921.* London, 1921.

Gutiérrez Santos, Daniel. *Historia militar de México, 1876–1914.* Mexico, 1955.—The author, a professor in the Escuela Superior de Guerra, limits himself to synthesizing what others have said. Of the four chapters in the book the second, which deals with the campaigns against the Yaquis and the Mayas and the army's role in the Cananea and Río Blanco strikes, is of particular interest.

Guzmán, Martín L. *The Eagle and the Serpent.* Translated by Harriet de Onís. New York, 1930.—Out of the heat of battle, this novel brings the Revolution down to the level of the common man.

Haight, Charles Henry. "The Contemporary Mexican Revolution as Viewed by Mexican Intellectuals," Unpublished doctoral dissertation, Stanford University, 1956.—Finds that generally speaking intellectuals have not been satisfied with achievements since 1945.

Hayner, Norman S. "Notes on the Changing Mexican Family," *American Sociological Review,* VII, No. 4 (August 1942), 489–97.—Significant observations on changes taking place in the family life of the urban middle sectors.

Hewes, Gordon W. "Mexicans in Search of the 'Mexican': Notes on Mexican National Character Studies," *The American Journal of Economics and Sociology,* XIII, No. 2 (January 1954), 209–23.— Mexican national character studies, with few exceptions have been "impressionistic, intuitive, or speculative." Some authors have been influenced by psychoanalysis and the social sciences.

Hoselitz, Bert. F. "Mexican Social Structure and Economic Development," *Economic Development and Cultural Change,* I, No. 3 (October 1952), 236–40.—This review article on *La estructura social y cultural de México,* Mexico, 1951, by José E. Iturriaga serves to point up some of the shortcomings of the social sciences in Latin America.

Humphrey, Norman D. "Ethnic Images and Stereotypes of Mexicans and Americans," *The American Journal of Economics and Sociology,* XIV, No. 3 (April 1955), 305–13.

Johnston, Marjorie C. *Education in Mexico.* Washington, D.C., 1956. —Useful primarily for the statistical material it contains.

Kneller, George F. *The Education of the Mexican Nation.* New York, 1951.—The Mexican education system in terms of the cultural inheritance of the people.

Lavín, José Domingo. *Petróleo; pasado, presente y futuro de una industria mexicana.* Mexico, 1950.—A strong defense of a national petroleum industry.

———. *Revisión de la industria petrolera mexicana.* Mexico, 1955.—A vigorous defense of expropriation. The petroleum resources of Mexico should be exploited by Mexicans for Mexicans.

Lombardo Toledano, Vicente. *Definición de la nación mexicana.* Mexico, 1943.—An address given in commemoration of Lenin.

López Alvarez, Francisco. *La administración pública y la vida económica de México.* Mexico, 1955.—The historical development of public administration in Mexico and the social and economic concepts it has reflected since 1917.

López Aparicio, Alfonso. *El movimiento obrero en México.* Mexico, 1952.—The most comprehensive study of the Mexican labor movement to date.

López-Portilla y Rojas, José. *Elevación y caída de Porfirio Díaz.* Mexico [1921]. A classic on the period.

López y Fuentes, Gregorio. *El Indio.* Translated by Anita Brenner. New York, 1937.—One of better known novels to come out of the Mexican Revolution.

Loyo, Gilberto. *Esquema demográfico de México.* Mexico, 1948.— Favors population increase if necessary through immigration.

Macín, Francisco J. *Los salarios en México.* México, 1947.—Wages, cost of living, and suggestions for improvement of conditions for the workingman.

Madero, Francisco I. *La sucesión presidencial en 1910.* 3d ed. Mexico, 1911.—The work that aroused the middle groups to action against Díaz.

Méjico revolucionario, a los pueblos de Europa y América, 1910-1918. Habana [1918?].—Manifestoes and decrees signed by Emiliano Zapata.

Mendieta y Núñez, Lucio. "La clase media en México," *Revista mexicana de sociología,* XVII, Nos. 2-3 (May-Dec., 1955), 517-31.—The middle sectors, which are highly fluid, are the conservators of national qualities and consequently it is necessary to strengthen their position.

———. "Ensayo sociológico sobre la burocracia mexicana," *Revista mexicana de sociología,* III, No. 3 (Sept.-Dec., 1941), 63-111.—Deals with the bureaucracy within the administrative framework, its composition and characteristics. The conclusion is that the bureaucrat in Mexico leaves considerable to be desired.

———. *La administración pública en México.* Mexico, 1943.—Quite critical of corruption in government, this is one of the outstanding studies on public administration to appear on Latin America.

Mexican Year Book; the Standard Authority on Mexico, 1920/21-1922/24. Los Angeles, 1922-24.

Mexico. Constitution. *The Mexican Constitution of 1917 Compared With the Constitution of 1857.* Translated and arranged by H. N. Branch. Philadelphia, 1917.—Highly useful supplement to the *Annals* of the American Academy of Political and Social Science.

———. Departamento de la Estadística Nacional. *Censo general de habitantes, 30 de noviembre de 1921.* 16 vols. in 3. Mexico, 1925-28.

———. Departamento del Trabajo. *Policies of the Present Administration of Mexico.* Mexico, 1936. Official statement of achievements during the first year of the "Six Year Plan" of the Lázaro Cárdenas administration, with particular attention to labor policies.

———. Ministerio de Hacienda y Crédito Público. *Anuario de estadística fiscal, 1911-1912* [. . . *1912-13, 1918-1919*]. 4 vols. Mexico, 1913-1922.

———. Secretaría de Economía, Dirección de Estudios Económicos. *Desarrollo de la economía nacional, 1939-1947.* Mexico, 1947.

———. Secretaría de la Economía Nacional. *Revista de economía y estadística.* Mexico, 1933—.

————. Secretaría de Gobernación. *Seis años de gobierno al servicio de México, 1934–1940.* Mexico, 1940.—Review of the accomplishments of the Cárdenas administration.

————. Secretaría de Relaciones Exteriores. *The Mexican Government in the Presence of Social and Economic Problems.* 8 vols. Mexico, 1936.

————. Suprema Corte de Justicia. *Decision Rendered by the Supreme Court of Mexico in the Oil Expropriation Case.* Translated by Attorney Oscar Rabasa. Mexico, 1940.

Mexico, Dirección de Estadística Económica. *Aspectos estadísticos de un quinquenio, 1921–1925.* Mexico, 1927.

Mexico, Dirección General de Estadística. *Anuario estadístico de los Estados Unidos Mexicanos.* Mexico, 1893–1907.

————. *Censo de funcionarios y empleados públicos, 30 de noviembre de 1930.* Mexico, 1934.

————. *Quinto censo de población, 15 de mayo de 1930.* Mexico, 1932—.

————. *Primer censo industrial de 1930, resúmenes generales por entidades.* Mexico, 1933.

————. *Segundo censo industrial de 1935.* Mexico, 1936–37.

————. *Tercer censo industrial de los Estados Unidos Mexicanos, 1940.* 4 vols. Mexico, 1943–44.

————. *Cuarto censo industrial de los Estados Unidos Mexicanos . . . 1945;resumen general.* Mexico, 1953.

————. *Segundo censo comercial de los Estados Unidos Mexicanos, 1945; resumen general.* Mexico, 1950.

————. *Cuadro sinóptico y estadístico de la República Mexicana . . . año de 1900.* Mexico, 1901.

————. *Séptimo censo general de población, 6 de junio de 1950; resumen general.* [Mexico, 1953.]

————. *6° censo de población, 1940.* Mexico, 1943—.

————. *Memoria de los censos generales de población agrícola, ganadero, y ejidal, 1950.* Mexico, 1952.

Mexico (City), Universidad Nacional, Escuela Nacional de Economía. *La intervención del estado en la economía.* Mexico, 1955.—A collaborative work that provides a cross section of center and left-of-center thinking on state intervention.

————. *Niveles de vida y desarrollo económico.* Mexico, 1953. The Mexican economy in national and international terms by a number of contributors.

Millán, Verna Carleton. *Mexico Reborn.* Boston, 1939.—An unusually keen sense of developments in Mexico under Cárdenas, who is warmly defended.

Molina Enriques, Andrés. *Los grandes problemas nacionales.* Mexico, 1909.—One of the works that most profoundly affected the thinking that came out of the Revolution. The sections dealing with politics are particularly perceptive.

Moore, Wilbert E. *Industrialization and Labor: Social Aspects of Economic Development.* Ithaca, N.Y., 1951.—Chapters IX, X, and XI offer some significant insights on the social conditions arising from industrial development in Mexico.

Morton, F. Rand. *Los novelistas de la revolución mexicana.* Mexico, 1949.—A major portion of the volume is devoted to well-known writers. A short conclusion seeks to establish the social, historical, and literary worth of the novels.

Mosk, Sanford A. *Industrial Revolution in Mexico.* Berkeley, 1950.—An expert diagnosis of the strengths and weaknesses of Mexico as it girded itself for moving ahead industrially.

Myers, Margaret G. "Mexico," in *Banking Systems,* Benjamin Haggott Beckhart, ed. New York, 1954. Pp. 573–607.—Useful discussion of practices and policies of national and private financial institutions up to 1950.

Navarrete, Alfredo, Jr. "Productividad, ocupación y desocupación en México: 1940–1965," *El trimestre económico,* XXIII, No. 4 (Oct.-Dec., 1956), 415–23.—The author leaves little doubt as to the problem Mexico faces in providing employment for the 250,000 who enter the labor pool each year.

Niemeyer, E. V., Jr. "Anticlericalism in the Mexican Constitutional Convention of 1916–1917," *The Americas,* XI, No. 1 (July 1954), 31–49.—Concerned with the debates which led to the writing of the anticlerical articles 3, 24, and 130.

Palavicini, Félix F. *Grandes de México.* Mexico, 1948.—Personalities of the twentieth century who played a leading role in the creation and implementation of Mexico's social and economic policies.

———. *Historia de la Constitución de 1917.* 2 vols., Mexico, 1938.—Contains debates held during the writing of the constitution.

Palermo, Angel. "Notas sobre la clase media en Mexico," in Pan American Union, *Ciencias sociales,* III, Nos. 14 & 15 (April-June, 1952), 18–27; No. 18 (December 1952), 129–35.—The author holds that the middle classes of Mexico during most of the nineteenth century were a carry-over from the colonial period. The middle sectors that began to develop under Díaz consciously imitated Europe and the United States.

Pan American Union, Department of International Law. *A Statement of the Laws of Mexico in Matters Affecting Business.* 2d ed., Washington, D.C., 1955.

Partido Nacional Revolucionario. *La democracia social en México: historia de la convención nacional revolucionaria.* Mexico, 1929.—A statement of the original objectives of the party.

———. *The Mexican Government's Six Year Plan, 1934–1940 . . . and General Lázaro Cárdenas' Nomination Address.* Mexico, 1934. —Written on orders of Calles, the plan became the basis for Cárdenas' "radical" administration.

Partido de la Revolución Mexicana. *The Second Six Year Plan, 1941–1946.* Mexico? [1939?].—A statement of objectives for the Camacho administration. Official plan plus several documents and speeches.

Peña, M. T. de la. "La expropiación de los ferrocarriles nacionales de México," *El trimestre económico,* IV, No. 3 (1937), 195–226.—Nearly equal attention is paid to the historical antecedents of expropriation and the consequences, especially financial and administrative, therof.

Phillips, Richard Baker. "José Vasconcelos and the Mexican Revolution of 1910." Unpublished doctoral dissertation. Stanford University, 1953.

Portes Gil, Emilio. *The Conflict Between the Civil Power and the Clergy; Historical and Legal Essay.* Mexico, 1935.—A statement by a past president and at the time of writing a high officer in the Mexican government. Church-State relations were tense.

――――. *Quince Años de política mexicana.* 2d ed. Mexico, 1941.—Some background material but largely a defense of the author's presidency.

――――. *The Railroads of Mexico.* Boston, 1921.—History and administration of the Mexican railroads. Good statistical data.

Powell, J. Richard. *The Mexican Petroleum Industry, 1938–1950.* Berkeley, 1956.—Expropriation cannot be judged from only an economic point of view.

Prewett, Virginia. "The Mexican Army," *Foreign Affairs,* XIX, No. 3 (April 1941), 609–20.—The development of the Mexican army after 1920 as a basis for judging its ability to contribute to hemispheric defense and its role in government.

Quirk, Robert E. "Liberales y radicales en la Revolución mexicana," *Historia mexicana,* II, No. 4 (April-June 1953), 503–28.—Compares the political, economic, and social convictions of Carranza, Villa, and Zapata, especially during 1913–16.

Rabasa, Emilio. *La constitución y la dictadura; estudio sobre la organización política de México.* 3d ed. Mexico, 1912.—Dictators may bring material progress without resolving basic political problems.

Radvanyi, Laszlo. "Ten Years of Sample Surveying in Mexico," *International Journal of Opinion and Attitude Research,* V, No. 4 (Winter, 1951–52), 491–510.—Experience gained in carrying out eighty-six surveys in Mexico, mainly Mexico City. Sample surveying has great potential in the area.

Ramos, Samuel. *El perfil del hombre y la cultura en México.* Mexico, 1934.—Mexican culture analyzed. The author finds a strong tendency for the Mexican to look abroad for his values. Highly recommended.

Rivera Marín, Guadalupe. "Los conflictos de trabajo en Mexico, 1937–1950," *El Trimestre económico,* XXII, No. 2 (April-June, 1955), 181–208.—Seeks to establish the number of strikes, reasons for them, and the government's role in the settling of labor-management disputes.

Robles, Gonzalo. "Noticia sobre la industrialización de México," *El trimestre económico,* XI, No. 2 (July-Sept., 1944), 256–83.—Industrial development is viewed historically from the pre-conquest era. A good brief account.

Roeder, Ralph. *Juárez and His Mexico.* 2 vols., New York, 1947.—The fullest study of Juárez in English.

Rolland, Modesto C. *Desastre municipal en la república mexicana.* 2d ed., Mexico, 1939.—Asks for new laws to control politicians at the municipal level. Questions the adequacy of the civil service system, and seeks a refinement of the tax structure with a view to relieving the pressure on the working groups.

Romanell, Patrick. *Making of the Mexican Mind.* Lincoln, Neb., 1952. Surveys philosophical thinking in Mexico during this century through the writings of a number of recognized Mexican authorities.

Ross, Stanley R. *Francisco I. Madero; Apostle of Mexican Democracy.* New York, 1955.—A well-written and objective account of the man and his times.

Sedwitz, Walter J. "Mexico's 1954 Devaluation in Retrospect," *Inter-American Economic Affairs,* X, No. 2 (Autumn, 1956), 22–44.— Frequent devaluation in Mexico seems to mirror certain weaknesses in monetary and fiscal policy rather than long-run structural difficulties.

Serrano, Gustavo P. *La minería y su influencia en el progreso y desarrollo de México.* Mexico, 1951.—Brief examination of the economic, demographic, and cultural impact of mining.

Servín, Armando. *Las finanzas públicas locales durante los últimos cincuenta años.* Mexico, 1956.—Statistical. Compares expenditures at the local, state and national levels.

Sierra, Justo. *Evolución política del pueblo mexicano.* Edited and annotated by Edmundo O'Gorman. Mexico, 1948.—First published in 1901, this synthesis has attained the stature of a classic among Mexican social documents.

——. *Mexico, Its Social Evolution; Synthesis of the Political History, Administration, Military Organization, and Economical State of the Mexican Confederation.* 2 vols in 3, Mexico. 1900–1904.

Silva Herzog, Jesús. "La epopeya del petróleo en México," *Cuadernos Americanos,* XII, No. 1 (Jan.-Feb., 1953), 7–63.—Pronouncedly antiforeign. Objects to permitting U.S. petroleum development companies to return to Mexico.

——. *Meditaciones sobre México; ensayos y notas.* Mexico, 1948.— Essays on a variety of subjects. A strong anticlerical bias is apparent.

——. *Nueve estudios mexicanos.* Mexico, 1953.—Essays on geography and economics with a view to determining the status of the Mexican Revolution.

——. *Petróleo mexicano, historia de un problema,* Mexico, 1941.—A strong defense of expropriation.

——. *Un ensayo sobre la revolución mexicana.* Mexico, 1946.—Seeks to explain the growth of the revolutionary ideology in Mexico.

Simpson, Eyler N. *The Ejido; Mexico's Way Out.* Chapel Hill, N.C., 1937.—Strong on statistics and somewhat weak on interpretation.

Simpson, Lesley Byrd. *Many Mexicos.* 3d ed. Rev. and enl. Berkeley, 1952. A "tough" objective history of Mexico from pre-conquent times to the present. Highly recommended.

Strode, Hudson. *Timeless Mexico.* New York [1944].—Primarily concerned with the period since 1910, the author is quite friendly to Cárdenas.

Sturmthal, Adolf. "Economic Development, Income Distribution, and Capital Formation in Mexico," *The Journal of Political Economy,* LXIII, No. 3 (June 1955), 183–201.—An excellent pulling-together of materials relating to some recent economic developments in Mexico. The most urgent economic need is to reduce agricultural underemployment.

Tannenbaum, Frank. _Mexico, the Struggle for Peace and Bread._ New York, 1950.—Acute insights into Mexico's basic social and economic problems by an "old pro." The author's implied recommendations on the future orientation of industry aroused a storm of protest in Mexico.

———. _Peace by Revolution; an Interpretation of Mexico._ New York, 1933.—It may be that no one sensed the meaning of the Mexican Revolution as well as did Tannenbaum at the time he wrote this volume.

———. "Personal Government in Mexico," _Foreign Affairs,_ XXVII, No. 1 (October 1948), 44–57.—"The government of Mexico is the president. There is no other way of expressing it."

———. "Technology and Race in Mexico," _Political Science Quarterly,_ LXI, No. 3 (September 1946), 365–83.—Primarily concerned with developments in the numerous villages where the Indian and mestizo predominates.

Thomson, Charles A. "Mexican Challenge to Foreign Capital," _Foreign Policy Reports,_ XIII, No. 11 (August 15, 1937), 126–36.—Largely background to the expropriation issue.

———. "Mexico's Social Revolution," _Foreign Policy Reports,_ XIII, No. 10 (August 1, 1937), 114–24.—The stress is upon the economic aspects of Cardenas' social program.

Townsend, William C. _Lázaro Cárdenas; Mexican Democrat._ Ann Arbor, 1952.—Although on the adulatory side, this book has considerable value in that the author was a personal friend of Cárdenas and thus was able to include many personal anecdotes in his study.

Tucker, William P. _The Mexican Government Today._ Minneapolis, 1957.—Comprehensive and generally optimistic of Mexico's political future.

United States. Tariff Commission. _Mining and Manufacturing Industries in Mexico._ Washington, D.C., 1946.

United States Department of Commerce, Bureau of Foreign Commerce. _Investment in Mexico, Conditions and Outlook for United States Investors._ Washington, D.C., 1956.

Uribe Romo, Emilio. "México y las implicaciones demográficas de la postguerra," _Revista mexicana de sociología,_ IX, No. 3 (Sept.-Dec., 1947), 315–40.—Mexico has many problems but the biggest one is the incorporation of the Indian into the Mexican nationality.

Vasconcelos, José. _Apuntes para la historia de México, desde la conquista hasta la Revolución de 1910._ Mexico, 1943.—Concludes that the ills of Mexico are the Indian, the mestizo, a form of government too advanced for the people, poverty of the government, the influence of the United States, and the persecution of the Catholic Church. Mexico needed a strong paternal government.

———. _Breve historia de México._ 6th ed. Madrid, 1952.—Almost but not quite recommends a return to Spanish colonialism.

Vasconcelos, José and Manuel Gamio. _Aspects of Mexican Civilization._ Chicago [1926]. — Vasconcelos concerns himself with the Latin

American basis of Mexican civilization; Gamio with the Indian basis.

Villoro, Luis. *Los grandes momentos del indigenismo en México.* Mexico, 1950.—The Indian in the Mexican conscience from Córtes to the present.

———. "Raíz del indigenismo en México," *Cuadernos Americanos,* XI, No. 1 (Jan.-Feb., 1952), 36–49.—Considerable attention is paid to the Indian in terms of his contribution to the formation of the mestizo element of society.

Whetten, Nathan L. *Rural Mexico.* Chicago, 1948.—Perhaps more optimistic for the future of Mexico than the evidence warranted. A storehouse of facts and figures.

———. "The Rise of the Middle Class in Mexico," *Materiales para el estudio de la clase media en la América Latina,* II, 1-29. Unión Panamericana, La oficina de ciencias sociales, Departamento de asuntos culturales. Washington, D.C., 1950.

Wythe, George. "Farms or Factories: Three Views of Mexico's Industrial Revolution," *Inter-American Economic Affairs,* IV, No. 1 (Summer, 1950), 35–43.—Brief examinations of the studies of Mosk, Whetten, and Tannenbaum.

Zavala, Silvio Arturo. *Aproximaciones a la historia de México.* Mexico, 1953.—Local and foreign factors contributing to the formation of the Mexican nationality.

———. "El mexicano en sus contactos con el exterior," *Cuadernos Americanos,* XI, No. 6 (Nov.-Dec., 1952), 75–92.—Objective. In its relations with the remainder of Latin America, the United States, and Spain, Mexico has considerable to gain and in turn much to contribute.

Zea, Leopoldo. *Apogeo y decadencia del positivismo en México.* Mexico, 1944.—Reasoned examination of the political philosophy that had such a profound impact upon social and economic development during the last two decades of Díaz' rule. A sequel to the author's *El positivismo* . . .

———. *Del liberalismo a la revolución en la educación mexicana.* Mexico, 1956.—Good on the nineteenth-century background of the educational system that developed under the Constitution of 1917.

———. *El positivismo en México.* Mexico, 1943.—The most mature study yet to appear on the conditions in Mexico that led to the rise and fall of positivism.

———. *El occidente y la conciencia de México.* Mexico, 1953.—A survey of the development of the Mexican mentality with considerable attention to the Revolution of 1910.

CHAPTER 8

The entries in this section are concerned chiefly with Brazil in the twentieth century.

Alexander, Robert J. "Brazilian Tenentismo," *Hispanic American Historical Review,* XXXVI, No. 2 (May 1956), 229–42.—Examination of an indigenous, radical, nationalist movement within the military during the 1920's, certain leaders of which continue significantly to affect Brazilian national politics.

———. "Brazil's CP: A Case Study in Latin-American Communism," in United States Information Agency, *Problems of Communism,* IV, No. 5 (Sept.-Oct., 1955), 17–26.—History and current status of the Party, then the largest in Latin America.

Amoroso Lima, Alceu. "The Direction of Brazilian Thought," *Life and Letters Today,* XXXVII (June 1943), 113–27.—The views of an outstanding Catholic layman.

———. "An Interpretation of Brazilian Politics," *Social Sciences,* XXVI, No. 4 (October 1951), 202–14.—Concise statement.

[Amoroso Lima, Alceu.] *Política.* 3d ed. Rio de Janeiro, 1939.—The last four chapters deal specifically with Brazil. The final chapter outlines the social, political, and economic responsibilities of Brazilian Catholics.

Andrade, Almir de. *Aspetos da cultura brasileira.* Rio de Janeiro, 1939. —Four thoughtful essays with considerable attention to the writings in the fields covered. Points to the lack of uniform development of Brazilian culture.

———. *Contribuição à história administrativa do Brasil, na República, até o ano 1945.* 2 vols. Rio de Janeiro, 1950.—Highly useful. Historical treatment of government actions on behalf of various economic commodities.

Aranha, Oswaldo, *A revolução e a América.* Rio de Janeiro, 1941.—A defense of Vargas' foreign policy by a high official of the Brazilian government.

Avila, Fernando Bastos de. *Economic Impacts of Immigration: the Brazilian Immigration Problem.* The Hague, 1954.—The author, a Catholic priest, holds that his country stands to gain much economically from immigration but that ultimately the economic factor is not acceptable as an appropriate criterion in determining scales of value.

Azevedo, Fernando de. *Brazilian Culture.* Translated by William R. Crawford. New York, 1950.—Monumental. Traces Brazil's cultural development from the colonial period to the 1930's, with considerable emphasis upon education. The first Portuguese edition, *A cultura brasileira* appeared in 1943.

Azevedo, Thales de. *Les élites de couleur dans une ville brésilienne.* Paris, 1953.—Social mobility among various ethnic groups in the city of Salvador da Bahia. Scholarly.

Baleeiro, Aliomar. *Rui, um estadista no Ministério de Fazenda.* Rio de Janeiro, 1952.—A brief, sympathetic account of the well-known statesman's contribution in the field of finance.

Baratz, Morton S. "The Crisis in Brazil," *Social Research,* XXII, No. 3 (October 1955), 347–61.—Background of events preceding Vargas' suicide and a brief glimpse into the future of Brazil.

Barretto, Castro. *Povoamento e população; política populacional brasileira.* Rio de Janeiro, 1951.—A general examination of demographic problems. Lacks depth.

Barros, Jayme de. *A política exterior do Brasil (1930–1940).* Rio de

Janeiro, 1941.—For all intents and purposes an official statement of Brazil's role in Western Hemisphere affairs during the first decade of Vargas' stewardship.

Bastos, Humberto. *A economia brasileira e o mundo moderno; ensaio geopolítico sobre a estruturação do capitalismo brasileiro*. São Paulo, 1948.—Scholarly. Traces Brazilian economic development from the colonial period and calls attention to current problems.

Bazzanella, Waldemiro. *Estratificação e mobilidade social no Brasil, fontes bibliográficas*. Rio de Janeiro, 1956.—A selective annotated bibliography of books and articles which deal with various aspects of the problem of social mobility and stratification in Brazil. A majority of the items have appeared since 1930.

Bello, José Maria. *História da república (1889–1945): adenda- 1945– 1954*. 3d ed. São Paulo, 1956.—An analytical synthesis of Brazilian political evolution since the founding of the republic. The finest objective treatment of Brazilian political dynamics after 1930.

———. *Panorama do Brasil: ensaio de interpretação da vida brasileira*. Rio de Janeiro, 1936.—Highly stimulating ideas.

———. *A questão social e a solução brasileira*. Rio de Janeiro, 1936.— Concerned primarily with development in the social and economic field between 1930–35.

Bishop, Dwight R. *Brazil: Agricultural Production and Trade Statistics*. Washington, D.C., 1951.

Brazil, Comissão Censitária Nacional. *Sinopse do censo demográfico, dados gerais*. Special ed. Rio de Janeiro, 1947.

———. *Sinopse do censo industrial e do censo dos serviços, dados gerais* (Recenseamento geral do Brasil, 1° de setembro de 1940). Rio de Janeiro, 1948.

Brazil, Conselho de Imigração e Colonização. *Revista de imigração e colonização*. Rio de Janeiro, 1940—.

Brazil, Conselho Nacional de Estatística. *Boletim estatístico*. Rio de Janeiro, 1943—.

———. *Sinopse estatística do município de São Paulo, Estado de São Paulo*. Rio de Janeiro, 1951.

Brazil, Constitution. *Complete Text of the Brazilian Constitution of 1934*. Translated by Ernest Hambloch. São Paulo, 1934.—Also contains the Brazilian Constitution of 1891 as amended in 1926.

———. *The New Constitution of the United States of Brazil, 1938*. São Paulo, 1938.—Although it was never given the force of law, the philosophy expressed in the document became, for the most part, that of the Estado Novo.

Brazil, Directoria Geral de Estatística. *Annuario estatístico do Brasil (1908–1912)*. 3 vols. Rio de Janeiro, 1916–1927.—Since 1936 this publication has been continued by the Instituto Brasileiro de Geografia e Estatística.

———. *Recenseamento do Brasil realizado em 1 de setembro de 1920*. 3 vols. Rio de Janeiro, 1922–1925.

———. *Recenseamento geral da república dos Estados Unidos do Brasil em 31 de dezembro de 1890*. Rio de Janeiro, 1895.

———. *Synopse do recenseamento realizado em 1 de setembro de 1920*.

Rio de Janeiro, 1924.—Coefficients of the Brazilian population by sex, civil status, and nationality in 1872, 1890, 1900, and 1920.

Brazil, Escritório de Propaganda e Expansão Comercial do Brasil no Estrangeiro, New York. *Corporations, Labor, and Tax System in Brazil.* New York, 1944.

Brazil, Instituto Brasileiro de Geografia e Estatística. *Estatística municipal; distribuição da população brasileira, segundo o domicílio.* Rio de Janeiro, 1950.

——. Conselho Nacional de Geografia. *Boletim geográfico.* Rio de Janeiro, 1943— —Useful for articles, legislation, notices, and bibliography.

Brazil, Ministério das Relações Exteriores. *Brazil, 1939–40.* Rio de Janeiro, 1940.—In English. A worthwhile compilation of pertinent statistical data.

Brazil, Ministério do Trabalho, Indústria, e Comércio. *O Ministério do Trabalho no Estado Novo.* Rio de Janeiro, 1941.—Report of the activities of the departments, services, and institutes in the years 1938, 1939 and 1940.

Brazil, Serviço de Estatística Econômica e Financeira. *Mensário estatístico,* Rio de Janeiro, 1951—.

Brazil, Serviço Nacional de Recenseamento. *Recenseamento geral do Brasil, 1. de julho de 1950. Sinopse preliminar do censo demográfico.* Rio de Janeiro, 1951.

——. *Recenseamento geral do Brasil, 1950. Sinopse preliminar do censo industrial.* Rio de Janeiro, 1952.

——. *VI [sexto] recenseamento geral do Brasil (1.-VII-1950):* Selected Tables of the Population Census. Rio de Janeiro, 1953.

Brazil, Tribunal Superior Eleitoral. *Dados estatísticos,* III, Pts. 1 and 2, Rio de Janeiro, 1957?—Part I contains statistics on federal, state, and municipal elections held in 1952, 1954, and 1955. Part 2 deals with federal and state elections held during 1954 and 1955.

Buarque de Hollanda, Sergio. *Raízes do Brasil.* 2d ed. Rio de Janeiro, 1948.—Highly perceptive. Brazilian development is painted in bold strokes, but urbanism and the shift of power from rural to urban areas receive more detailed treatment.

Calmon, Pedro. *Brasil e América, história de uma política.* 2d ed. Rio de Janeiro, 1944.—Largely relations between Brazil and the United States, but the influence of the remainder of Latin America and Europe upon those relations is not overlooked. Pleads for hemispheric unity.

——. *História da civilização brasileira.* 2d ed. ("Biblioteca Pedagógica Brasileira," 5th ser., vol. 14.) São Paulo, 1935.—A social, economic, administrative, and political synthesis, written for classroom use.

——. *História social do Brasil.* 3 vols. ("Biblioteca Pedagógica Brasileira," 5th ser., vols. 40, 83, 173.) São Paulo, 1937–39.—The second volume deals with the empire, the third with the republic to 1922. Treatment is chronological and as much political and economic as social.

Calogeras, João Pandía. *A History of Brazil.* Translated by Percy A.

Martin. Chapel Hill, N.C., 1939.—A standard reference work for the period to 1930.

Camacho, J. A. *Brazil: An Interim Assessment.* New York, 1952.— A useful reference.

Carneiro Leão, Antonio. *Os deveres das novas gerações brasileiras.* Rio de Janeiro, 1923.—Points up the need for broader education without sacrificing the best from the past.

——. *O sentido da evolução cultural do Brasil.* Rio de Janeiro, 1946. —The first chapter seeks to compare and contrast developments in the New World colonies of England, Spain, and Portugal. Three chapters are devoted to Brazilian education, the area of the author's special competence. One chapter is given to the problems of rural society.

Carvalho, Hernani de. *Sociologia da vida rural brasileira.* Rio de Janeiro, 1951.—Broad in scope. Pleads for greater recognition of the rural inhabitant both because of his backwardness and because of his inadequate contribution to national development.

Carvalho, Orlando M. *A crise dos partidos nacionais.* Belo Horizonte, 1950.—Calls attention to the need for a clearer appreciation of Brazilian political institutions.

——. "Os partidos políticos em Minas Gerais," *Revista brasileira de estudos políticos,* I, No. 2 (July 1957), 99–115.—A careful analysis of voting trends and the composition of political party leadership in Minas Gerais since 1945.

Castro Barretto. *Estudos brasileiros de população.* 2d ed. Rio de Janeiro, 1947.—Brazil's demographic problems within a world framework. Chapter I, "A criança é o melhor imigrante," and chapter VIII, "Formação das elites," are particularly relevant to the present study. Chapter VIII emphasizes education.

Coelho, Levindo. "Depoimento de un velho político mineiro," *Revista brasileira de estudos políticos,* I, No. 2 (July 1957), 116–31.—An account of political party organization and activities in Minas Gerais from 1900 to 1934 by a leader of the Partido Republicano Mineiro.

Conjuntura econômica. Rio de Janeiro, 1947—. Published by the Fundação Getúlio Vargas.—Articles are of generally good quality.

Costa, Affonso. *A marinha mercante no Brasil.* Rio de Janeiro, 1910.— A proposal for the reorganization of the merchant marine.

Cultura política; revista mensal de estudos brasileiros. Rio de Janeiro, 1941—.—Articles tend to be short, cover a broad area; well-established names contribute.

Cunha, Euclydes da. *Rebellion in the Backlands.* Translated from *Os Sertões* by Samuel Putnam. Chicago, 1944.—A critical account of conditions at the end of the nineteenth century.

Davis, Horace B. "Brazil's Political and Economic Problems," *Foreign Policy Reports,* XI, No. 1 (March 13, 1935), 1–12.—Monoculture, foreign capital, foreign debts, revolts, the Church are criticized. The Vargas regime is shown to be a failure in most respects.

Duncan, Julian Smith. *Public and Private Operation of Railways in Brazil.* New York, 1932.—More concerned with public than with private operations.

Fischlowitz, Estanislau. *Revolução contemporânea na política social.* Rio de Janeiro, 1951.—May be considered an official statement on labor, laboring classes, and public welfare.

Freyre, Gilberto. *Brazil: An Interpretation.* New York, 1945.—A brilliant interpretation of the Brazilian milieu except for one chapter in which the author moves out of his field of specialization and assumes the cloak of an authority on Brazilian international relations.

————. *Nação e exército.* Rio de Janeiro, 1949.—A veiled warning that the Brazilian military has tremendous political influence and must use it discreetly.

————. "Relación de la literatura moderna de Brasil con los problemas sociales brasileños," *Cuadernos Americanos,* IV, No. 3 (May–June, 1945), 114–33.—Art and letters to about 1900 were based upon European models. Satire was used effectively. Since the 1930's a new school has grown up that has intellectual and cultural spontaneity.

————. "Slavery, Monarchy, and Modern Brazil," *Foreign Affairs,* XXXIII, No. 4 (July 1955), 624–33.—The views of an outstanding social thinker.

Furtado, Celso. *A economia brasileira (contribuição à análise do seu desenvolvimento).* Rio de Janeiro, 1954.—A serious study with proposals that warrant attention.

Ganzert, Frederic William. "The Baron do Rio-Branco, Joaquim Nabuco, and the Growth of Brazilian-American Friendship, 1900–1910," *Hispanic American Historical Review,* XXII, No. 3 (August 1942), 432–51.—Furtherance of Pan-Americanism through close United States–Brazilian relations.

Gouvêa de Bulhões, Octávio. "Economia e nacionalismo," *Revista brasileira de economia,* VI, No. 1 (March 1952), 91–117.—Nationalism, which is discouraging economic growth, thrives because its advocates are still thinking in terms of the nineteenth century. They refuse to recognize that in this century national states have been able better to control foreign capital and to see that it produces for local consumption.

————. "Inflation and Industrialization," in *Four Papers Presented in the Institute for Brazilian Studies, Vanderbilt University.* Charles Wagley *et al.,* eds. Nashville, 1951. Pp. 33–55.—Inflation, foreign capital, and private enterprise as factors in the industrial process.

Great Britain, Board of Trade. *Brazil: Economic and Commercial Conditions in Brazil,* in "Export Promotion Department: Overseas Economic Surveys." London, 1954.

————. *Brazil, Report on Economic and Commercial Conditions in Brazil,* in "Export Promotion Department: Overseas Economic Surveys." London, 1948.

Great Britain, Department of Overseas Trade. *Report on Economic and Commercial Conditions in Brazil.* London, 1920.

Hamilton, D. Lee. "The Brazilian Scene," *Yale Review,* n.s. XXXVIII, No. 1 (Autumn 1948), 109–27.—Seeks to fit the intellectual into the post–World War II Brazilian complex.

Haring, Clarence H. "Vargas Returns in Brazil," *Foreign Affairs,* XXIX, No. 2 (January 1951), 308–14.—Informed comment on the election of October 3, 1950, and Vargas' return to the presidency.

Harris, Marvin. *Town and Country in Brazil.* New York, 1956.—The rural-urban dichotomy in terms of specific Brazilian institutions and values. Based on extensive field work.

Hermann, Lucilla. "The Middle Class in Guaratinguetá," *Economic Development and Cultural Change,* II, No. 2 (June 1953), 83–108.— The middle class in a *município* of the State of São Paulo is viewed historically as it passes through several economic cycles. Valuable observations on social mobility and the changing function of the middle class.

Herring, Hubert. "Brazil," *Yale Review,* n.s. XXXVI, No. 2 (Winter 1947), 304–19.—A well-written summary of the Vargas regime, the dictator's ouster, and the role of the United States, first, in keeping Vargas in power after 1938, and, second, in his overthrow.

Hill, Lawrence F., ed. *Brazil.* Berkeley, 1947. One of the University of California's United Nations Series.—Articles, by a number of Brazilian and United States scholars, are of varying worth and are generally sympathetic and optimistic.

Hutchinson, Bertram. "Social Grading of Occupations in Brazil," *British Journal of Sociology,* VIII, No. 2 (June 1957), 176–89.—Based upon the responses of several hundred first-year students at the University of São Paulo in 1955. Finds that income is an important factor in social grading of occupations and professions.

Inman, Samuel Guy. "Which Way Brazilian Economics?" *World Affairs,* n.s. V, No. 4 (October 1951), 479–89. An examination of economic policies as Vargas returned to the helm in 1951.

James, Herman Gerlach. *The Constitutional System of Brazil.* Washington, D.C., 1923.—A legal treatise.

James, Preston E. "Forces for Union and Disunion in Brazil," *Journal of Geography,* XXXVIII, No. 7 (October 1939), 260–66.—Excellent.

Jobim, José. *Brazil in the Making.* New York, 1943.—Factual with the stress on manufacturing industries.

Joint Brazil–United States Economic Development Commission. *Brazilian Technical Studies.* Washington, D.C., 1955.—Recommendations with special reference to the formulation of plans designed to overcome transportation and electric-power shortages.

———. *The Development of Brazil; Report with appendixes.* Washington, D.C., 1954.—Outlines bases for mutual cooperation looking to the economic development of Brazil. Some experts have felt that the *Report* was somewhat too optimistic. The Brazilian edition contained the full details of 41 projects prepared by the Joint Commission.

Joint Brazil–United States Technical Commission. *Report . . . with appendixes, approved by the Central Commission at Rio de Janeiro, February 7, 1949.* Washington, D.C., 1949.—Also referred to as the John Abbink Report, this small volume contains extremely valuable materials on Brazil's economic status and its future potential.

Kafka, Alexandre. "Brazil," in *Banking Systems,* Benjamin Haggott Beckhart, ed. New York, 1954. Pp. 49–118.—Brazil's monetary institutions in need of a thorough overhauling.

Kuznets, Simon S., *et al.,* eds. *Economic Growth: Brazil, India, Japan.* Durham, N.C., 1955.—Contains six chapters on contemporary Brazil by highly competent authors: George Wythe (Industry); Preston E. James (Agriculture); T. Lynn Smith (Demography); Bernard J. Seigel (Social Structure and Economic Change); Henry William Spiegel (The State and Economic Growth); and Stanley J. Stein (The Cotton Textile Industry).

Levy, Herbert Victor. *O Brasil e os novos tempos; considerações sôbre o problema de reestruturação política, económica e social do Brasil.* São Paulo [1946].—Examines democracy as it was besieged by the extreme Left and Right, and makes recommendations, based upon the wartime experiences of the United States, which might be expected to lead to strengthening the democratic process.

Lins de Barros, João Alberto. *Memórias de um revolucionário.* Rio de Janeiro, 1953.—Recollections of one of the leaders of the Prestes Column. A stirring account of revolutionary activities between 1922 and 1930, almost wholly devoid of political interpretation.

Lipson, Leslie. "Government in Contemporary Brazil," *The Canadian Journal of Economics and Political Science,* XXII, No. 2 (May 1956), 183–98.—Thoughtful analysis of what happens in politics when government reform must be adjusted to rapid economic change and a slow rate of social change.

Loeb, Gustaaf F. "Números índices do desenvolvimento físico da produção industrial no Brasil, 1939–1949," *Revista brasileira de economia,* VII, No. 1 (March 1953), 31–66.—Based on the industrial censuses of 1939 and 1949.

Loewenstein, Karl. *Brazil Under Vargas.* New York, 1942.—Legalistic and, as a legal interpretation of the early years of Vargas' rule, it still has validity.

Lowrie, Samuel H. "The Negro Element in the Population of São Paulo, a Southernly State of Brazil," *Phylon,* III, No. 4 (1942), 398–416.—Concludes that races in the State of São Paulo are not mixing as rapidly as is generally assumed.

Machado, F. Zenha. *Os últimos dias do govêrno de Vargas, a crise política de agôsto de 1954.* Rio de Janeiro, 1955.—Reportage. Contains several documents concerning the events preceding and immediately following Vargas' suicide.

Manchester, Alan K. "Brazil in Transition," *South Atlantic Quarterly,* LIV, No. 2 (April 1955), 167–76.—Comparison of conditions before and after 1930 and characteristics of the Vargas regime.

Melo Franco, Afonso Arinos de. *Estudos de direito constitucional.* Rio de Janeiro, 1957.—A collection of articles, speeches, and reports to the Brazilian Congress presented between 1949 and 1956. The author, a liberal, examines Brazilian political development from both practical and legalistic points of view.

Mendonça, Renato. *Breve historia del Brasil.* Madrid, 1950.—A survey largely lacking in interpretation.

Morazé, Charles. *Les trois âges du Brésil: Essai de politique.* Paris, 1954.—A penetrating study of Brazilian politics since independence. Getúlio Vargas' success in the 1930's and his return to office in 1951 were owing to his ability to exercise the "moderative power," which had been developed into a fine art by Emperor Pedro II. Considerable attention is paid to the political rise of the city after World War II.

Morse, Richard M. "São Paulo in the Twentieth Century: Social and Economic Aspects," *Inter-American Economic Affairs,* VIII, No. 1 (Summer 1954), 3–60.

———. "São Paulo Since Independence: A Cultural Interpretation," *Hispanic American Historical Review,* XXXIV, No. 4 (November 1954), 419–44.—The cultural impact of a burgeoning economy.

Mortara, Giorgio. "A distribuição da população do Brasil, segundo ramos de atividade," *Revista brasileira de economia,* I, No. 1 (September 1947), 75–105.—Article is based primarily on the demographic census of 1940. Seeks to establish the changes that took place between 1940 and 1947.

Normano, João F. *Brazil: A Study of Economic Types.* Chapel Hill, N.C., 1935.—"All history in new countries is economic history." In this case types and tendencies are treated typologically.

Nunes Leal, Victor. *Coronelismo, enxada e voto; o município e o regime representativo no Brasil.* Rio de Janeiro, 1948.—An unusually perceptive account of Brazilian politics at the municipal level.

O observador econômico e financiero (Rio de Janeiro, 1936—).—Brazil's *Fortune.* Social and political implications of economic developments are too often slighted.

Oliveira Vianna, Francisco José de. *Evolução do povo brasileiro.* 2d ed. São Paulo, 1933.—Interpretation of Brazilian development based upon highly controversial assumptions regarding the human races.

———. *Instituições políticas brasileiras.* 2 vols. São Paulo, 1949.—The treatment of the "clan" in politics is particularly interesting.

Palmer, Thomas W., Jr. "The Locomotive and Twenty Empty Freight Cars," *Inter-American Economic Affairs,* IV, No. 2 (Autumn 1950), 53–94.—Factual justification for the claim that the State of São Paulo keeps Brazil alive economically.

Paulding Associates. "A Summary Review of the Brazilian Economy, 1955." Rio de Janeiro, 1956. (Processed.)—Up-to-the-minute statistical information.

Pierson, Donald. "The Educational Process and the Brazilian Negro," *American Journal of Sociology,* XLVIII, No. 6 (May 1943), 692–700.—The loss of prestige on the part of African culture has, in many instances, reached the point where families are divided.

———. *Negroes in Brazil, A Study of Race Contact at Bahia.* Chicago, 1942.—Valuable insights on social determinants in northeastern Brazil.

Pinto, Luiz. *História do povo brasileiro.* Rio de Janeiro, 1948.—Essentially a synthesis with a marked social and economic orientation. Seeks to evaluate the contributions of the writers of Brazilian history. Pleads for more interpretation.

Prado, Caio, Jr. *Evolução política do Brasil.* 2d ed. São Paulo, 1947.— *"Interpretação materialista"* of Brazilian history. Highly critical of earlier writers on the subject.

——. *História Econômica do Brasil.* 2d ed. "Coleção 'grandes estudos' Brasilienses," vol. 2. São Paulo, 1949.—A pioneer work with a definite Marxist orientation. Offers a good panorama of Brazil's economic development to about 1930.

Prestes, Luiz Carlos. *Os comunistas na luta pela democracia.* Rio de Janeiro, 1945.—A report to the National Committee of the Communist Party of Brazil by the party's leader.

Price, Paul H. "The Brazilian Population at Mid-Century," *Inter-American Economic Affairs,* X, No. 1 (Summer 1956), 66–78.—Largely statistical.

Price, Paul H., and J. V. Freitas Marcondes. "A Demographic Analysis of the Population of the State of São Paulo, Brazil," *Social Forces,* XXVII, No. 4 (May 1949), 381–91.—Based primarily upon the Brazilian census of September 1, 1940.

Putnam, Samuel. "Brazilian Culture Under Vargas," *Science and Society,* VI, No. 1 (Winter 1942), 34–57.—Vargas is portrayed as a Fascist dictator.

——. *Marvelous Journey: A Survey of Four Centuries of Brazilian Writing.* New York, 1948.—Contains much social and cultural history.

——. "Race and Nation in Brazil," *Science and Society,* VII, No. 4 (Fall 1943), 321–37.—Based largely upon Euclydes da Cunha's *Os Sertões,* which Putnam had translated.

Revista brasileira de economia (Rio de Janeiro, 1947—). Published by the Getúlio Vargas Foundation.—Contains articles on both domestic and international economics. Considerable attention is paid to demographic and employment problems and to education.

Revista brasileira de estatística. Rio de Janeiro, 1940—. The official organ of the Conselho Nacional de Estatística of the Instituto Brasileiro de Geografia e Estatística. Supersedes the *Revista de economia e estatística,* which began publication in 1936.— Contains a wealth of material on agriculture, industry, and demography.

Revista brasileira de geografia. Rio de Janeiro, 1939—.—Organ of the Conselho Nacional de Geografia. Major articles are summarized in several languages. Useful maps.

Rippy, J. Fred. "A Century of Railway-Building in Brazil," *Inter-American Economic Affairs,* VII, No. 3 (Winter 1953), 29–35.—Considerable attention is paid to the contribution of foreigners.

Salgado, Plínio. *Psicologia da revolução.* 4th ed. Rio de Janeiro [1953].—The author is the leader of the extreme Right Wing Popular Representation Party.

Segadas Vianna, Renato. *O sindicato no Brasil.* Rio de Janeiro, 1953.—Published by the Ministry of Labor, Industry and Commerce and dedicated to President Vargas, the volume was prepared in order to better inform the workers upon their rights and privileges. Useful for the laws and regulations it contains.

Siegel, Bernard J. "Themes and Variations in Brazilian Culture," *Pacific Spectator*, VI, No. 1 (Winter 1952), 98–112.—National similarities and regional differences.

Silva, Carlos Medeiros. *Public Functionaries and the Brazilian Constitution*. Rio de Janeiro, 1954.—Historical. Public office and public servants in seven Brazilian constitutions.

Simonsen, Roberto C. *Brazil's Industrial Evolution*. São Paulo, 1939.— A brief survey prepared for a visiting mission from the United States.

————. *A industria em face da economia nacional*. São Paulo, 1937.— Largely recommendations for the creation of an economic policy, by a leading industrialist and public servant.

Singer, H. W. "The Brazilian SALTE Plan : An Historical Case Study of the Role of Internal Borrowing in Economic Development," *Economic Development and Cultural Change*, I, No. 5 (February 1953), 341–49.—The problems and importance of internal financing of developmental projects.

Smith, T. Lynn. *Brazil; People and Institutions*. Rev. ed. Baton Rouge, La., 1954.—A highly useful source book. Includes data to 1950.

Smith, T. Lynn, ed. *Brazil: Portrait of Half a Continent*. New York, 1951.—Nineteen essays, several of them stimulating, by eighteen authors. Examines a wide range of social, political, and economic problems.

Souza Campos, Ernesto de. *Educação superior no Brasil*. Rio de Janeiro, 1940.—Official and historical.

————. *Instituições culturais e de educação superior no Brasil. Resumo histórico*. Rio de Janeiro, 1941.—A quality handbook for higher education and cultural institutions of Brazil, with good historical background.

Spiegel, Henry William. *The Brazilian Economy; Chronic Inflation and Sporadic Industrialization*. Philadelphia, 1949.—Scholarly. All major economic areas receive attention.

————. "Income, Savings, and Investment in Brazil," *Inter-American Economic Affairs*, I, No. 1 (June 1947), 113–30.—A careful study which finds many danger signals in Brazil's economic future.

Stein, Stanley J. "The Brazilian Cotton Textile Industry, 1850–1950," *Inter-American Economic Affairs*, VIII, No. 1 (Summer 1954), 69–91.—This fine study in expanded form appeared as a book, Cambridge, Mass., 1957.

Sternberg, Hilgard O'Reilly. "Agriculture and Industry in Brazil," *Geographical Journal*, CXXI, No. 4 (December 1955), 488–502.— The resource bases of agriculture and of industry allow for considerable expansion. Harmonious integration of the two economic sectors is vital.

Teixeira, Anísio. "La escuela brasileña y la estabilidad social," in Pan American Union, *La educación*, No. 8 (Oct.-Dec. 1957), 5–14.—By a champion of basic educational reform. Reviews the role of State-supported higher education in the formation and perpetuation of a social elite at the expense of the Brazilian public.

Torres, Alberto. *O problema nacional brasileiro.* 3d ed. São Paulo, 1938.—First published in 1912, mildly antiforeign, fears for the culture of Brazil in face of the inroads made by materialism.

Torres, João Camillo de Oliveira. *O positivismo no Brasil.* Petrópolis, 1943.—The conditions under which positivism became a major political-religious movement in Brazil in the late nineteenth and early twentieth centuries.

United Nations. Department of Economic and Social Affairs. *Analysis and Projections of Economic Development: II. The Economic Development of Brazil* (E/CN.12/364/Rev.1). New York, 1956.— Projections to 1962 on the basis of relatively detailed study of developments since World War II.

——. Economic and Social Council, Economic Commission for Latin America. Fourth Session, Mexico City, 28 May 1951. "Recent Developments and Trends in the Brazilian Economy" (E/CN.12/217/Add. 2). Mexico, 1951 (Processed).

United States, Tariff Commission. *Mining and Manufacturing Industries in Brazil.* Washington, D.C., 1949.—Very useful.

Vargas, Getúlio. *A campanha presidencial.* Rio de Janeiro, 1951.— Approximately eighty addresses given during a bitterly waged campaign.

——. *O govêrno trabalhista do Brasil.* 2 vols. Rio de Janeiro, 1952–54.—Largely campaign addresses and messages to congress. Valuable as an outline of Vargas' stated objectives as he sought to rebuild his political fortunes.

——. *A política trabalhista no Brasil.* Rio de Janeiro, 1950.—Addresses, messages, and press interviews between November 1945 and March 1947 by the ousted dictator and future president.

Viana, Luiz. *A vida de Rui Barbosa.* Special Centennial Edition. São Paulo, 1949.—A reasonably objective account of one of Brazil's truly outstanding statesmen, by an obvious admirer.

W. A. T. "Brazil and Her Expanding Economy," *The World Today,* X, No. 9 (September 1954), 397–406.—Optimistic.

Wagley, Charles. "Brazil," in *Most of the World,* Ralph Linton, ed. New York, 1949. Pp. 212–270.—Masterful summary of the principal characteristics of the major regions of Brazil and of the nation as a whole.

——. "Regionalism and Cultural Unity in Brazil," *Social Forces,* XXVI, No. 4 (May 1948), 457–64.—Excellent summary.

Wagley, Charles, ed. *Race and Class in Rural Brazil.* Paris, 1952.— The results of an extensive research program by the author and three student-colleagues. Three rural communities of the State of Bahia and one in the Amazon Valley are studied.

Washington, Samuel Walter. "A Study of the Causes of Hostility Toward the United States in Latin America: Brazil." Washington, D.C., 1956 (Processed).—An External Research Paper, Department of State.

Werneck Sodre, Nelson. *Formação da sociedade brasileira.* Rio de Janeiro, 1944.—The last four chapters of this survey are concerned with the modern period to 1929.

Willems, Emilio. *Assimilação e populações marginais no Brasil.* São Paulo, 1940.—A study of the Germans in Brazil by one of the republic's outstanding sociologists.

———. "Some Aspects of Cultural Conflict and Acculturation in Southern Rural Brazil," *Rural Sociology,* VII, No. 4 (December 1942), 375–84.—Scholarly.

———. "The Structure of the Brazilian Family," *Social Forces,* XXXI, No. 4 (May 1953), 339–45.—Only the family as it relates to the privileged groups is known in Brazil. It is dangerous to generalize from such information. Suggests that among the lower classes the family lacks many of the characteristics that are of major significance in the middle and upper classes.

Wyckoff, Theodore. "Brazilian Political Parties," *South Atlantic Quarterly,* LVI, No. 3 (Summer 1957), 281–98.—A quite good review, with optimistic overtones, of decision-making, interest groups, and the role of political parties in transmitting pressures from interest groups to decision-makers.

Wyler, Marcus. "The Development of the Brazilian Constitution (1891–1946)," *Journal of Comparative Legislation and International Law,* 3d ser., XXXI, parts III-IV (November 1949), 53–60.—Highly useful.

Wythe, George. *Brazil, an Expanding Economy.* New York, 1949.— A quite useful examination of the debits and credits with which Brazil would face the future.

Index